# The Life of a Stripper

Romana Van Lissum

# 50 Exotic Dancers
# Confess Their
# Personal Experiences
# in the
# *Adult Entertainment Industry*

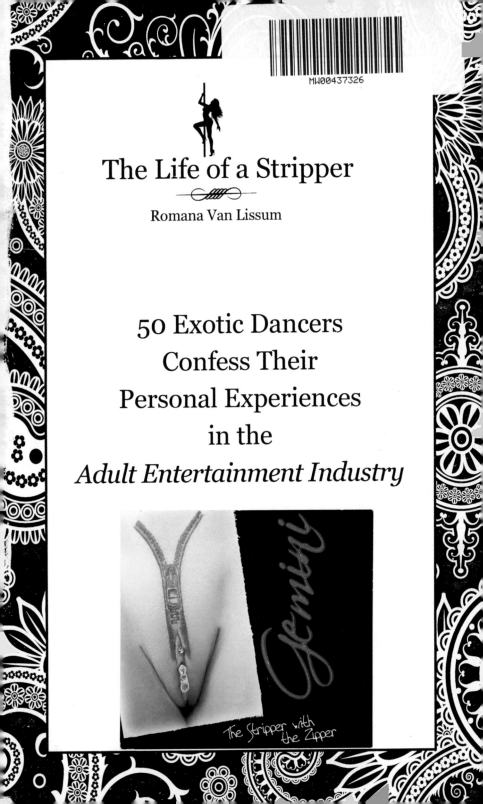

Gemini

The Stripper with the Zipper

# The Life of a Stripper
## 50 Exotic Dancers Share their Personal Experiences in the *Adult Entertainment Industry*

First Edition
ROMANA VAN LISSUM

Disclaimer: These are true stories, and the characters and events are real. However, in some cases, the names, descriptions, and locations have been changed, and some events have been altered, combined or condensed for storytelling purposes, but the overall chronology is an accurate depiction of the authors' experiences. You may also be uncomfortable with some of the language and content.

Romana can be contacted at:
howtobeawaitress.com, thelifeofastripper.com and
romanavanlissum@yahoo.ca

# Dedication

This book is dedicated to Marsha, who was an icon in the Western Canadian exotic dance industry, and to all the dancers I have had the privilege of knowing over the past 17 years; the rookies, the veterans, the retired and the deceased.

I especially want to dedicate this book to the 50 girls who bared their souls to me so that I could expose their experiences and secrets. Thank you for giving us a peek into your world – the crazy, unpredictable and misunderstood business of stripping.

*You already possess everything necessary to become great.*

– Crow

# Contents

# Acknowledgments

My heartfelt thanks go out to each and every one of these girls for opening up to me and sharing their stories. Without your time, honesty and patience this book would not be possible.

Thank you to my editor and new friend, Carnation, for ensuring the stories were told with grace and, whenever possible, humour. A big thank you to an old friend Aqilla Aziz (or for those of you in the front row, Pleasure) for using her graphic design skills to create my cover the way I envisioned it. I'm also grateful to my daughter Kelsey Van Lissum for doing the photography, and for her unwavering support. And of course I can't forget to mention my best friend and husband of 21 years, Rod. *xo*

Thank you to my friend and long-time regular, Mr. L who gave me the idea to use the names of flowers. You know who you are, *wink wink.*

# What Others Say About This Book

A very informative and juicy read! After over 10 years in this industry it was eye opening to read these women's stories and get THEIR perspective of an industry that I knew only a small part of. Once you open this book make sure all appointments are cancelled because time will fly by.

Dave Shannon
DJ/bartender

Great book, easy read. Truly gives a person a much better perspective that not all dancers come from the same mold. Shocking and educational stories all rolled into one nice package!

Karli
Entertainer

This book offers a peek into the private world of the strong, beautiful women who have chosen to become Exotic Dancers. Each unique, personal story in her own words! A fascinating and eye opening read!!

Dennis
Sales

This is a very interesting read for everyone, but very beneficial to anyone who wants to get into the business. I love the idea of the life stories of dancers and reading this book. I have come to respect these women. Every story is different; some sad with a hard life and others with a good head on their shoulders, very driven women. It really takes you through their experiences and you realize that these girls have feelings, hopes and dreams like everyone else. I love it!

Carrie
Homemaker

Romana's Bouquet of flowers is a fascinating read. Just like the flowers they have chosen, each woman is different but still the same. Each has her own colors and characteristics, strengths and weaknesses. Each grew differently. As you read you will find each is her own person but just like the rest of us, each is really two people. One, the person she is and two, the job she does. You will find they are not the stereotypes many would dismiss them as.

A book long overdue and a look into a world which is misunderstood and pre judged.

Mr. L
Retired

Romana has done an amazing job getting these girls to open up to her. You're getting every thought, hope, regret and dream from each of the dancers. Great insight into a profession that most times is greatly misunderstood. A great read!

Mike M
Business Owner

There's a reason that tabloid magazines sell by the millions; other people's lives are very interesting! Romana takes this to an ultimate level by using the real life stories and struggles of exotic dancers. Who wouldn't get hooked on reading these confessions!

Alisa Clarke
Owner of Horsd'oovers

The first story I read surprised me – it was so moving and heart-warming! Not everyone's tale is like that, but I appreciated the dancers' candid sharing. Enlightening!

Tammy
Artist

This book is the most inner look into the life of a "stripper" and the intimate details of how they began their profession of exotic entertainment. The saying, "Never judge a man before you've walked a mile in his shoes," rings true in these wonderfully illustrated stories. Whatever thoughts you may have had before about this line of work, I guarantee it will change your point of view.

Shari
Server for over 10 years

Put your handkerchiefs away – you won't need them. While some of the dancers who give us a glimpse into their lives here have undoubtedly suffered a few hard knocks along the way, as a group they are a bunch of tough cookies. Young (mostly) and beautiful, they are making some of the best money of their lives, and rather than being desperate to escape exotic dancing, they are managing their careers and banking their earnings. An eye-opening read.

Cam Braithwaite
Retired musician

Love the background as told by each dancer. It reinforces that everyone has a story ... if only we'd take the time to listen to it.

Carrie-Anne
Mother and homemaker

Van Lissum writes with frank honesty which will be appreciated by those looking to learn more about the exotic dance industry and the human condition alike. Her sincerity and empathy for her subjects and their personal stories is immediately apparent. There isn't any sensationalism here, just a woman providing the straight goods on a profession not often examined from the inside out.

Clara Cole
Communications Expert

Romana has a writing style that I enjoy. It is light and fun; I always want to keep reading. There is enough substance to make me coming back to it. A reference, if you like. Discussing exotic dancers is certainly a topic of interest to me. Some say they are artists and others disagree. Some strippers are natural dancers, some well trained dancers, some natural entertainers and some are disappointing. They have good days and bad days (as do we all).

When you see a good dancer who has good training and is a natural entertainer on her best day, you will have no doubt that you have had artistic experience. They are truly a joy to behold.

I highly recommend this book to you. Learning more about these artists is certainly worthwhile. Read this book with an open mind. Enjoy it. Give a copy to a friend. I will!

Roger G. Welch
Former President
Maple Ridge Pitt Meadows Arts Council

If you want a real inside look at the world of exotic dancing... well, look no further. You've found it! A lot of people think the dance world is what they see in movies, on TV or music videos. But the truth is NOTHING like what you think you know. There are dancers from all walks of life; all ages, races and sizes. Some are mothers, students, artists, business owners... the list goes on.

This is an excellent read for anyone interested in learning about the people involved in the exotic dance industry.

Miss Rosa
Exotic dancer

"The Life of a Stripper" has opened my eyes to such a misunderstood world. To know that these women are just as vulnerable, wise and "normal" as anybody else should be common knowledge. It must take a tonne of street smarts to handle such a hard job. The artistic licence that Romana has handed to them is the best way to tell all these different stories and perspectives. The samples I have read leave me itching for more! I can't wait to secure my own copy!

Judy Chung
Lab Assistant, UBC

Enormous and brilliant... crammed with characters unbelievably alive. Touches all human emotions; love, hate, hope and despair. See for yourself. This is truly a book to get lost in.

France
Business Owner

Wow! What an incredible read! Fascinating to get a peek into people's lives and their different journeys that have led them to the world of exotic dancing. A profession we often look upon with great judgement. Some stories make you smile, while others truly make you cry. Thank you Romana for putting this together. Your book is a real eye opener.

Ronaye Ireland
Author of "How to find trouble free horse boarding, even if you're new to horses"
www.HorseBoardingSecrets.com

What amazing stories! I worked with Romana in the strip bar industry for eight years and met some amazing girls and lifelong friends. Ro your stories are funny, heart warming and some are truly heartbreaking. Good job friend!

Kimberly Williams
Hair stylist

Very compelling stories! The more stories I read, the more I realized that all the dancers want is the same as anyone...the best they can do for their families and themselves. They all lead lives that are different than mine and that is what makes this book so interesting and hard to stop reading!

Brian
Retired

I have had the joy of working with Romana for nearly eight years, serving in the same exotic show lounge. I was so excited when Ro first told me her idea. The anticipation has been killing me while I've watched her interview several dancers after shift over the past couple of years. I know many of the girls in this book personally and to see the sharing of their intimate stories is touching. Everyone is curious to know about the 'life of a dancer,' and in this book, Romana has executed that wonderfully.

Katherine Romero-Blackwell
Server for 8 years

Romana manages to move us in this truly powerful and provocative collaboration of engaging stories. Think of it as a Chicken Soup for the Exotic Dancer's Soul. It's depth of inspiration and intelligence is an admirable book you have never read before.

Sarah Lawrence
PR

# A Word from the Editor

I remember my first time on stage. I don't know what I thought. I guess I was waiting for the fear to hit – the realization of what I was doing. But it was something different instead. The lights flashed and I was on fire. By song three, however, the adrenaline was gone and it had sunk in that soon I would be naked on a stage. For forever, in a way, because once you've done it you can never take it back. I didn't hesitate, though. I pulled my gear off and didn't look back. I was home.

Looking back on that moment now, what feels like hundreds of years later, I'm proud of that girl. She did it. We've all done it, and that's what sets us apart from everyone else. We will all be, in some immutable way, on that stage forever. Dancing absolutely changes you, for better and for worse, but if you're smart and lucky you will get out with some money, some good stories and only a few battle scars.

Editing these stories has been a privilege. I knew it would be interesting, but who knew I would feel as proud as I do of my fellow dancers. Although we are all different; came from different backgrounds and made our way to the stage individually, I see a similar spirit in each one of us, in each of the beautiful wild women I've danced with all across this country. It's this inner strength that makes me proud to count myself among these nomadic, furious, fiery hellcats. Thanks for the stories, ladies.

Written by Carnation

# A Word from the Author

For 17 years, I have been a server at a popular Vancouver strip club. Throughout the years, I have always wondered what a girl's motivation was for taking her clothes off for a living. Is it out of desperation? Can they truly enjoy dancing naked in front of strangers? Is it the money? The attention? What road do these women travel to end up on that stage?

Although I'm not a dancer, I feel that it is my duty to bring these women's stories to a broader audience. During the course of this project, I asked my questions and lent an ear, all without judging or scrutinizing. I feel honoured to be entrusted with this confidential information, and to be able to act not only as their storyteller, but also as a confidante and friend. My mission is to do these women justice by helping them find their voice.

This book will open your eyes, as it did for me. I apologize in advance for the vulgar language and vivid explanations. The stories are written here as they were told to me. You will quickly realize that the stories are not sugar coated, and you may find, as I did, that some weigh heavy on your heart. That being said, I encourage you to keep an open mind and refrain from judging these women. They are wonderful human beings just making a living.

The main question that couldn't be answered, by myself or the dancers I interviewed, was about judgment. Why are people (especially other women) so focused on judging and criticizing strippers? It's easy to judge this profession as a whole and not take into account the individual paths that a person takes to get here. Dancers pay taxes (like the rest of us) and most of them work six and sometimes seven days a week. They do make a good living, but in my opinion, they deserve to make the big money. I definitely don't want to do their job!

Most people are convinced that every dancer has 'daddy issues' and comes from a broken family. This is far from the truth. As the reader, you have a front row seat to see exactly why these women made the choices they did. It is important for people to realize that 'strippers' are just like everyone else. Yes, some of them have an alcoholic father or come from a broken home, but this is also the case in the general population. Many of the girls in this book have parents that are still happily married. In this life, each person is ultimately responsible for making decisions about what they will do, and those decisions sometimes can't be tracked. Do they end up homeless, wandering the streets high on drugs, or accomplish something with their life such as becoming a doctor, car salesman, teacher, or even an exotic dancer.

In the end, you will come to realize that each woman has walked her own unique journey. They arrive from different roads but have all ended up at the same destination – a tough business, full of long days, late hours, rough customers and most of the time, living out of a suitcase.

For privacy purposes, I have chosen to keep the dancers' names (and stage names) confidential by substituting them with the names of flowers. I feel that it is my responsibility to keep stage names and private information confidential because it's too easy for an unstable individual to hunt down a girl through their agency's website. Also, using an alias allowed these women to be totally open and give us their insider secrets.

You will find that some of the stories have been written by the girls, and the rest of them were written by me after I interviewed them. During my interviews, I spent many long hours chatting with these women (my longest interview was over four hours long!) and later transcribed our conversations, but the girls had complete control of what was published. During the editing process, some information ended up being pulled by the girls or the editor to protect their privacy.

I've been asked how I picked the girls for the book. It was based simply on which girls happened to come through our bar that week. I also contacted girls I knew who were retired, with families of their own. Some of them chose to participate, but most declined, mainly for their family's sake. Frankly, most of the retired girls I talked to were happy to leave this world in their past.

I hope this book helps you to better understand the exotic dancing industry – and the women working in it – in a positive way. I look forward to you learning about these remarkable women as much as I enjoyed spending time with them and putting this unique book together. It's been an incredible journey!

All the best,
Romana


*"Be yourself, everyone else is already taken."*

– Oscar Wilde

# African Daisy

My friend and I were working at a pub and she decided to give dancing a try. Six months later, she was back and she told me how great it was. So, I cut back some of my shifts at the pub and started working for a company that sent girls out for stags and bachelor parties. The money was fantastic! I figured that if I started stage dancing, I would make double the money. I didn't realize that I was already making some fantastic money at the company since stag parties were usually on the weekends and I still continued to work in the bar through the week.

I was 22 when I started dancing and have been dancing now for three years. Because I had been working for the company that provided girls for stag parties, I was already comfortable with getting naked in front of strangers, so my first day on the job was not too uncomfortable. My only worry was about what people thought of my dancing.

My parents, sister and older brother know what I do for a living. Although my mom says that she is fine with it, I know she would prefer that I did something else. Dad was upset when he found out and now he treats me differently. He used to call me on my phone everyday and now he doesn't feel comfortable talking to me. My relationship with my brother has changed as well. I know he doesn't like the fact that I am a dancer. We used to talk and hang out on the weekends but now we don't and it seems as if we have grown apart.

Growing up, I have never had any issues with my dad. Although my parents are divorced, my mom was a wonderful, strong parent. My dad was not in my life for a long time because of his drinking. He has tried to make it up to my brother and I in our teenage years. The saddest part of my childhood is that when I was 15, my cousin and I were molested by a family friend. It was a big deal because it ended up on the news where the guy committed suicide right before the court case. Because of the molestation, I hate men.

There are some things I like about my job. I like the freedom and the fact that we are able to pick our own hours. I met some really good friends in this business and many nice people. I have been able to travel to places I never could have without this job. Working in this industry has opened up doors and opportunities for me. The money is okay; it is what you make of it.

Aside from that, I hate the fact that my privacy is compromised. When I started out in this business, I was expecting to keep my dancer life and my private life separate, but that wasn't what happened. Also, some people in the industry are pretty shady. They are never what they seem to be so it's hard to trust them.

It's especially hard to deal with the jealous girls. I became friends with a certain group of girls and I was told by quite a few people that these girls were crazy and always causing drama. The girl in this group who was supposedly my best friend ended up putting an old dancer photo of me on a website along with my real name, first and last. She also posted that I was a drug addict. I've known of many other dancers who are on this website as well. It's very hurtful and embarrassing since it's not easy to remove. It's sad to know that my co-workers and friends would do that to me.

When that same girl and I were still friends, we were driving to an out of town booking during the first week of December in her truck. It had bald tires, but we thought we could make it. She was hung over and sleeping, so I was the one stuck driving, and I didn't even have a driver's licence at the time! I had been driving for 15 hours and I was exhausted, so when I stopped for gas I woke her up and told her it was her turn to drive.

Five minutes later while she was making an illegal turn on the highway, we got t-boned by a semi-truck. We spent two days in the hospital as a result. This episode basically ruined our friendship. Two weeks after the car accident, I had moved out of my apartment building because I didn't want to be connected with her since she was always lipping someone off and causing a big scene. She is truly a psycho. A couple of months ago, she showed up at the club I was working at and ended up punching me in the throat. Not too long ago, she showed up at another club I was working at and while I was giving a lap dance she got into the dancer change room and smashed all my make-up. It was $400 worth of brand new make-up and the bar wouldn't cover it. She's one person I want to stay far away from.

I also hate all the unfairness in the industry, especially with agencies. They pick and choose their favourites and they'll bump you out of work for their favourite.

One of the scariest times of my life was when I used to be addicted to percs and oxys. I was spending $500 a day on pills and falling behind on my bills. I had to work like crazy and took no time off so I could make money to support my habit and pay bills. It was hurting my family since they didn't know I was into the drugs and they couldn't understand why I was working my ass off and losing my possessions. I went to see a drugs and alcohol counselor and with a lot of hard work and help, I am now clean.

As for crazy customers, I just dealt with a stalker. A friend of mine brought a friend of his (a 35 year old good looking guy) to visit me at the bar I was working at. Right from the start, I had told this guy that my boyfriend had just died and I wasn't looking for a relationship. He called me the next day and asked me to go with him to the fair, so I did. He also took me out for breakfast. Afterwards, he said that he was going to say good-bye to me since we wouldn't be seeing each other again.

That wasn't goodbye though. After he left, he started texted me saying how much he missed me, which was pretty unnerving and creepy. He texted me to say that he wanted to come out to the bar I was working at that week. I told him not to, but he came out anyways. I was not impressed. At one point while we were outside, he started to rub my arm and get a little too friendly with me. After leaving, he sent me almost

30 text messages saying that he wanted to be with me and that he knows that I want to be with him too. I told him to leave me alone but he still messages me, so I just ignore him. If it continues, I may need to call the police.

My weirdest experience was when I was dancing and my cousin came in. I noticed him sit on the other side of the room but I'm still not sure whether he saw me that day or not since there were four other dancers dancing. Also, I recently found out that my brother and his friends went to a club I was working at. They didn't see me but when they sat down, they checked out the flyer on the table and saw my name on it. They bolted out the door!

My weirdest customer is this guy who many of the other dancers hang out with. When I come to his town, he takes me out to dinners and lunches and buys me presents. He knew I had a boyfriend, yet he seemed to get too attached to me. Last year I had crashed my car and it was towed to the impound yard. I had to pay $2000 to get it back and since I didn't have the money, he said that he would pay the bill. I told him that I would pay him back. While it was a lot of money for me to pay back at once, he said that he would be happy if I could pay him $150 a week. I agreed and told him how much I appreciated it.

Things started to get weird and uncomfortable when I would sit with him and he would get mad when other customers would stop and talk to me. I wanted to disconnect myself from him and told him I was going to pay him all the money back right away. He got pissed off! Staff from another bar told me that he said that he wanted to kill me. I found out that he went into a club where my agent was one night and he slapped my agent in the face, yelling at him for not firing me. Shortly after, I dropped out of the circuit for two months. I haven't seen him since.

One of the weirdest gifts I received came from a customer who bought me a dress from a popular women's clothing boutique. It was by far the ugliest dress on the planet. It was an 80's style prom dress – in salmon pink! And of course he wanted me to wear it. I lied and said it didn't fit me, so then he offered to have it altered for me. I gave it back to him and told him I wouldn't wear it anyways. Some of the nicest gifts I received over time were chocolates and flowers. I had a customer that used to bring me amazingly delicious baked goods (even a birthday cake) from an Italian bakery. The biggest tip I got on stage was $700.

My best customer is an older gentleman that is in his 60's. He takes me out to dinner all the time, buys me shoes for work and other items when I need them. He will lend me money if I am short for bills, however he won't cross the line. I know that he is hoping that someday I will change my mind and want to be with him in a more romantic way.

Here's my embarrassing story: at one strip club, the poles are very close to the edge of the stage (about two inches from the edge). I was buck naked and twirling upside down when my hair got in my face. I thought that I was on the inside of the stage but I wasn't. I flipped over and landed in the lap of a customer. It was such a violent fall that I broke a couple of nails and knocked over his beer. I was so embarrassed, and I apologized like crazy! I even offered to buy him another beer. I guess my apology wasn't good enough for the rude jerk because he called me a 'stupid bitch,' which embarrassed me even more!

Something that you would find interesting about me is that I went to university for four years to be a police officer. I know this will sound a little strange to some people, but I refuse to work on the island because I'm scared of the ferry. The island also freaks me out and I get a weird energy from it. Four things I won't leave home without are my hairbrush, sunglasses, camera and carwash kit.

One thing that surprised me about this industry is after hearing all the rumours about all the drugs and prostitution, I realize it is definitely true after I have witnessed it at some of the strip clubs.

Before I got into this industry, I wish I knew how much mental and physical stress was involved. I always thought that I would go in, do my job and leave. That is impossible because if something is happening in the dancer change room, for example, you're involved in all the drama and bullshit whether you like it or not.

I also wish I knew how hard it is to get out of the business once you've started. Once you get used to making a certain amount of money, it's almost like a disposable income. It's really hard to go back to a regular job.

My boyfriend had passed away a couple of months ago and everything about the industry reminds me of him. I always talked to him about getting out of this business. He agreed and said that I should do something good with my life. I started applying at oil camps for a job and my plan is to move to Alberta and start over because nobody knows me there. I have four weeks of bookings left and then I am done with being a dancer. I am looking forward to moving and making a change in my life.

I am not ashamed of my job. The only time I felt a bit bad was when my boyfriend's parents found out what I did for a living. After they knew they treated me differently, and I know they are disappointed. I hate when they make comments to me like, "It's not a very respectful job. How long do you expect to have a life from this?"

Do I regret getting into this business? Yes and no. Yes, because it is so hard to get out once you get in, and also because of the drug scene. No, because of some of the great people I have met.

My advice for new girls is that if you have other options (another job), stay out. But if you have to and you end up dancing, stay smart. Stay out of the drama, the drugs and the partying. Don't make it your life since it's easy to get caught up in the lifestyle. And save your money!

# Ayanna

I was 19 when I moved out with a room mate. Shortly after, I met my friend's cousin and he asked me if I would be interested in dancing after he explained that I could make enough money to furnish my apartment. I was curious, so my friend and I went with him to a local strip club.

He pointed at the stage and asked me if I could dance and take my clothes off for money. I said I could. Then he took me shopping for new clothes and shoes, and even a car so that I could get to work. That same night he took me to a club. I wasn't sure what I was getting into at this point but I clued in that he was a pimp. I thought it was a business deal, more or less. He informed me that he would take all the money I would make in the month and he would give me a lump sum at the end. After a month of working, I didn't see a penny of the money I made other than the small amount I set aside for myself in secret.

Meeting his 'other girls,' I noticed they also had cars bought for them. He paid all their bills and he even paid to have their hair and nails done. I remember my first day on the job and how scared I felt because I was wearing outfits that were pretty revealing and attracting a lot of attention. I wasn't used to it. I barely made any money that first day because I had a hard time talking to the guys and asking them to buy private dances. I got rejected a couple of times and that hurt me to the core of my soul. I only did one table dance that night.

My 'boss' was never abusive towards me but I did see him beat some of the other girls. He pressured me to turn tricks but I refused. I continued to work harder by working 14 hour days. I would work the day shift at one club and then I would drive to another club to work the night shift. At every club, the other dancers knew I was 'his' girl. The senior girls that worked for him were always watching me, too. If they noticed something they didn't like, or thought any of his girls were trying to leave him, the senior girls would threaten them or beat them up.

One day, I got really sick and I couldn't work. He forced me to work anyways and I ended up quitting. He took back all the clothes and shoes, and I went into the hospital for the weekend.

Prior to going into the hospital, I met a dancer from BC. She told me to come visit her, so I did. She had another girl staying with her at the time and we started to hang out. One day the two of us took off for the day and by the time we got back, we were basically kicked out and locked out. The dancer refused to give us our luggage or clothes back and we were told to not come back. We were given some bullshit reason and to this day we don't know why she kicked us out that day. We returned home to the east.

Months later, I came back to BC because I liked it and needed a change. I also wanted a fresh start and I was planning on enrolling in university. I got into dancing the circuit instead because I wanted to make some easy money.

Growing up, I had a childhood that anyone would want. I had a great education, family vacations every year and I was involved in sports and extra curricular activities. My family and friends still don't know what I do for a living; the only person who knows is my best friend. My family is very religious and I know they would have a heart attack if they knew what I was up to. They think that I do clerical and administration work.

I hate the jerks I meet in this industry. Some of the guys are such losers and they don't respect women. These are guys that expect so much for nothing and because they paid me for a lap dance, they feel as though they own me for those three minutes.

Regardless of the negative aspects, I enjoy performing in front of an audience and I like the amount of money I can make while dancing (the biggest tip I ever got was $500).

Many dancers receive gifts from the customers. I've got to say that one of the strangest gifts I received came from a sweetheart of a customer. He pulled a steak wrapped in tin foil out of his back pocket and told me that he brought me dinner.

I had a scary episode when I was working the floor one day doing VIP dances. The customer wanted more than just a private dance and I told him that I was not doing anything extra. He refused the dance and walked away. Then he approached me again for a dance with a promise to behave. He paid up front and I started my dance. During the last song, he tried touching me. I told him I was finished as I grabbed my purse and headed for the exit. He yelled at me that he wanted his money back and I refused. Then he grabbed at my purse and I panicked and pulled it towards me. I had a friend's cell phone on me and I was scared he was going to steal it. He threw me down on the couch and started to punch me in the face as I screamed at the top of my lungs for help. A couple of other VIP dancers and their customers came running into the room. The customer told management that I told him it was okay for him to touch me and that I changed my mind in the end. They believed him over me so I never went back to work at that club again.

While picking my dancer name, I chose a name that I elongated from a popular TV series. Another personal thing about me is when I leave for the day I won't leave home without my lip gloss, phone and hand sanitizer.

My most embarrassing moment would be when I got my period on stage. I also had a professor show up unexpectedly twice in two different clubs I worked at.

Before getting into this line of work, I wish I understood the value of money since I made a lot in the beginning and I spent it foolishly. Getting into this industry, I was surprised to find out how pimps operate and that there are other businesses that operate in the clubs that the general public is unaware of.

At 19, I started in this industry and I've been dancing now for four years. I'm not sure how much longer I will be dancing as I have some goals set for the next two years and it really just depends on whether I meet them or not.

I do not regret getting into this business because I was able to better myself. I discovered my independence and learned a lot about people, especially the crazy ones! I also realize that I make more money than most people my age. I'm not ashamed of telling people what I do for a living but I am aware of who people think I am. Also, I know that those who matter to me the most know who I really am.

My advice for new dancers coming into this business is to just be aware of who you are socializing with. You have to be careful because there are many wolves in sheep's clothing, you can't trust anyone. Also, don't work for anyone but yourself and stay focused on your goals. Finally, just stay true to yourself! It's not what you do; it's how you do it.

# Azalea

Before I started dancing, I worked in nursing homes and also with children who had ADD disabilities. It was work I enjoyed a lot and found very rewarding, but I wanted to see what else was out there, so from 2002 to 2004, I started competing in wet t-shirt contests. It was fun and I almost always placed first. It was easy money and I would always go home with anywhere from $300-$500! I was inspired by the dancers I saw on stage, so I started freelancing, and stuck with it for nine months.

My first day on the job, I was 20 years old and was doing an amateur contest. I was freaking out but also nervous and excited at the same time. The agent who came to pick me up and drive me to the contest was wearing a funky hat and chains. As I sat in his car, I remember thinking to myself, "What the hell did I get myself into?!"

After my first week of dancing, I told my parents. This caused a big problem between us and we basically had no relationship for almost three years. My dad was especially upset and he didn't talk to me for two whole years. I come from a wealthy family, so my parents questioned why I would pick dancing to earn a living. I keep my job secret from the rest of the family, just to avoid upsetting them. Some of them think I work in bars as a traveling waitress, and that I also do photo shoots from time to time.

My favourite part of working as a dancer is the money and the fun I have working with different girls every week. The best feeling in the world for me is when I get to dance to my favourite music! I also love to travel and my favourite trip is in the summer when I drive between Edmonton and Vancouver. BC is my favourite place to work even though the money isn't as good as Alberta. I see working in BC like a little paid vacation where I'm not expected to do any private dances if I don't want to. It's pretty laid back and I like that.

There are a few things I don't like about this industry and those are all the rules, mostly the cap on dancers regarding pay. It is also mandatory in many Alberta clubs for dancers to do forty private dances during the week and the rules have changed from where you didn't have to stay on the floor all night, to now you have to.

I don't have any weird or crazy customer stories because I basically keep to myself. I never want to get into any unsafe predicaments.

An awkward experience for me was the day my dad's best friend (they have been friends since before I was born) showed up unexpectedly at the club I was working at. I was extremely uncomfortable so he said he would leave but he didn't. He stuck around watching my show! I told my dad about it and it hasn't been brought up since.

I have to say that one of my favourite customers is an older guy who is around 50. He takes me to rock and roll concerts and gets us the best seats he can and we spend our time rocking out and talking about music. He's a really nice guy who treats me like a friend, not a dancer, so we always have a blast when we hang out.

I received a very sweet gift from a customer once; a necklace with a diamond pendant in the shape of a cross. It is very special to me because it was given to me at Christmas by a customer that understood my belief in God.

Something that most people would find unusual about me is that I probably have about 150 hoodies. My favourite brand is Bench and since I am a hoodie freak, my weakness is to buy a hoodie once a week.

Three things I won't leave home without are make-up, straightener and a joint.

When I was in the process of picking a dancer name, I always loved this one name. My parents were going to name my baby sister that but then changed their minds. Years ago I was talking to a waitress and she said I should pick that same name but I had already settled on it before she even told me. To this day, she thinks that she was the one to give me the idea. I just didn't have the heart to tell her that I had already decided on it beforehand.

The one thing that surprised me about this business is the bruises you get from working on the pole and crawling around on the stage. I also didn't realize how many good memories I would have because of all the great girls I work with every week. Before getting into this line of work, I wish I knew how hard of a time it would be getting out because the money is so good.

I've been a dancer now for eight years and my plan is to dance for another five. I've been volunteering at a nursing home for the past three years and my plan is to go to school and work with seniors full time.

I'm not ashamed to tell others what I do for a living. I feel I have to be upfront about it because people might recognize me. I was at an interview for a senior home job once and I recognized some of the nurses from the club and they recognized me too.

My advice for new girls getting into this business is to stay clear of the drugs and the party scene. Make sure you are doing it for the money and doing it to meet your goals. The most important thing I can pass on to new girls is to stay true to yourself. Don't let dancing change who you are as a person. I'm basically the same girl I was in high school, just grown up.

Regarding any regrets I have getting into this business; I would say yes and no. Yes, because you have a hard time getting out and you feel like you're trapped. You also have to deal with the judgment from others. I lost a lot of high school friends when they found out I became a dancer. At the same time, I have no regrets because of the money, the experiences and the traveling. It has helped me become a better person and I appreciate what I have.

# Bella Donna

I was 17 when my girlfriend and I started going to this nightclub that had stripper poles on the dance floor. We used to go there all the time and practice doing pole tricks. I always thought that strippers were famous and super cool. A year later, we met a stripper who was hanging out at the nightclub and she told us to check out the strip club she worked at, so we did.

I was 18 when I started and have been dancing now for four years. My first day on the job was so nerve wracking. It was a training day and I felt so nervous. I really had nothing to be nervous about, since we only had to get naked in front of five or six other girls, and we were all friends. I don't really remember the first few months I danced since I usually drank a mickey a day. I had to drink in order to feel comfortable socializing and talking to the guys.

My parents know what I do for a living. Although my mom is supportive, my dad wants to kill me. He can't stop me, though, because I don't live at home. My parents split up because my mom was a crack head (we only started to get along two years ago). My dad is a biker and he raised me. I was a crazy teenager, and partied way too much when I was young. I was on drugs from 13-16, and then got clean. I only drink alcohol now.

I love the attention, money and free drinks I get as a dancer. I love dressing up in fancy outfits and high heels since I'm a huge show off anyways. I love the attention. The sisterhood with the other dancers is great, and the instant VIP status I get when I say that I'm a stripper. I love the independence I have and the fact that I have met a lot of people and made a lot of friends. I have been lucky to travel and see two provinces.

I hate that this job is a constant party environment. This job is stressful and is full of old men, rude guys and many of the guys are always trying to grab you. I hate the drunk guys, drug addicts, cocky girls and the bitchy staff that work at some of the clubs.

I refuse to work at certain clubs, one in particular, because the competition there is so stiff. The girls that work at that bar are hookers on the side and I am not. I don't work at any bars where the staff disrespects me or where I don't get paid enough.

My stalkers are a group of three guys (one of them is a virgin) who follow me to many of the local bars. They tip me $5 when I'm on stage and always buy me a drink after my show.

Lap dances can get scary sometimes when guys try to grab you even though you have already explained that the dance is no contact. I have been grabbed and held down, while having my hair pulled. I have also been bit on the shoulder! This same guy followed me home, so I called the police. This has happened to me on more than one occasion.

With the bad, comes the good. I met a guy in the bar and we dated for two years (my ex-boyfriend). He falls into my good customer category.

I have a regular who buys me everything and doesn't try to sleep with me. He has helped me when I got in trouble once. I had no money and was stuck in Alberta. He paid for a plane ticket so I could get home.

One of the weirdest gifts I got was a bathing suit that was way too big for me, with some dollar store jewellery. The guy sat at front row and tipped me little chocolates wrapped in $5 bills. The nicest gift I got was a huge Guess shopping spree.

The biggest tip I ever got was $100. One time I saw a girl get almost $700 all in $20 bills stacked on top of each other like a house. She acted like it was nothing. I was blown away!

I have had a few embarrassing moments. Once, I was wondering why no one was clapping during my show, then I looked down and my tampon string was hanging out! No wonder it was a quiet show! Another time I was dancing hammered out of my mind. I fell off the stage backwards, cutting my leg and landing in a customer's lap. I was crying and bleeding for two more songs and I ended up getting $200 in pity tips!

I don't know who this is more embarrassing for, me or them, but I have had cousins and an uncle show up in towns they don't live in with girls other than their wives! Also, some of my girlfriends' boyfriends have shown up at bars I'm working at when I know full well they are not supposed to be in strip clubs at all.

The one thing that surprised me about this industry was how desperate some girls can be. I know that some people do drugs, party and have sex. That's fine, to each their own, and I am certainly not one to be judging anybody. But it is disgusting how some girls get so drunk they take off with a group of guys from the club to do God knows what. I heard one girl got gang banged and the whole thing was videotaped. And she didn't even get paid, she just did it because she is drunk and they were buying her drinks. You can get guys to buy you drinks in a normal bar and they don't expect a filmed gang bang! Check your head, ladies. These girls will lower themselves and suck off or screw some guy just so that he will give them some money or buy them drinks. It's also sad that some girls spend every penny they make on drugs.

I wish I knew how hard it would be not to drink. The temptation to drink is there all the time and everyone is offering you free drinks all day and night. I also wish I knew how it would screw with my head to have men always want to touch me. It's weird, but now I don't really like to be touched by anybody, even in my daily life. I'm surprised by how much I hate men and how some of them think it's perfectly fine to make vulgar comments like wanting to fuck me up the ass. It still shocks me.

Some personal things about me you would find interesting is that I am a third generation dancer. My grandma was a burlesque dancer and my mom was a table dancer in Toronto. Also, I am open to meeting guys in bars but most guys are too scared to approach me in the first place. My favourite part of the day is playing with my two hamsters. Three things I can't leave home without are my hairbrush, cell phone and pot.

I am proud of telling people, actually bragging, to them about what I do for a living. I don't regret getting into this business because I am twenty one years old and I have my own place, my own car, security and a lot of really nice things. I plan on dancing for another five years because I have a lot of money invested in it. It also depends on the industry.

My advice for new girls coming into this business is to maintain your dignity (translation: don't be a whore). It gives all dancers a bad name and the girls won't like you. You won't get any respect from the other dancers, the staff and especially from the patrons.

# Bird of Paradise

Five years ago, my husband and I brought a stripper pole home, mostly just for a laugh. I had always been intrigued by pole dancing and so after we got the pole I was determined to learn how to do it. At first, I just checked out some pole dancing videos online, and learned what I could from them. Then it happened; I discovered pole dancing competitions! I loved it! I did competitions for a few years and got pretty good at it. I was a tax consultant by day and because my work was seasonal, I needed to find something else to bring in some money. Today, I am a pole dancing instructor and a dancer.

I was 18 when I started dancing. Nobody asked to see my identification at the time. I started in a club that didn't serve alcohol, so 18 was considered legal in that establishment. At this same club two years earlier, there were rumours that a 14 year old was dancing there after showing fake ID.

The best way to explain my first day on the job is that I almost died because I was so nervous! Every time I was on stage, I sprinted across the stage from pole to pole instead of walking. I had it in my head that the faster I walked, the more impressive I looked. By the end of the day, I was so out of breath that I could barely move!

By the age of 19, I was dancing the circuit. When I leave for work every morning, the three things I won't leave home without are my wedding ring that I love with all my heart (my husband had it custom made for me which is diamond shaped like Hello Kitty; I collect Hello Kitty everything), my Hello Kitty necklace and my gold sneakers.

Some things you would find interesting about me is that every pair of shoes I own are gold in color. Also, I'm very health conscious as I don't drink and I don't do drugs. I don't even take Tylenol. You might not expect it, but I have a great relationship with both of my parents and my brothers. They are completely supportive of my job. My husband has no problems with it either. I love that he stays at home and is the 'stay at home dad' with our baby daughter while I get to go to a job that I enjoy. It works out well for us.

What I love about the business is that I get to meet many interesting people and work with some pretty cool dancers all the time. My favourite customer is a guy who makes me intricate origami with five dollar bills. He's made me an avatar bird and a mermaid. He has turned out to be one of my best friends as we send Christmas cards and cookies to each other during the holidays and he now does all my promotional materials for my job.

Although I meet some great people, I also meet the odd balls. One of the weirdest customers I've met is a guy with a foot fetish who gave me socks and wanted me to wear them for a week. Then he wanted me to give them back to him! I've had some embarrassing moments too. I recently had my most embarrassing moment on stage where my tampon string was hanging out and a customer pointed it out to me while I was spread eagle!

Apart from meeting creeps, another thing I hate about this industry is the misconceptions people have, thinking that all dancers are alcoholics, drug addicts and prostitutes. It's the opposite. The women in this industry continue to amaze me. Some do have problems, but most of them are definitely not substance abusers or pros, they are extraordinarily strong and resourceful.

To protect our privacy, dancers need a stage name. The first part of my dancer name has a historical meaning. It was a Celtic war cry when they wanted the queen to be murdered. I was kind of disappointed when people didn't understand that, and kept referring to a district near my city. As for the second part to my name, it just seemed to fit the best and it's basically a play on words for something private. We essentially construct another personality. Before I got into this line of work, I wish

I knew that if I was going to tell a little white lie, I should keep the story straight because customers talk to each other.

I absolutely do not regret getting involved in this business because I am having the time of my life and will always have the proof that I was young and beautiful!

My advice for any new girls wanting to get into this business is to be respectful to the other dancers because if you get on their bad side, they will eat you alive and you'll get a bad reputation. A bad attitude gets you nowhere.

# Blue Lotus

I used to look in the newspaper all the time under the adult section. There was always the same ad saying you could earn $300-$500 per day as a dancer. This ad appealed to me because I would have given anything to have money and be considered beautiful. When I was a kid, I wished upon a star every day that I would be beautiful and skinny.

When I was about 16, I overheard a group of guys talking about one of the girls at school. She was thin, blonde, confident and a stripper! She was in grade 12 and just old enough to work in the adult industry. The guys were all hyped up and going on about how hot and 'loaded' she was. At that moment, I knew that I would become a stripper too. I wanted to be the girl that guys talked about like that. Not only did they acknowledge her existence, but they saw her as someone special.

Throughout high school, I didn't have many friends and I went unnoticed for the most part. It wasn't completely my fault since my mom raised me and my sister by herself and we were one step above welfare. She was a broken soul who turned to religion as a way of coping. This wasn't a normal church, though. It was a lesser known faith where the women aren't allowed to wear pants, cut their hair, watch TV, listen to the radio or do anything at all really. So, everyday I went to school with a long, ratty skirt that was full of holes. It was the only skirt I owned and I had about three or four ugly shirts. My mom could only afford to buy me one outfit a year. The other students called me 'skirt girl.'

To make matters worse, I was on medication until grade eight for my epilepsy and was being given too strong of a dose. I couldn't communicate with the other kids because I couldn't even understand what they were saying. This was due to the high dosage of medication. I had no friends and I hadn't said a word all year. One day a new girl said to me, "How are you?"

and I panicked. I couldn't understand what she meant or how to respond to it.

I had a deep longing to be liked by everybody. I wanted people to notice and care whether I was there or not. My upbringing gave me such a complex. Even today, I think you have to be beautiful to be considered special.

Before I became a dancer, I worked my way into the adult world. I tried to get into porn with little luck. I would go to meet local amateur producers but they never called me back. I stopped trying for a bit when I turned 19.

I worked as a VIP dancer at a strip club and it was there that I learned how to talk to people. It took me a little over a year to get on the circuit even though I still wasn't very attractive at this point. They paid me $35 per show to work out of town, even though most girls were making more just working in town. I stuck with it regardless. I learned how to do my hair and my makeup and I worked my way up to a normal show price. I got the show price by switching agencies.

At this point, I was working all the time by bouncing between the local strip clubs. It was getting to the point that I needed to buy a car with all the travelling I was doing. I wanted a car as soon as possible and I was short on money for the down payment so I tried to get into porn again. I don't want to mention names but all the locals hate the man I first did a scene with. I went home crying after the scene and was physically sick. He purposely pushed my boundaries. I swore to myself I would never do porn again, but I broke that promise. A year later I got a call from a producer and was talked into it. He promised me that I would be treated right and that he would do whatever he could to make me feel comfortable. After the hour long phone call, I decided to go through with it again.

About a month after that, and about 10-20 scenes later, I got my tits done and had hair extensions put in. I also got some really nice promo done. I asked my dancing agent for a raise, and usually all of these improvements would entitle me to a raise (especially the implants), but my agency wouldn't book me above $45 a show. I was really upset and said, "fuck dancing." I was sick of the disrespect. I wanted glamour.

I moved to L.A. and made it as a porn star. I married someone in the industry but for legal reasons we had to move to Canada. We had a lawyer working on getting me a visa as his wife. Before it was all approved, our marriage fell apart. He told me that I wasn't allowed to dance or even leave the house. I stayed with him for four years even after he broke my nose because he thought I was checking out some DJ at a club. Now that I have left this loser, I have a new appreciation for life and for my independence.

I'm so happy to be dancing right now. I love what I do and love having control over my life. My wish did come true! I may not be in California but I have everything I could ever want. I'm going to school to get a degree so that I can spend the rest of my life surfing the waves in Hawaii!

Written by Blue Lotus

# Buttercup

For two years, I used to clean houses for people. I was also working at a temp agency and went to school at the same time. I found it hard to juggle this heavy work load with only four hours of sleep, especially when I was making such shitty money!

My cousin and I signed up to take a free course in pole dancing at a strip club. After the course was done, you had the option of working there as a VIP girl, which is what I did. My cousin quit. I decided to stay on, so my cousin helped me pick my stage name.

Doing private dances felt very awkward and weird at first. Although there is no contact, you dance very close to the customer. I hated getting all the weird and stupid comments from them. In time you get used to it and learn to grow a thick skin. I worked there for two and a half years and it was great to make some pretty good money. After that amount of time, the money just didn't seem as good as it was in the beginning. So, a few of us girls quit and took off to Alberta. We tried it out and eventually came back. My girlfriend was a month shy of turning 19, so we waited for her to turn of age and then we signed up with an agency. We wanted to work together, so we were booked at all the clubs at the same time.

The agent wanted me to start with some amateur contests and I refused. I told him that I wasn't an amateur anymore as I had been dancing as a VIP girl for two and a half years. He agreed and didn't argue.

I have been dancing now for four years and my mom is very supportive as long as I don't party and do drugs. We are very close and I refer to her as my best friend. She was a single mom on welfare while raising me. When I was little, my dad committed a crime and got sent back to Fiji. He was in jail and got murdered. Just before his death, my grandma passed away (we were very close). To this day, I think that I am still upset about my grandma's passing. Then my grandfather passed away shortly after. I was around eight years old and with three important people in my life passing away around the same time, it affected me in a big way.

This industry is pretty good, but it definitely has its moments. I love meeting new people and hearing their stories. You also get to experience things in this business that a regular person doesn't. I also love building close friendships with the girls. My favourite customer is an older gentleman named John who is very polite and fun to hang out with. He always leaves tips on the stage for all the dancers and he brings the party to life when there is no party! Mr. L is another one of my favourite customers.

One time, I was on stage doing my show when a customer at gyno asked me what my favourite kinds of baked goods are. I told him that I liked cinnamon buns. After my show, he disappeared and showed up later with two containers of cinnamon buns! He explained to me that he worked in a bakery. The biggest tip I ever got on stage was $300.

The one thing that I can't stand about my work is the cattiness from some of the girls. We all work together for the week so we should just get along. The other thing that makes me mad to know is that exotic dancing is considered prostitution. It's classified as the same; in the sex trade.

There is only one place I refuse to work on the circuit and it is because of all the creepy stories I hear from the other girls. I don't need to check it out for myself, I'm happy to learn from their mistakes.

My embarrassing moment was when my heel broke on stage and I danced like that for my whole show. Thank goodness, I have never had a male friend, uncle or dad show up where I work unexpectedly but once my landlord came into the strip club and I think he recognised me. That was pretty weird.

Some personal things I don't mind sharing is that I am a

very down to earth kind of girl. One of my favourite things to do is to curl up at home and watch movies. I also love animals and one day I would love to work with them in rescue. When I was going to school for modeling and acting, I spent $15,000 on my training and education. The one thing I can't leave home without is one very important item worth mentioning, my phone!

Before getting into this business, I wish I knew about the mind games that screw with your head. You feel that you always have to look your best, you shouldn't have any cellulite and that you need to have fake boobs. The industry definitely changes you as a person. I have always said that I was going to be an all-natural kind of girl, but I got caught up in the whole image thing and got my lips done, dyed my hair blonde and now I'm even thinking of getting a boob job. It's hard not to cave in to the demands of this industry. There's one area where I won't bend my rules; I'm proud to say that I held my ground and stayed away from the drugs and crazy partying lifestyle.

I am not ashamed to tell people what I do for a living. If they don't like it, that's too bad. It's not my fault they live in a bubble. Everyone gets naked every day; the only difference for me is that I do it in front of a bunch of people and I get paid.

This industry has been a big part of my life, and I do not regret getting into it. I'm glad I had the opportunity to do it. I learned a lot and I am a good, strong person as a result. I was a very shy and innocent kind of girl before I embarked on my dancer journey and I wouldn't be who I am today if I didn't get into this industry. I plan on dancing as long as I possibly can.

My advice for new girls coming into this business is to listen to the older dancers. Not many girls will give you advice to help you out, so take it if it is offered to you. Try to be a strong person, not gullible or naïve. Some girls get roped in with the drugs and bad people which seem like the highlight of their life, then one day their eyes open and BAM! They realized that they have wasted some good years and a lot of money.

# Calla Lily

I grew up in a small town in the Maritimes and had always dreamed of moving to a bigger city; a place with more opportunities to make more money and have a better life. Throughout high school, the trend seemed to be to graduate and move to the west coast. The west coast was bigger, better, beautiful and of course it's where all of the great weed was! Moving to BC was *the* thing to do. You move there, grow dope, cut dope, sell dope and make tons of money. So, two weeks after I graduated high school, I made my move and took off to the west coast. Many people from home already lived here so I quickly became involved in the 'growing' world.

I met my boyfriend at a 'pick' and we started dating. He was involved in some business that wasn't exactly legitimate, so most of his meetings with his 'business associates' took place in exotic show lounges. He always seemed to be going on and on about the dancers, the strippers, the peelers, etc. Being the insecure 18 year old that I was, I was somewhat bothered by this (ok, I was really bothered by it).

What made those women better than me? At this point I had still never been inside a strip bar. It seemed as though he thought that strippers were the be-all and end-all of women. As his girlfriend, I wanted to feel like I was the greatest woman in his world, not these faceless girls from the strip club. I'm sure any woman wants to feel this in their relationship, no matter how young or old.

We went on a cross country trip, back home to the Maritimes for business and to visit family. With 42 pounds of dope in the truck, he decided to stop overnight in Montreal rather than play it safe and drive through. Montreal, the strip club capitol of Canada. Gee... I wonder why he wanted to stop there? Anyway, I decided to be the cool girlfriend and join him in the club, instead of my usual routine of sitting in the car waiting for him. We were on vacation after all!

Two things happened. First off, I instantly felt a great respect and appreciation for what these beautiful and confident, courageous and talented women were doing on stage. Dancing exotically, gracefully and artistically and further more making a lot of money! I had never had the privilege of earning money like these women were obviously doing.

Second, my boyfriend got up and left me at the table for half an hour to get private dances. There I was, all alone with my mixed emotions: fury, embarrassment and rage that my boyfriend was paying to have a beautiful naked woman dance for him. Strangely, this still didn't deter my appreciation for what I had seen earlier on stage. I stormed out of there and went back to our hotel and proceeded to smash his $400 custom glass bong into a million pieces. That was a start, but in my mind, that wasn't enough.

This little incident got me thinking. I was always an okay looking girl. I was always outgoing and I enjoyed being the center of attention. I then thought back to when I was younger and had won a dance competition. I knew that I had rhythm. My new plan clicked into place – revenge! If you can't beat 'em, join 'em!

I waited for the perfect time. I was secretly researching on how to enter this lucrative world of nakedness and found my answer. The ad read, 'Make up to $1500 a week as an exotic dancer.'

My boyfriend had been planning a trip back east to go to a friend's wedding. He didn't want me to go with him (needless to say, this relationship was on the rocks). He left for the trip and then off I went on my new adventure. A friend of mine had picked me up from my current job as a waitress and we made the trek downtown.

I had told myself that if I wasn't good at it, then I wouldn't continue. Turns out, I was really good at it. When my boyfriend got home from his trip, I had already transformed into a dancer. I kept it up for about a month after his return, working my waitressing shift, and then doing the hour long drive to the strip club to work my shift there, and he didn't notice. Finally, he accused me of cheating because I was out so late all the time. I wasn't getting home from the club until 3:30 am. I then handed him the strip club matchbook and the questions started flying! I told him exactly what I had done, and that I was proving a point. I told him that since he liked strippers so much, I thought I should become one to get his attention. He still didn't believe me so I pulled out my freshly purchased, yet already scuffed boots and the $1400 I had made the previous week and there were no more questions. Only a look of shock!

Revenge was sweet! It still is. Eight years later, with pictures published in *Playboy*, two awards for favorite floor show performer, and having met some of the greatest people I know, including my two best friends, I feel that this has been the most rewarding decision I've ever made.

I don't regret it one bit and I never will. If it wasn't for jealousy and my extreme need to prove a point (I'm an Aries, I can't help it), this would have never happened. Thanks to my ex-boyfriend for being a pervert!

I am truly a believer of life leading you to where you're supposed to be. I have a reason to believe this. When I was young, my father travelled for sports tournaments all over Canada. He gave me a stuffed bear when I was four from one of his trips. I carried that bear with me everywhere! When I moved to BC years later, my father decided he would send it to me as a cute memory. When he was wrapping it up for the mail, he remembered where he bought it – Vancouver. Funny how that bear spent its whole life with me, and then I brought it home.

My advice for new girls who are looking to get into this industry is to take it seriously, but still have fun with it. If you're going to become a dancer, do it right and go all the way with costumes, promo and professionalism. And only do it if it makes you happy!

Written by Calla Lily

# Camellia

I got into this industry 11 years ago. I was 18.

When my boyfriend and I moved to BC, I was going to school part time and working part time at a coffee shop. We moved to a little cottage on the beach but my boyfriend had lost his job and we could no longer afford the place. He didn't tell me about this problem until two days before our rent was due. I saw an ad in the newspaper and it said that a girl could make $300-$1000 per night dancing. I mentioned it to my boyfriend – I said that I could just do it for two days to make the rent money and then quit. He agreed, so I called the ad on Thursday and by Sunday I had made $1700. Guess who quit the coffee shop!

My first day on the job I wore a red snakeskin jumpsuit and I was truly terrified. I found the whole experience actually quite humiliating because I fell while trying to get it off in my heels. The only nice thing about the whole experience was that people still cheered and were nice to me.

I danced at that club for a year, and then one of the other dancers told me it was silly for me to be there since I could make better money elsewhere. I called the local agency and they told me to go do an amateur contest. I was told that if I got some gear and won the contest, then I would be guaranteed consistent work. I won! My boyfriend and I bought a new vehicle, rented a nicer place and we concentrated on his band.

I was just 19 when I hit the circuit and left home. My first tour was five weeks straight on the road which is a long haul but by the time it was over I had made $8000. After that I didn't mind hitting the circuit! My next move was to try travelling outside of BC but my boyfriend missed me too much, so I stayed local. He was a bit of a problem, though. He was a major pothead and when we had moved to our new city apartment, he lost one job after another.

When we moved to another apartment in the city, my

boyfriend had the idea that we should start growing dope. We lived in a rough part of town with helicopters constantly flying overhead. "Trust me, it'll be low profile," he said. But I came home from work one day and noticed that he hadn't taped up the windows. There was a glow from the lights in the basement like you wouldn't believe! We were not good at this new venture and scrapped the idea. The plants all died anyways.

My boyfriend was manically in love with me and said that he would kill himself if I ever left him. It was frustrating for me because he never seemed to have a job and always emptied my wallet for 'lunch money.' I couldn't support him anymore, so when he left for the day, I put half our stuff into a moving truck and left. I made my mom promise not to tell him where I disappeared to, but he still found me three months later. He fell to his knees and sobbed that he couldn't live without me. Although this was the six year mark of our relationship, I didn't go back to him.

My next relationship was way better. I met my husband at a tradeshow and soon after we met, I decided to quit dancing and focus on a new career with him. We got married, had kids, and started our own business in real estate. Things were going great until the market tanked. We went from making $120,000 to living on our credit cards and having trouble to make ends meet. I made the decision to return to dancing temporarily to pay some bills and help keep the household running. It's what I have to do to support my family, but it's not what I imagined I'd be doing at 29, years after retiring from this industry.

My family knew that I was a dancer before I met my husband. They don't know that I have gone back to dancing recently though.

My mom and dad separated when I was young. I say 'separated' but what really happened is that Mom and I were left for a 26 year old blackjack dealer at a casino. My father left one day after he completely emptied the house. He took everything, and only left us with two seat cushions. I was never abused but I do think that because my dad deserted us I may have some abandonment issues as a result.

My mom is a born again Christian. One of my sisters is an environmental scientist that has gone to university for 11 years and my other sister has been in university for four years. I am the black sheep of the family. I am always battling with myself over whether or not dancing is morally okay for me to do. Personally, I think I have a bit of an addiction to dancing.

I love the money (the biggest tip I ever got was $1000 on stage). I also love the sisterhood with the girls I work with. It's like a big party in the change room. I don't dislike the positive attention since I find it quite flattering.

There are only a couple things I hate about my job. One is when men are being really slimy and stick their tongues out at you doing the licking motion while you're on stage. The other thing I hate is that it's really hard to get into the character of my stage persona and get my 'fuck me' face on sometimes. I'm a wife and mother!

As for stalkers, Pockets is the closest to a stalker I've gotten. He travels around from strip bar to strip bar with a pocket full of flyers from other strip clubs. When I got back into dancing, I ran into him and he yelled my old stage name at me. He pulled a stack of flyers out of his pocket, leafed through them and pulled one out that had me on it from six years earlier with my old stage name! My weirdest customer is the sock guy.

Here's a scary story: I was a rookie, only two months into dancing, when a group of bikers came into the bar. One of them asked for a private dance and I was the girl he picked. He wanted me to dance for him in a hidden area in the corner of the bar. As I was dancing with my back to him, he had yanked his cock out and pulled me on top of him. I freaked out, fought him off and ran out. The manager shuttled me into a secret tunnel that ran under the stage ending at a secret room. He told me to wait there until they left. I sobbed until he came back a short time later. He said to me, "The guys are gone now, so you can come out. I want you to never mention what happened here to anyone. Now, get to work please." I was stunned that he would just sweep it under the rug and expected me to get back to business!

When I was about 19 or 20, I was working out of town. At the end of my first show a big bouquet of roses were thrown on stage for me. When I went outside, a biker was standing there waiting for me and said that he was the one who threw the roses. Every day after that, he would wait for me and ask me if I wanted to go for a ride on his motorcycle. I turned him down every time. One day, another one of the dancers asked me if I wanted to go to another bar for some drinks, so we headed over to the club. When we got there, the biker was there waiting for me with all his friends. That dancer had lured me there! Without even speaking to the guy, I left the bar and walked all the way back to the strip club. Other than that bar, I will work almost anywhere. I only refuse to work at bars that cancel shows because then I won't have a decent paycheque.

Something that you would find interesting about me is that I love gardening. I have an impressive garden full of veggies and flowers as a result.

Three things I won't leave home without are my cigarettes, pot and lip gloss.

When I was choosing my stage name, I remembered this foxy little French girl who had a thick accent. She rode a motorcycle, wore no make up and had sexy sandy blonde hair that fell out of her motorcycle helmet when she took it off and shook it all over. I thought she was hot as hell. I used her stage name.

One thing I wish I knew before getting into this business was how addictive this job is. After getting into the industry, I was surprised that who you know and how social you are has a lot to do with things like getting booked for work.

Am I ashamed of telling people what I do for a living? Absolutely! Only because of the circles I travel in now. I'm a soccer mom and I would be mortified if the other parents found out. I only regret getting into this business now that I'm a mother. God forbid my daughter got any scrutiny because of me. This job isn't main stream and when some people find out that I'm a dancer, they treat me like I'm a prostitute. I plan on dancing for a couple more weeks and then I'm out. I'm thinking of going back to school and study nursing.

My advice for new girls coming into the business is to keep your ears open and your mouth closed.

# Cannabis

Five years ago, I was a full time apprentice carpenter while I also worked the reception desk at a high end gym on Saturdays. A couple of women came into the gym and started teaching pole dancing. They gave me a free class, so I took it for the fitness aspect. I was hooked!

I was sent to the Okanogan for six weeks to go through some apprenticeship training. While there, I heard about some amateur contests that were held on Sundays at the local strip club. I went with a couple girl friends to check out my first strip club and I remember thinking, "I can do that!" Since I wasn't working for six weeks while I was in school, I thought that I would try it out. My first time on stage, I wasn't nervous but I had a few butterflies. There were only about 10 customers in the room and a few of my friends. While trying out some crazy pole moves and wiping out twice, the bar still liked me and asked me to come back, saying that they would pay me $35 per show. During those six weeks, I made $150 per week. After calling the local agency, they set me up to be a fill-in girl.

I was doing a job renovating a house. In eight hours, I would swing my hammer and make $100. Then I would shower, change, and go compete in an amateur contest in the evening. In that hour, I would usually win the contest and make $100!

I was getting restless in my construction job and I thought that I would go full time into dancing. I told my sister I would only do it for a year, mostly for her sake but I knew that I would be doing it longer. I was really open about my new career change with my sister, which ended up being a mistake. She told my brothers, and then my youngest brother (who was 19 at the time) sent a really long email to my mom, telling her about my plans. When mom contacted me about it, I denied it.

To this day, my mom doesn't know what I do for a living. I told her that I am a traveling hotel worker for a major hotel chain and that they have a new program where five of us are trained for the front desk. This little lie works because when my mom calls me and I am out of town, she thinks I am working at another hotel.

There are a lot of reasons I love my job. I love entertaining, being self employed, traveling, taking summers off and of course, the money. I also like being able to see the many different personalities and challenge myself to sell to each one. There are so many experiences to learn from in this industry or to have a good laugh at.

I also love the fact that you can work and keep living your life at the same time. For example, you can do a show and then take off to do your grocery shopping or do homework right after. The freedom is great!

I love that I am doing something different and unique from other people. I also like the hedonism (immediate satisfaction) that guys get from what I give them. I'm serving the erotic and exotic. Guys work hard and then come into the bar looking to let loose and I am giving them the gratification. In return I am making money for providing that satisfaction. In my opinion, there's nothing wrong with that.

On the other hand, I hate the stereotypes. I was at a restaurant not too long ago with a friend and the server asked us what we did for a living. I told him that I was an exotic dancer and his response was, "Oh, I should REALLY get your number!" It's like people think that we are skanks or hookers.

I hate that I can't be completely honest about what I do for a living. I'm in sales now and a business colleague told me that I wouldn't have been hired if I told the truth about my past at the interview (my boss knows now). It's too bad because working in this industry taught me a lot that helps me in my sales job.

There is one strip club that I refuse to work at. I was supposed to be there for a week and a half (Friday until two Sundays later). I only lasted half a week. When I showed up, I had to pay the bar $2 for a towel. They provided us with sheets and a blanket.

I went to the dancer house and I was totally creeped out. The mattresses were disgusting to the point of me not wanting to sit on them, let alone sleep on them! When I opened up the pink flannel blanket given to me, there was an enormous hole in it! I basically held the perimeter of the blanket in my hands. From that trip onward, I knew that I would always travel with my own bedding. When the DJ came to the house, I complained about the blanket and he responded with, "Well, what did you expect, The Ritz?" I said to him, "No, but I do want a blanket to cover me and keep me warm!" I also saw three mice in one day, so I can't imagine how many mice ran through the house that we didn't see. The house was really old and creepy and I was concerned for my security since everyone in that town knew it was the dancer house.

At that bar they did many theme shows. One of them was a flashlight show that was done a couple nights a week. They shut all the lights off and gave customers flashlights to shine at the dancers' vagina. I could not see, so I took tiny little steps in a circle and I basically just stood there during my show so that I wouldn't kill myself by falling off the stage.

Another one of their theme shows was the paint show. Dancers had to paint their naked body and right after, do a shower show. The bar had a garden hose that ran along the upper part of the ceiling and the DJ would roll out a three by three plexi-glass basin that you had to step into and wash the paint off your body. It was okay if you were the first girl, but the third girl was standing in all the filth from the first and second girl. I was lucky to be the first girl.

I couldn't handle the uncleanliness in the dancer house anymore so I asked the bar if they could put me up in a hotel. They said that they didn't have the budget for that, so I told them to pay me for my four days of work and I would leave. They fined me for two shows because I was leaving early and I only got paid for 10 shows instead of my 12. I remember asking the bar if it was mandatory to do the theme shows. Their response was that it was not mandatory, but if you refused to do them, you would be fined $50. That sounds pretty mandatory to me! It worked out in the end for me anyways because I ended up going to work at another club not too far away. They were looking for a replacement girl since someone had quit.

I wouldn't mind going back to that bar again but only if I stayed in my own camper or another hotel. It was a pretty sweet gig working from nine to two. When I was new to the business, the theme shows bothered me, but now they wouldn't.

Another crazy story was when I was working a Sunday night doing my first amateur contest. I hooked up with another dancer and since we clicked, she brought me under her wing. We partied all night which was great, but I had an exam for my construction school the next day. That morning she said, "I'm coming to class with you!" I was the only girl in the class and it was an advantage because nobody was going to argue with me bringing a stripper friend into class. Not only did she insist on taking the exam, she got 65 percent! During lunch break, we were doing bumps (coke) in the bathroom. When she got bored, she left. I told my instructor that I had to go home because I wasn't feeling too hot so he let me go.

My scary episode happened when I was brand new in the business and doing a fundraiser when my jealous ex showed up. At the end of the night when I was leaving, some of the staff and dancers were standing around in the parking lot. They were really alarmed and told me that some guy was hiding behind my truck, so the bouncer came out and told the guy to leave. We realized it wasn't a stalker, just my ex creeping around.

I don't have any creeper stories, just number one fans. There is a customer who is in his early 60's and he writes poems for the girls. He will drive three hours out of town to see his favourite dancers and stay overnight in a hotel. When he gets private dances, he moans my name during the entire dance. He always asks me if he can cup my bum, so I let him because he pays me $200. He is a very respectful and almost hesitant kind of guy who thanks me like crazy. He's very sweet, but in a creepy kind of way too (if that even makes any sense?!). The DJs are convinced that he is a pedophile.

Another one of my fans is a poor soul who seems down on his luck. He has asked me to go out on a date with him and he's even asked me to be his girlfriend once. I just like to be sweet to him because I feel sorry for him.

I met my weirdest customer when I was sitting with some guys once while shooting the shit. One of them asked me for a private dance and after I was done the dance, we started talking. We got on the subject of drinking pee. I thought he was screwing around with me until he said, "So, how much do you want if I were to drink your pee?" I was joking around with him and asking him how we would do it. I asked him if we would grab a tarp so I didn't pee all over the floor. He ignored the question but kept asking me numerous times how much money I wanted to let him drink my pee. I humoured him and told him $200. He agreed to it and said he would pay! Just the thought of this disgusting act was a pretty dominating thing. How many girls can say that they pissed on a guy and got paid to do it?

Then he said, "If it makes you feel uncomfortable, you can go to the bathroom and pee in a glass and bring it back to me." I was floored and not sure what to do. It would be a pretty easy way to make $200! I wasn't sure what I should do so I went to the DJ and told him of this plan, and asked if I was allowed to do it. The DJ screamed, "No!" I should have just done it and not told the DJ. I would've been $200 richer.

My best customers are the magpies! I don't like to toot my own horn, but I created them. They are a group of regular guys who know each other through the bar. It's a special men's club who hang out at the strip club together. When their favourite dancer goes on stage, they flock down to the stage and tip her $5. They love when I come up to their table and say, "Hello, my magpies!" It turned into a great little marketing gag at the bar.

The nicest gift I got was when a customer took me shopping and spent $1000 on me and then made me lobster. In one store he bought me a leather jacket, motorcycle boots, a big plush blanket, an entire luggage set, a purse and a scarf. After the shopping trip, I went to his house where he made me lobster. This is the only time I have ever gone to someone's home, only after I did some homework by talking to the owner and staff. I was told that he was a very nice regular and has been known for quite some time. As a precaution, I left a note on my table of this person's address, should I disappear. Other nice gifts I receive are poems and some quick sketches from the artists that come into the bar.

One of my favourite gifts came from the magpies on my birthday. They gave me a singing Southpark card (I love Southpark) that they all signed. Each guy gave me some random gift such as lotion, a mini lava lamp and ribbon that said, "Kiss me, it's my birthday!" Other than the $1000 shopping spree, I got a $100 bill on stage once.

My most embarrassing moment was when I got my period on stage. I got spotting on my legs so I grabbed my blanket and tried to wipe it off. I covered myself with my blanket and finished up my show. To make it even worse, some acquaintances of mine who I go to metal concerts with had come into the bar to see my show for the first time. We still haven't really talked since the 'period incident' as it was pretty awkward for all of us.

The one thing that surprised me about this business was how many girls I couldn't really relate to. Also, I became more jaded than I thought I would.

Before getting into this business, I wish I knew how tempting this job is. I constantly wonder how long I can push my luck by working my day job and still dancing without the owner finding out. My position is fairly high profile since I'm the owner's right hand woman. I am in charge of sales and marketing, dispatching the calls and he trusts me with all the company's information. He knows that I used to work as a dancer but I think that he may suspect I'm doing it now, because he pays me only $800 for the month and I obviously can't live on that. It's tricky to keep it quiet, but I think of ways. For example, I will be going to the island to do some training for my sales job. Since the company is paying for my ferry and hotel, I might as well work a few shifts at the local strip bar and make a few extra bucks!

Being busy is good in my books since I've always kept myself busy while dancing. I went to school for three and a half years, did construction, was a server at a trendy restaurant, worked in sales for a marketing communication firm for school and I made jewellery.

Something that you would find interesting about me is that when I was 18 months old, I pulled a tea kettle off the counter and spilled the scalding water onto myself. I got second degree burns all over my left arm and part of my face. In the beginning, the agency was concerned that this would be a problem, but actually the only people that seem to notice or even comment on it are people that have burns themselves, or the ones that are fascinated with scars. The other amusing thing about me is that I am a self proclaimed spreader! Three things I won't leave home without are baby wipes, shoes and CDs.

I'm not ashamed of telling people what I do for a living, but I hate that I can't tell everybody. It's not the shame, it's the stigma. It is understandable though as not everyone goes to strip clubs. I was 21 when I did my first amateur contest and I plan on dancing as long as I can swing it. I started on the circuit when I was 22 and I've been dancing now for five years. Why stop now?

My advice for new girls coming into this business is this: dancing is not going to last forever. You should always have something on the go and be ready for your next move. Save your money or do something with it, like buy a home or invest it. It's a good idea to track how much money you're making since it's easy to blow it all. By keeping track of your money, you can compare how much you make each year and how much at which bar.

I do not regret getting into this business because it's the best thing I ever did. It is the only thing I did in my life that I feel I was meant to do.

# Cherry Blossom

I grew up with my dad. He raised me so that I could have a normal childhood because my mom was a crack head. When I turned 14, I insisted on meeting my mom and I moved in with her. She was responsible when she looked after me, but things started getting too much for me when I would come home and find Jamaican drug dealers hanging out in our house. I even found out her transvestite friends were borrowing my clothes! This was too much for me to handle so I eventually moved out.

In high school, my best friend babysat for a couple who were strippers. She also babysat for another (retired) dancer who lived down the hallway from them. She suggested that I try dancing, so I did.

The year was 1997 and the two of us went to Quebec. It was the first bar I had ever set foot in as we walked down a set of creepy stairs to the club. Everyone spoke French except me. I showed the manager my dancer friend's ID so I could work; I was just 18, at that time, not of legal age.

At this club, I saw my first naked girl. She was dark black, dancing slowly on stage. She completely mesmerized me. In a daze, I went into the dressing room and I will never forget the smell of perfume, pot and body odour. My first day on the job, I was really nervous so I drank test tube shots. This was my first introduction to getting wasted. I was drunk and walked out onto the stage with my arms wide open and I thought I was a star. All I could think was, "Look at me, I'm so pretty and I'm naked. Everyone loves me!"

My first year of dancing, I got drunk every single night. It was insane. My girlfriend and I had a pretty crazy schedule working from noon until three in the morning. The bar had crazy events like mud wrestling and threesome nights. There were 50 girls working the floor at one time doing VIP dances.

The bar was always busy and a girl could easily make $1000 a night if she hustled.

I was almost 20 when I decided I needed a change from Quebec, so I went to work in Ontario. I met my kids' dad in a club and we fell in love. We started dating and he ended up going to jail for three months. When he was released he came back to me and started living off me. His brother was moving to BC to start a grow-op and told us to come with him, convincing us that we'd all become millionaires. I was four months pregnant at the time and we hopped on a greyhound bus and ended up living in an awful house infested with rats.

Shortly after, I got pregnant again and we moved again to run a bigger grow-op. My boyfriend and I fought a lot and had a very destructive relationship. While fighting one day, he broke my nose. He was a very evil person that would find it funny to trip the baby when he was learning to walk towards me.

I had taken the kids to the babysitter one night because we were supposed to have a party. The cops came and busted us, arresting everyone in the house. I had to leave, so I took my kids and went to stay with a girlfriend. It didn't last, though. My boyfriend sweet talked me back. So I moved back in with him and we moved again to start yet another grow-op. He was starting to act normal and stopped being psycho for about a month – until he got into crack. Then we got busted again. My oldest child was in grade one and the younger one wasn't in school yet. I was in jail for two weeks and I was terrified of losing my kids! When I got out, I told my boyfriend that I couldn't stay in this destructive lifestyle. He agreed and got a job as a truck driver and we moved into a basement suite. Unfortunately, he got addicted to crack even worse during this time and we were evicted from our home twice. That was it; I needed to make a change for my kids and myself!

I wanted to start dancing again to make some money, so I walked into the strip club and talked to the manager. I didn't have any money, clothes or shoes but he hired me anyways so I could do some VIP dances and start making money right away. Then I called my girlfriend who called her brother to come pick me up with my kids and one Tupperware bin full of the kids clothes. I left the rest of my stuff behind and basically disappeared.

I worked at the strip club for seven months. I later found out my ex was in jail for eight years because he robbed almost eight banks in one day. He even punched some of the tellers in the face!

I was now making money and had costumes, so I called the agency and spent three and a half hours on the phone with the agent. Aside from my VIP dances, I was working as a fill-in girl at my strip club for girls that were sick or late.

Three months went by and I met a guy at the club. He was a gorgeous artsy type who pretended to be a biker and who bought many private dances from me. He said he was off the tugboats for three weeks and came by to see me at my work almost every day. One night, I was at a nightclub with three of my girlfriends and he found us sitting with three hot guys. He slid up to talk to me and we ended up going to his after-hours club. He said he was engaged and also said he wanted to continue hanging out with me. When I went to work out of town, he followed me and told me his fiancé had mental problems. He mentioned that he didn't want to break up with her until she was done with school. True to his word, he split up with her when she finished her course, then he sold their condo and moved in with me and my kids.

Life was fantastic! He was a really attentive man who would draw me a bath with real lilies floating in it. We would never fight and he was never mean to me. Years later, my kids call him dad, we got married and he had no problem with me dancing.

I was still working, but more and more I looked forward to going home at the end of my shift and hanging out with my family. I didn't hang out at work anymore. It got to the point where I needed a change so I quit dancing and was a waitress for one and a half years.

Two days before my kid's birthday party, my husband tells me that he has something important to talk to me about. The day of the birthday party comes and goes and after the guests leave, we start to talk. I didn't know it, but from that point on, I would never trust a man again. He informs me he has been hanging out at the strip club getting private dances. Then he said that during the four and a half years we were together, he had 27 incidents with prostitutes! He gave me every detail – he said that some of them had no teeth, some were shaking from the drugs they were high on and one of them was shooting up. He said that he would jerk off to his social networking website while looking at photos of my friends. He insisted that he was a sex addict.

My mom told me to stay with him for the security until the kids grew up and left, but all of my best friends told me that I had to leave him. I knew I couldn't be with him any longer. I couldn't even stomach looking at him! He didn't want me to leave him and said he would do anything if I would go through counselling with him. I wanted to fuck him up so I said I would go through the counselling with him if he paid for my boob job. At the time of this writing, I go for surgery tomorrow!!

He was active with the kids for a bit and his mom babysits them from time to time. I didn't want to disrupt their lives too much, but I did move them out of his place. We are living with one of my girlfriends and her daughter. I can continue to work when he takes them, so I benefit as well. Every second week I get to hang out with my kids and friends. I still can't look at him, let alone trust him. He hurt me too bad. Recently, he is threatening to sue me for a TV and has stopped being so active with the kids.

My mom and I have not really spoken much in years but my sister knows what I do for a living. My dad and his wife (she's like a mom to me) have no clue what I do for a living. I don't think he'd be disappointed, but I know he would expect more from me. They don't know about the boob job I'm getting tomorrow and since they're coming to visit next week, I will definitely be hiding under my hockey jersey.

I was 18 when I started dancing and I am now 32. It has been 14 years with some time off, so technically I have been dancing for eight years. I'm a spur of the moment kind of girl so I don't know how much longer I plan on dancing. I quit dancing and started waitressing on a whim so who knows what I'll do day to day.

I'm on stress leave from my waitressing job right now. When I started there, I clicked with the manager and loved working with the staff. I got the hang of the job with no problem and I really enjoyed working there. Although I am dancing right now to make some good money, I plan on going back there soon since it's a job I really enjoy and have fun at.

I love working in this industry because I love the people. I get along with everyone. I love the freedom to come and go; 20 minutes of work and then I can take off until my next show. I don't have to answer to anyone if I want a day off – I just book it. I also love the glory and how pretty I feel when people applaud for me.

It seems like every place I work at, I don't like something. Depending on the bar, I hate the distance I have to travel there, the schedule, the big breaks between shows or the $50 show price caps! Another thing I've noticed is the catty dancers. Years ago, the girls weren't into sabotage. Not too long ago, I witnessed a girl pissing into another girl's suitcase. Scratching another girl's CDs on purpose out of jealousy is also unnecessary bullshit.

The closest I got to having a stalker was this one guy I danced for at an out of town strip club. During the dance he said he was in love with me and asked me out to dinner. I said no, but he followed me everywhere anyways. I just ran away from him and was able to get away because he was so slow.

A creepy episode was when I was giving a man a private dance and noticed that the guy was jerking off while I danced for him!

I would say that my favourite customers are the magpies, Pockets (a guy who fills his back pockets with the little flyers from the local strip clubs) and the sock guy (who buys your used socks for $10 and gives you a new pair). Some gifts given to me over the years from customers are teddy bears thrown on stage and a t-shirt from a stag party. The biggest tip I got was $300 from a guy who just threw it on stage.

My most embarrassing moment was when I was on stage filling in for a girl. I looked down at the customers in gyno and noticed my landlord sitting there! I tripped on my skirt, fell on my knee, fell on my other knee and then fell on my face. It was less than graceful.

Something amusing about me is that I'm a soccer mom and proud of it! When I leave for the day, three things I can't leave the house without are my smokes, weed and car keys.

Before getting into this business, I wish I would have taken a makeup course because I could have used it back then. I find that many rookies don't know how to do their makeup properly.

I am only ashamed to tell other kid's parents what I do for a living because I don't want to involve my kids or embarrass them.

My advice for new girls coming into this business is to quit and don't even bother starting out. I find that there is no more money in this industry anymore unless you go to Alberta. The dancers seem to get nastier to each other and are always attacking one another by ripping each other off. It's just not worth it.

Even so, I don't have any regrets getting into this business. I love it and it has made me a stronger person.

# Clover

I was 17 when I moved out of my parents' house and in with my boyfriend. He dumped me and left me with my first apartment. I knew I couldn't live off of minimum wage, so I went down to the local strip club and they trained me after hours. This club didn't serve alcohol, so it was legal for a girl to work there at the age of 18. I started doing VIP dances on my 18th birthday!

My very first lap dance, I didn't know that the guy was supposed to prepay me. After the dance was over, he jumped up and ran out the door and down the street. The out of shape doorman ran after him but lost him. I was stiffed $25 for my first lap dance ever, and to top it off it was on my birthday! First lesson learned; no matter what, the customer must always prepay.

My first day on the job, my body was physically shaking and I couldn't stop sweating. I was nervous at first to get naked, but it was actually not that bad once I had taken all my clothes off. I made $600 that first night.

At $25 per dance, I was making about $500 a night. I was good at my job and made a lot of money, so that pissed off the other girls and they wanted to get rid of me. I found out from management that some of the girls were emailing the bar and pretending to be my parents. I explained that my parents didn't know that I was dancing so that wasn't possible. These girls even followed me home, broke into my apartment and stole some of my stuff. The bar told me that I was too much trouble, so they were letting me go. I got some fake ID and went down to the local agency. They hired me and put me on the circuit.

My family knows what I do for a living. My dad is nice but acts awkward around me on the subject, mumbling to me to be careful. I know that my mom doesn't like it but if she wants a relationship with me and my son (he's five months old now) then she has no choice but to accept it. However, she doesn't want me dancing in my hometown, where she lives. I have no choice because I am limited by the number of clubs available to me since I do not travel out of town because of my baby.

My parents split up when I was three. When I was six years old, my dad was 'bad' and went to jail so I didn't see him for a few years. My mom was a wonderful woman who never drank or did drugs. I was raised with manners and strict rules. She made sure that I took school seriously and I did since I got straight A's throughout high school.

My sister helped me choose my stage name, and she doesn't mind my job at all. I was hanging out with my older sister and some of her friends one night and they all threw names at me until we came up with one that I liked.

I love dancing and the creative integrity of being able to choose my own music, theme and costume. It's funny when customers assume that all dancers are trained because the majority of us are not.

I hate the fact dancers don't get tipped by customers anymore because they think that we make a lot of money. Many people don't realize that most clubs already have a price cap of $50. We have to hope that some of our shows aren't cancelled which really affects our paycheque, and then on top of that we get deductions just like everybody else. Our deductions are for music usage, HST, 'manager' fees, accommodations and of course the agency's percentage. We also have costumes, makeup and shoes to pay for. We pay for our traveling fees (gas, ferry or plane fare) and hotel, not to mention eating out all the time. So, unless we get tipped, in reality we're not making a whole lot for taking our clothes off!

I hate it when guys try to lick my boobs when I get close to them in a private dance. Last month I must have had about ten guys lick me! I react by taking the heel of my hand and slamming it into the side of their head.

Some nights it's all worth it, though. I especially love the nights I make a shit load of tips. I cram it in my bag and when

I get home, I dump it on the floor and find out I made $800. It makes me excited and gives me comfort as well as security.

My best customer is a guy who bought $700 worth of half hour private dances, all in one night. I told him that I got my learner's permit that week and I wanted to buy a car. He told me that he hoped that I would use that money to buy a car. I did!

A few times, customers have tipped me $100 on stage. There was one guy that I didn't even notice or really flirt with during my show. I didn't even make eye contact with him, but he set $100 down on the stage on his way out the door. About half an hour later a guy was pointing a gun at him (possibly to rob him). My tipper ended up grabbing the gun out of the gunman's hands and beating him with it. The gunman died. I heard about it on the news. Another time, I had a total of $350 set on the stage for me during one of my shows by several customers.

I have a 60 year old customer who told me that he was sick and had a lot of surgeries for much of his life. He brings me tonnes of bottles of vitamins all the time.

I refuse to work at one strip club because it's only a two day gig, Friday and Saturday night, and then they make you come back after 11:00 am on Sunday to pick up your measly $300 cheque! It's annoying because the club is out of the way so a girl can waste her day off just dealing with picking up her pay.

There's another club I won't work at because the owner is a nut. He grabs your hand and drags you to a table trying to convince the guys to buy a private dance from you. It's so embarrassing! When he leaves, I always apologize to the group and have to try to salvage the situation. He also convinces customers in the bar to buy him shots! The last time I was there, one of the other girls was in my room and we heard the owner stumble into the hallway in his drunken state. Because the doors to both of our rooms were open, we saw him stagger into my friend's room and pat down her bed calling her name. When we saw him turn around and head for my room, we jumped up from the bed and hid in my closet. He roamed my room calling my name and walked right by the open closet where we were standing, then finally went back downstairs. It was creepy as hell so I will never go back to that bar.

I have fallen off stage three times. The first time was when I was working my first week on the circuit. I did a spin around the pole and as I was reaching for it, I realized it wasn't there! I was so far forward – I knew I was going to fall. I ended up jumping over a customer's head in my seven inch platforms and landing on the floor on my feet. The crowd cheered, so I crawled back on stage and continued my show, laughing.

My second fall was at that same bar and I pulled the same move, except this time I landed sitting my ass in an empty chair by the stage!

My third fall happened when I was joking around with a server who was standing at the bar. I was walking, looking over my shoulder and continued to walk right off the edge of the stage! I landed in a customer's lap (lucky him).

The ultimate embarrassing moment was this one busy night at work. I was onstage wiping down the poles just before my show trying to be cute, shaking my booty while I did it, just fooling around and being silly. I threw my cloth down and turned around. Imagine my horror...there was my dad! He didn't know that I was a stripper – well, he did now. He was hammered and just sat there with his mouth open. I ran off the stage and in my hurry I left my stage bag behind, that's how panicked I was!

I told the DJ my predicament and thankfully he postponed my show for half an hour to make sure that my dad was really gone. When I finally did go on for my show, I didn't know if he had left or not so it was probably the least sexy performance of my career. I hoped he had left! That would be pretty fucked up if he stayed! A week later, I called him up about something else and he said to me, "So, I saw this girl that looks like you and..."

I stopped him mid-sentence and said, "Dad, don't!" He

laughed awkwardly and left it alone. Eventually he brought it up again but in an awkward way only saying, "I just want you to be safe and look after yourself." Fair enough!

The one thing that surprised me about this industry that I knew nothing about in the beginning is that I thought that there would be contact allowed with customers, but it is just the opposite.

The one thing I wish I knew before getting into this line of work was how stressful it is to be booking myself for work. I have to stay on top of calling my agent. If I don't stay on top of it, no one will be doing it for me. I also wish I knew how few bars there are to work at in town since I can't travel out of town because of my son.

Something the reader would find shocking about me is that I have been an avid horseback rider since I was nine years old. Three things I won't leave home without are a diaper bag, cigarettes and my cell phone.

Also, when I was pregnant, I worked until I was four months along. I took five months off and my son was born a month early. It took me only four weeks to get back into my dancing body. I went from 170 lbs back down to 115 lbs in a month. My agent said that I had by far the fastest recovery after having a baby in the history of any other dancers at the agency.

I have been dancing now for two and a half years. I plan to save money and buy a farm or riding stable in the east within the next five years (by the time I am 25). Then I want to run it for five years and hopefully by then (at 30) I can get out of the industry and make money just from my riding stable.

I am only ashamed of telling people what I do for a living when it concerns my son, such as with doctors or education funds.

My advice for new girls coming into this business is to go away and leave us alone. Plain and simple! There isn't enough work for the dancers here as it is. We need more bars to work at, not more girls.

I do not regret getting into this business because it basically saved my life. I've always been a person with a lot of ambition and I could never imagine slaving away for minimum wage. I have worked for $8 an hour and it just doesn't cut it. I thought of either going to university or becoming a dancer. There is no need for university to run a stable, so I chose the latter. Dancing has got me to a higher place in life. I have a very nice life and I thank this industry for all of it!

# Daffodil

How I became a stripper. Hmmm, it's really pretty pathetic and a little cliché, but here it is!

I grew up in the system, going from foster home to group home until I finally had enough of it and struck out on my own. I was on 'kid welfare' for a year, but got cut off when I turned 18. I tried to get on grown up welfare and go back to high school but I burned that bridge when I dropped out.

So, my friend and I got a guy to boot for us. We sat down with our $10 bottle of wine and discussed our future. We ruled out selling drugs and working at McDonalds pretty much right away. That left us with only two options. Not wanting to sell our tender teenage bodies, we walked down to the local strip club and told the bartender we wanted to be strippers. We lasted two days before the manager tried to force my friend to fellate him. Calling random strip clubs all over the city, we finally got in touch with an agent willing to ship us out to another city where we were of legal age.

It was rough; mean girls and rude customers. The only easy part was the dancing nude which surprisingly never bothered me. Before I was taken away from my parents, they were big fans of a local nudist beach, so public nudity was never taboo. Probably the worst part of my rookie year was the fact that I wasn't very fit or glamorous and my friend was a knockout. Some lasting self-esteem issues there!

Now, I guess I'm a 'career stripper.' I've been dancing steady for 14 years. It's been good, bad, hurtful, liberating and hilarious! I started so young I don't really know any other life, so I'll never know if I'm traumatized or not.

As for advice for new girls, I'd say to any young girl starting out, SAVE YOUR MONEY and better yourselves – go to school, travel, take care of your body.

This will probably be my last year. I'm going to school to be a palliative care aid. I'll miss stripping, though. The only thing about my job I regret is not saving more money!

Written by Daffodil

# Dahlia

I'm a 23 year old dancer from BC, and I have been dancing since January 2008. I started in this business by working a week or two per month, then nothing, then another week or two. Then I was on the road every week. Currently, I'm on a break until spring. I often leave the industry to have some 'time out.' There's no pressure for me to stay as I have other ways to make money. I see dancing as a fast and fun way to make money, but way less fun than some of my other ways of making a living.

I've always been intrigued by strip clubs. I'm not sure what sparked this fascination but from there it was a natural progression. I started going to a local strip club on the weekend as a patron, and started taking pole dancing lessons on the side. It was awesome! I was going to enter the amateur contest at the strip club, but was stopped at the time by my reluctant boyfriend. My friend won the contest and we started dancing together (after my boyfriend and I broke up).

My first gig was a booking to cover a dancer fired for bad behaviour. Zero to 12 shows in three days. I jumped right in!

I love this job because it encourages me to be charming and sexy. My day as a dancer involves a one hour shower, doing my hair and makeup at the beginning of the day, 10 minutes to get dressed, 10 minutes to get from the dressing room to the DJ booth, onto the stage for a 16-19 minute show, get dressed and cool down, chill, wash, rinse and repeat!

I get to dress up, dance to my favourite music and make easy money. It's creative and I have time to do things that I want to do when I'm not working (like focusing on a hobby or passion). It's fast money, good exercise and I choose when and where I want to work. I feel stronger, wiser, and more powerful – an ultra-seductive superwoman!

The downside of this job is that I began to resent men. This industry is full of seedy men and bastard club owners. Because I'm a dancer it's automatically assumed that I'll go home with you and your boyfriend/girlfriend, and because I'm a dancer it's assumed that I'll give you a complete anatomy lesson of my pussy.

It's hard on the body and mind. The long hours of being at the top of your game can be extremely tiring. It affects my body image and at times, my self-worth. Being around so many gorgeous women constantly nitpicking at their looks is horribly infectious. It's a bug that never really shakes off.

Dancing is a gateway career to a lot of bad habits. You can always come back to work and the drugs and alcohol are free and waiting. Also, there's no job security – you can be booted out a full weeks work with no remorse or consideration from the agent, and sometimes no pay from the club.

Depending on how much you work, there isn't much of a private life aside from time after a shift. On the road, you're sharing a room with another girl. If you're on the road for a few weeks at a time, you start to lose connections with friends and family. It's hard to keep friendships strong when you're travelling across the province. My best friend was always there for me – cell phones are amazing! I did lose a few strong connections with friends because I was out of town so much. Growing apart sucks, but sometimes it's a good cleanse.

As for romantic relationships, I was never really into the idea. It's just too complicated. Usually a guy is super-stoked about the idea of having a dancer girlfriend. He's 'totally fine with it.' I do honestly believe there are some men who are genuinely turned on by the idea, but most men can't stand it. When it does bother them, they lose it. They get emotional, jealous, mean, vindictive and spiteful. I also think that some men just can't handle the idea of the woman making the majority of the money.

I know that the popular views of stripping do not accurately represent my profession. People think I'm a desperate dumb bimbo who is flakey and slutty; a money crazed wild woman. I doubt the views will change anytime soon, especially with conservative government, seedy venues and a connection to underground criminal activity. In order to change the stigma against stripping, we need to create nicer venues, a union mentality with support for the industry workers and liberal laws. Change is slow; I've noticed the current economic climate has an effect. More dancers are coming back out of retirement, and girls getting into the business at a younger age. Hey, why not! Everyone else is making minimum wage and working 12 hour days.

Dancing is so different from other professions though. Think about it – I get naked in a sexual manner to please the male population! It is also different because I have a lot of power. I choose when and where I want to work. I choose what I dance to and what I wear. I have the ability to be the best or worst I can be and still likely get a booking (within reason).

There are similarities to other jobs too – the need for people skills, business sense and the desire to make money. I get up, put my game face on and make it happen. As in many professions, my image reflects the establishment that I'm working from.

Ultimately, I dance for myself. I make it appear as though I'm dancing for the erotic pleasure of men – it's being an actress. When I dance, I become my alter-ego. She's fierce, tough, ultra sexy and uses those traits in her power to seduce. She also has no problem telling someone off if they displease her.

I felt my most powerful when I was doing stage shows. I choose my own music, costumes and how far I want to go in terms of what I want to show off. I can't control what people think of me, but I take pride in the fact that I can draw an audience's attention with my mystique. It's a great feeling – there's definitely a lot of power to be had when dancing around a bunch of men. They are stunned and become putty. They'd be glad to help you with something, be it a drink, massage or some 'help.' Tips aren't that great in BC, but the tips I do make are usually inspired by an entertaining show.

I really disliked private dancing because it is the complete opposite power exchange. The guys would seem like they were doing you a favour by getting a dance from you. Three and a half minutes for $40. Rip-off. They know that, especially when it's a no contact dance.

I wouldn't recommend this profession to everyone. But for smart, confident girls who don't care what people might think or say it can work. Being a money hungry person helps and this is where I lack. I see beautiful women sell themselves short everyday just to make a sale.

Dancing is funny. It can definitely be a completely thankless job that makes you question your existence, but sometimes it's an ultra-gratifying profession where people treat you like a rock star and love you wildly.

My advice for new girls starting out in this business is to start saving money as soon as possible! Pay yourself first before paying 'the man.' Also, stay healthy.

Written by Dahlia

# Daisy

Working as an exotic dancer has been a crazy rollercoaster. For me it all started when I was 18 and working as a shooter girl at a strip club in Alberta. Seeing all the tips the dancers were making made me extremely curious, not to mention, dancing looked easy... little did I know!

I've always been known for having a more 'taboo' side. I never really went with what society deemed the right way, so dancing just seemed like the natural next step. As soon as I decided to look into dancing, I called my mother to inform her of my great plans. At this point in time we weren't on the best of terms so I'm sure she took it as a direct hit. At first, my family told her I was just trying to get a rise out of her but it didn't take long for them to start to believe it and shut me out. My mother didn't take long to come around. At first she was mad but it turned more into fear for me. After many years and lots of hard work, I can truly say that she is my best friend. We talk almost every day and she still tells me how she can't wait for me to leave the business. But after all my hard work of persuading her that I am truly happy, she has come to be extremely supportive.

Within a few days, I got in touch with the agency. Next thing I knew, I was on a late bus to my first booking in Alberta. It was a complete hole in the wall but the tips and customers were awesome! The bar was right in the middle of an industrial park, not to mention, it was when the Alberta boom was really starting to get crazy. When I got on the bus to head out there, I remember hugging my boyfriend and not wanting to go anymore but I got on the bus and was on my way. When I got there, it was in the middle of a stormy winter night and the bus station wasn't open so I had to stand outside all alone and wait for a cab. Needless to say, I was freaking out and by the time I arrived at the motel I was terrified.

My first few days were great! I was working with probably still to this day, one of the most diverse line-ups I have ever seen. One girl in particular who is still my favourite entertainer really helped me out with costumes, promo and helpful hints on stage.

Later in the week, I met one of the dreaded agents that I will leave nameless. After I had met with him, he told me that my next booking was extremely picky and that I wasn't what he had expected. The following week turned out to be great and the bar loved me! It wasn't until a few weeks later when I was at the sister bar that the owner saw me and my problems began. I soon found out that in this guy's mind, the perfect woman was 10 pounds, long blonde hair and big implants. At the end of the week, he even cut my show price without telling me. And of course, when I called the agents all they did was yell at me and belittle me.

Obviously, I then started to compare myself to the blondes, their implants, the costumes, etc. When I first started dancing, I was okay with who I was but between the bar owner and the agent I acquired low self esteem and one hell of a body complex that will probably haunt me for the rest of my life.

After just a few weeks working in Alberta, I was broken and ready to leave dancing because I couldn't handle working for my agents anymore. I didn't realize that they weren't the only agency I could work for (amazing how agents make themselves look like the be-all and end all). But after I did some internet research, I found another agency that represented Manitoba and northern Ontario, so I went off and learned the ropes! I traveled all over Canada and even stopped back at my old agent's office once (that meanie even gave me a compliment!).

Over my five years in this business, I have dealt with all the games and comments of the agents. With them, one day you're hot and the next day you're not. As much as I love some of the agents, sometimes it's all just one big irritating game that we all unfortunately have to play.

Between gigs, show prices, contests and other girls, you are always playing a game. Sometimes I find myself looking at the dancers now and thinking, "You get paid how much?" Girls and show prices are such a pain in the ass – especially when you're an all natural girl with a great show and you have to sit back and watch the girls with implants and boring shows make more money. She could have the most boring show on the planet but she will get paid more than me because there's thousands of dollars on her chest just screaming, "I get what I want!" Obviously this isn't always the case, but if you ask me it's the way the agencies want it. There are so many things about the business that drive me insane. If I had to use just one word, it would be 'vanity.'

Life has stayed pretty calm for me. Granted, there are some huge changes in how certain people view you but eventually you get used to it and realize who and what is really important. For the most part, my privacy has been kept intact up until recently when an employee at my gym gave out my personal information. This caused some serious problems for me. At first I was completely in shock and people who knew me said I looked like a ghost. As of right now I am trying to not think too much about it and have done everything I can about the situation. When I am out in public, I try to keep a low profile and I have a big difference in the way I do my hair, makeup, dress, etc, than when I am in the club.

As time went on, I definitely saw my fair share of funny to downright disgusting things on the circuit. Some of my personal favourites would be the old men dancing and creating their own symphony to the music the girls would dance to. Though for me the worst times are when customers 'go off' about my stage blanket (my hockey team). I have been called a wide range of offensive comments; the most common being a separatist bitch. This always blows my mind considering in my team's town you wouldn't be called out for wearing another team's gear. One guy even went as far as to throw something at me and repeatedly scream, "Get the hell out of Canada!" For the most part, this is pretty amusing to me but the odd time I get in a huff and want to move back home.

Customers to me are all pretty much the same. Obviously we have the regulars which many girls will love but other girls will despise. For the most part ALL regulars love gyno row and the more you show, the more they throw. I have met many girls who will refuse them and walk away empty handed. This can be irritating, considering we are here to dance and not give a medical lesson on the female anatomy. For me personally, making the regulars happy is easier, not to mention extremely beneficial versus having an argument and the pain of dealing with them on future bookings. In BC, it is key to realize that the regulars do go to many of the bars and they can find out who is working where on the agency web page.

Personally I would rather dance for older men then the young boys. My mom once said she gets creeped out thinking of all those really old gross men. "Doesn't it bother you?" she asked. I truly laughed and said, "Mom, if that's the only customers the bars had, we would be rich!"

The trend of strip clubs bringing young guys and an obscene amount of young girls into the club is what bothers me. Girls can be so bloody mean! Sometimes I hear them say, "Oh the splits? I can do that! She's hanging upside down. Big deal, anybody could do that!"

One time a girl was criticizing me to no end and actually had the nerve to say, "You need to smile more!" I truly don't know how it happened but my leg just went a bit too far off the stage and her drink went into her lap! Needless to say, she was not happy but after 15 minutes of her being rude, who could blame me.

Traveling has been one of my favourite parts of this job. All the places I have experienced at my age are amazing. Not many people can say that they have been all over Canada many times at the age of 23. This business has given me the opportunity to learn a side of life that no other job could offer. I have been introduced to some of the most amazing and brilliant people who I believe have helped shape the person I am today. All the good, bad and ugly experiences I have had are truly a gift and I wouldn't give them up for anything in the world.

When I started, I was only dancing in western Canada, but I also had the advantage to know what dancing in southern Ontario, Québec, and the Maritimes was like. Out west you will always hear about how dirty Montréal is but the bottom line is that Montréal has the perfect system. They have every type of club you can think of. Montreal is called the 'sin city' of Canada for a reason; you can get whatever you're looking for there. There are the basic non contact clubs in the west where songs are a fully nude table dance ranging $8 a song (most girls have a minimum amount of songs). The tourist district has light contact (you WILL see this in some clubs in Alberta and certain bars in BC) where the girls DO NOT remove their underwear during these dances – no ifs, ands or buts. Then you get to the French district where contact varies, but still the laws are no extras; underwear stays on and contact is usually full with all areas being grabbed except the girl's cookie.

Like everywhere in the world, there will always be a girl to break the rules. When you leave the island of Montréal, more contact comes into play and there are plus clubs. To me, this is brilliant because no girl who wants to do extras will waste her time in a straight club downtown and risk getting beaten up or charged. This setup keeps girls where they want to be and nobody steps on anybody's toes. Also in these clubs, you go on stage once or twice a night for two songs to advertise yourself. There is no pay for this. You can feature in some clubs and be paid but this also means no floor time. Featuring is not what it used to be out there as there are fewer clubs who will pay for a dancer when they can have a porn star.

In Ontario and Québec it is legal for many girls to be on stage, so at least once a night you will see a duo show ranging from soft core to XXX. The girls do them for free and in the long run get many dances – hence the slow fall of the feature dancer.

Newfoundland can be extremely good as well. It's basically the same idea with different rules in each club. Ontario is a whole new game where they do full contact dances with underwear off and once again each club varies in the rules. The further out of the city the more that happens. I would suggest that any girl interested in working in these areas should research the clubs before going and know as much as you possibly can or it can get sticky (no pun intended).

When I go away, whether it's a week or two months, I never leave without my Sponge Bob blanket, Napoleon (my stuffed dog given by my fiancé) and tonnes of movies to keep me company between shows. For the most part, I try to avoid being in the clubs between shows unless it's mandatory or a place that I feel extremely comfortable in. It's been just over a year that I have been completely sober so I still try to avoid the party scene situation. Because I am on the road so much, I try to get a lot done when I am at home. It is hard because usually I am so burnt out when I get home that all I want to do is relax.

I try very hard to keep the romance going with my fiancé. Sometimes it can get interesting, but we find ways to make up for the distance. I got extremely lucky with him. In his line of work, he has to travel for long periods of time and he doesn't have the week-to-week option like I do. He is very understanding because he makes a point of coming to visit wherever I am on weekends and we try not to be apart for more than two weeks. I like to book the bar with longer hours and stricter rules the first week and then when he arrives the next week, be in a calmer setting where we have time together in the day. I pick the clubs that don't mind if he sits in the back corner during my shows so we can take off and do something after. This has worked very well. I find most bars are good about the boyfriend as long as they don't know. The ones who strictly say no boyfriends are the ones you wouldn't want your boyfriend to come to. Between the volume of shows and the earning potential there really is no point.

For any girls thinking about joining this business, whether it is part time or full time, the best advice that I could give would be to never compromise yourself for money. Keep the people who love you as close as you can and just because one person doesn't like the way you look, it doesn't mean that there isn't people who do!

Exotic dancing, or as I like to call it 'exotic walking' or 'monkey climbing' (for all the pole dancers out there), can be a very positive experience if done with dignity. But it can be a very dark path if you're not careful. Trust me I know! Always try to keep in mind that the agent is making money off you so don't let them be mean to you! Work your way up and good things will come.

As of now, I have been dancing for over five years and recently moved to BC with my fiancé whom I actually met while dancing. We will be getting married early summer. Recently, I started a home business, as well as got myself going in school for the future (as much as I like to think I will never get old, it will happen). I am also hoping to purchase a second house with my fiancé this following summer as a rental property.

Dancing has been a wild ride with many ups and downs but it's an experience that I wouldn't trade for the world!

Written by Daisy

# Danica

I was 19, working hard to save a bunch of money for a month long backpacking trip through Australia with my boyfriend. For six months, I worked at a high end coffee shop from 6:00 am- 1:00 pm, and then I would run off to my office data entry job from 2:00-7:00 pm.

The trip was fantastic! When it was over, we came to the realization that we had to get jobs again and get back to making money. I wanted to try dancing (I think this idea came from the movie Showgirls) since I was always involved in many genres of dance and I used to compete in ballet. So, I started to do some research on the internet and came upon a website from a girl who was a dancer. I liked what I found out so I approached my boyfriend with the idea. He was okay with it, so I marched into a club in Sydney and started.

My first day on the job was four years ago. Although I was nervous, I still felt really confident. When I look back, I don't know where I got all the confidence I mustered that day! I had my ballet background, but I had never taken any pole dancing or stripping lessons. I had zero inhibitions about my naked body so I didn't have a problem with the naked part of this job. At first, I didn't like the idea of showing my vagina to strangers, but after I did it once, it was no big deal.

I had a regular childhood with no sexual abuse and my whole family knows what I do for a living. My dad had a mental breakdown at first and my mom was disappointed. After I told them the amount of money I make, they now understand why I do it. They are okay with it as long as I'm smart with my money and keep a level head by staying away from the drugs and partying. I am not involved or interested in that aspect of dancing anyways.

I love the opportunity that dancing has given me to make large amounts of money as a young person. It has also made me feel more confident in some aspects of my life, such as nudity and talking to men. This job definitely makes me feel sexy and has gotten me in touch with my sexy feminine side. It has also made me realize that I need a career working for myself, but I need to make good money doing it. This job has given me the opportunity to travel all over the world and I am introduced to some of the most amazing people. Dance is an outlet of artistic expression for me. It's a form of artistry; everything from the dancing, to pole work, to designing your costumes and picking your music.

I hate that dancers are treated with disrespect. Since this job requires me to play a role while dancing, many men judge me and see me as a stereotype (hooker or drug addict). I'm not taken seriously, which I can understand to a certain extent, but many dancers are educated and smart, and people don't realize that. This is a very misunderstood industry. When I was moving out on my own, it was nearly impossible for me to rent an apartment. As soon as I told the apartment manager that I was a stripper, they invariably made comments like, "There are absolutely no parties and no drugs allowed!" I am not a party girl and I have no desire to sleep around. During my time off, I like relaxing quiet time with my family, not a loud environment like work. I did end up renting an apartment but I had to tell the manager that I was a book keeper!

A woman becomes very critical with her body in this industry. I was very insecure about my small chest for a while and the more I worried and cried about it, the more I would get comments like, "If you had bigger boobs, I'd give you all my money" or "Why are your boobs so small?" When I stopped worrying about my chest and had more confidence in myself, I started getting comments like, "You look great! Don't ever ruin yourself and get a boob job!" I believe in the law of attraction because it works!

To me, it seems as though the more time you spend working in this industry, the less confident you get with your self image.

It's an industry I don't want to work in for the rest of my life because of how people see dancers. You are judged on your body alone; you are seen as just body parts. I want to be a respected, dignified human being. As a dancer, I can't help but be critical of my body. You have to be critical of everything – I worry about the size of my boobs, the shape of my bum and even what my vagina looks like. I'll even tuck my labia in before going on stage!

Hustling the customers to get them into the private dance room and the fake flirting is definitely the part I like the least about my job because it's very hard to do and extremely draining.

Girls can end up hanging out with the wrong kind of crowd while working in this industry and get into some messy situations. Like the time I got roped into drugs during the first three months of my dancing career. One night I was hanging out with some gangsters and I stayed up for four days straight without any sleep, while snorting and smoking any kind of drugs that were offered to me. I was on E, ice, you name it. I passed out beside one of the guys and woke up in the morning to his fingers up my vagina!

After this four day binge, one of the guys wanted to go on a road trip to the next state over from Australia. I was hallucinating and freaking out so bad that he put me on a plane by myself and sent me home. I was hearing voices and thought people were trying to break into my apartment. It was awful!

Another scary experience was when my girlfriend and I worked for a full month straight with no day off in Alberta. We had saved up $20,000 each and we kept the money hidden away in our safe. After we went to work, we got a call from one of the dancers saying that the dancer house was broken into. My friend's safe was uncovered and stolen. It was devastating! We think it was an inside job.

I've never had any stalkers, just regulars who follow me to different clubs. I refuse to work a certain strip club because I don't like the aura of the bar and I feel degraded working there. The girls that work there provide full contact lap dances and I'm not comfortable with that. One time a customer pushed me with full force and I fell to the floor in my stripper gear, platforms and all. I think that turned me off of the bar as well.

I met my rudest customer when I was doing a VIP dance in a private room. The guy poked his finger at my anus! I was pretty new to the job and didn't know what to do so I kept on dancing. If this happened now, I would handle the situation much differently. I was not as assertive with customers in the beginning but now I stick up for myself. Customers don't get away with anything anymore!

My weirdest customer was the guy who paid me $350 to go in the private dance room for the hour and take the heel of my shoe and jab it into his collar bone as hard as I could!

It's not all weirdos, though. I love talking to customers who teach me about many different things. It's fantastic to get some free education.

I met this amazing customer just recently who became totally obsessed with me. He was a very polite Indian man who said that he really liked me. He barely wanted any private dances. He just wanted to hang out, link arms with me and talk. He came by to see me almost every day for three weeks and paid me $2000 per day ($360 an hour) just to sit with him and chat.

In Australia I met a guy who gave me $1000 to go out and have dinner and drinks with him. It was a treat because he was a wonderful person who took me to the classiest restaurants and lounges.

Some of the strangest gifts given to me from customers have been dildos and vibrators. The biggest tip I got on stage was $300.

My most embarrassing moment was when I got my period all over my white underwear. I was doing a private dance and I had flipped over upside down. I didn't know that I had blood all over my legs and crotch, and the customer didn't say anything.

Another time I farted once in a private dance room and it smelt pretty bad.

Something that you would find interesting about me is that I had a marijuana addiction for 10 years. I have now successfully quit because I wanted to change my life. I'm hanging in there and don't feel any need for it anymore.

I did some modeling as a teenager. I also had an eating disorder from the ages of 17-19, probably from ballet. I was trying to keep up with the 34-24-34 measurements. Dancing freed me from this!

My sister and I are both saving up money so that we could possibly open a sandwich shop in the future. I also took training in makeup artistry for film and television because I might want to do something in that field one day.

Three things I won't leave home without are my iPhone, my favourite plumping lipgloss and mascara.

When I was picking my dancer name, I named myself after my favourite porn star. For my last name I picked a name that sounded feisty.

I wish I knew how hard it was to get out of this industry after you started because the money is too good. It scares me because I'm 23 now and I know my career is coming to an end. I want to be an educated adult and not like some of the other girls who are still dancing even after they feel their time is done. Some of these girls have no other choice or any other skills. This is a supply and demand industry where men will always want to see naked women and these women will take their money to show them. It's sad because a lot of the dancers I have met are really sweet, hard working women. I would never have guessed that before I became a dancer myself!

Do I have any regrets on getting into this business? I want to say no, but parts of me say yes. I kind of wish I went to school first and had a normal life. Then I wouldn't be so focused on my appearance and I would be less insecure about silly things that are not important. This job concentrates too much on vanity.

On the other hand, I am glad that I got into this business because it's shaped who I am and I'm still happy with myself. I believe that everything happens for a reason and I've had many amazing experiences. I plan on dancing for a couple more years, tops!

Although for the most part I am not ashamed to tell people what I do for a living, I am reluctant to tell some people. I feel they are judging me and looking at me as a stupid slut who is not smart. I want to be seen as someone worthy of respect.

My advice to new girls coming into the agency is to save your money and work hard while you're in this business. Be confident and be yourself. Don't let the idiots out there affect you with their stupid, negative comments. Remember that this industry focuses on fantasy. If you're in this industry, better yourself and stay strong and happy!

# Delphinium

I got the idea of being a stripper in my early 20's. I was in Toronto working toward my undergraduate sociology degree in university. The focus of my research in school was the sex trade – prostitution, pornography and stripping. The research piqued my interest about stripping and because I was a broke student I started to wonder if I had the guts to do more than just study dancing. However, I felt guilty about dancing because I still got some financial support from my parents, so I didn't end up entering the industry at the time. I kept the idea in the back of my mind though. Looking back, I'm glad I didn't start dancing back in Toronto because I'm sure I wouldn't have been able to handle it. From what I've heard, the line between prostitution and stripping is a little blurry in Ontario, and there is far more competition between dancers than in BC. I would likely have been traumatized if I started dancing there.

After I finished my degrees, I moved to BC and worked an office job for two years. It didn't pay particularly well and it came with lots of stress from the big work load. Because I didn't take a break after high school, I was severely burned out from going straight into university for six years (it took me five years to get my BA and another year to get my Masters) in social sciences. I realize now that it was too much for me and I should've taken some time off after graduation to figure out what I really want to do with my life. I was groomed by my parents to go to university, and I didn't want to disappoint them, so that was all I thought about doing after high school.

I was 28 years old and it was time to bite the bullet and start dancing. I got back into my research mode and I found an online community for exotic dancers. Because I'm a safety net girl, I researched the whole industry and found that I could make more money stripping than doing my office job. Girls wrote gig reviews and gave their honest opinions about the industry in the forums, which was really helpful.

I was very cautious about the industry and wanted to be well prepared, so I started taking pole dancing lessons. Then I called the local agency to ask if I could do an amateur contest. I chatted with the agent and he booked me at the strip club where I won my first contest.

I was still working my office job during the day when I did the first contest. Entering this business was such a culture shock to me, as I had only been to strip clubs a few times before and didn't know anyone personally who had worked in the industry. I did three or four more contests and then I gave my office job notice that I was quitting. After that, I started dancing full time on the circuit.

Financially, dancing is totally worthwhile because I paid off my student loans and credit cards, and I was able to save some money. More importantly, I love that I met my very best friends in this industry. The other perks of this job are dancing to my favourite music, performing on stage, wearing the gorgeous costumes and working on my strength and fitness. It's a great feeling when you put on a good show and the crowd appreciates it by cheering like crazy. My middle two years of dancing were my favourites when I absolutely loved my job! I had everything all figured out and I did lots of private dances and made tons of money in tips.

I hated lying to my friends and family about what I did for a living (for the five years I danced, they still thought I had my office job). My parents wouldn't understand if they knew the truth because as their only child, they envisioned me as a lawyer or doctor. My parents have always been extremely loving and supportive of me, but if they knew I was working in this industry, they would feel ashamed and think it reflected poorly on them as parents.

I was an only child and I had a very normal childhood. My parents are still together and I have a great relationship with them. As for the stereotype that dancers have 'daddy issues' or were abused, nothing could be further from the truth in my experience. My dad is a wonderful man who never mistreated me in any way. My parents saw my potential and always encouraged me to go to school. I had a white picket fence upbringing. Perhaps their only short coming was that they were very overprotective of me, kept me on a short leash and didn't let me make my own mistakes as I was growing up.

I know that they would think my job is dangerous and dirty. I felt worse in the beginning because I wasn't used to lying to them and I was always scared that someone would tell them my little secret. But after a while, lying became a normal part of my life. I'm very lucky they didn't find out by coming across one of my posters, or a website with my picture on it, because I worked in the same city as them every few months.

Dancing definitely takes a toll on your personal life as boyfriends have a hard time dealing with it. My ex had some trust issues and would express his frustration by calling me names, punching walls, etc. He pretty much did everything short of physically abusing me. I exhausted myself by constantly trying to prove to him that I was committed to our relationship. He said that he was okay with it except for the private dances which I only did when I felt like making some extra money and I was never doing them to pick up guys.

I have a new boyfriend now that treats me right. We are starting a family together! I quit dancing four months ago because I am pregnant. I finally told my agent about my pregnancy last week. I am 26 weeks pregnant and lucky that my guy supports me so I can spend time with our baby after he is born. After the baby is born, I have plans to go into nursing. There is a two year nursing program at the local university.

It's a bit of a relief to stop dancing because I was always second guessing myself wondering if the money was worthwhile, given the havoc my job was creating in my personal life. It was really draining for me to deal with all the jealousy and to justify what I do for a living on a near daily basis.

I hate dealing with the ignorant attitudes from people when the conversation is focused on this industry. Many customers assume that dancers are uneducated, have suffered some form of horrible abuse, or have nothing else going for them except stripping. Dealing with such attitudes was really stressful and demoralizing for me. I have more paper on the wall than most of these guys! I also hated being around drugs. Being offered them and seeing people abuse them depressed me a lot as time went on.

I was 28 years old when I started dancing and I danced for five years. My first day on the job I was really nervous yet it didn't cross my mind to drink before I went on stage. In the beginning I know I must have looked like a deer in headlights and I found it difficult to interact with the customers. My first time on stage I told myself to stick to what I learned in my pole dancing classes, which didn't work all that well because there is more to putting on a good show than doing pole tricks. I was aware of my nakedness but that went away very quickly within the first month of dancing._

I never refused to work at certain bars without working there first. In the beginning, I was sent to small town bars but I didn't go back if the accommodations were unreasonably dirty and/or unsafe. I quickly learned to stop expecting a lot in regards to cleanliness. Most bars are filthy and you just have to get used to it.

I had a guy do a belly dive onto the stage while I was doing a show once. Another dude told me he'd been struck by lightning as a child and had the ability to do "healing massage" ever since. I think this is something he invented to tell dancers so he could cop a feel for free!

Twice, I had a guy throw up and pass out while I was giving a lap dance. I had joked around and said, "I'm so good, I could make you throw up in there!

One of my scary incidents was when I was working out of town one week and had a couple of customers knock on my hotel room door. There was no security so I just ignored them, and they eventually went away. It really freaked me out and made me realize how completely vulnerable we are when we go out of town to work.

I grew to be able to identify the stalker types quickly and made sure to stay away from them. I didn't have a problem with those types of people since I usually kept to myself.

My favourite customers are the ones that tip consistently and the ones that are genuinely interested in me as a person and not a stripper.

I have been given gift certificates to the spa and the mall. I'm usually not that comfortable accepting gifts from customers, but the people I did accept gifts from didn't expect anything sexual in return from me. One guy left a bag of super tacky lingerie on stage for me once. He looked like a homeless person and I was quite certain he'd stolen these items from the sex shop down the street. The biggest tip I ever got on stage was $500. Five guys each handed me $100.

I had a few embarrassing moments in my dancing career. I went through a phase of drinking quite a bit at work. Somehow I never fell on stage from being drunk, but I definitely had quite a few sloppy moments, and at times was probably more belligerent with customers than I should have been.

Once there was a guy in front row who was seated in a wheelchair. Unfortunately I didn't realize this and gestured at him repeatedly to stand up so I could give him a poster. I was mortified when I finally realized he wasn't standing up because he couldn't stand up! Thankfully he was cool about the whole thing.

I got my period on stage when I was new to dancing, something every dancer seems to experience at some point.

It was my second week of dancing and a co-worker from my previous job showed up at the club I was working at. We were both mortified. A couple weeks later he ended up bringing other co-workers from the office to see me strip! The whole thing was super awkward and very weird.

One thing that surprised me was how awesome and open minded dancers are and the many talents they have as artists, singers, writers, etc. I also grew to understand how truly moronic men can be when they are drunk. I also learned not to take the job too seriously and to stop expecting fair treatment.

I used to get propositioned for sex all the time at work. When I was new to dancing this would enrage me. In time, I grew to expect this sort of thing as part of working in a sexualized environment where alcohol is served to horny men. I wish I knew the necessity of having a thick skin. It took me a long time to develop one. It used to really upset me when I was criticized or insulted at work, and when customers would proposition me for sex. I used to get all huffy and defensive, and the guys would see how upset I was, which just made the situation worse. Eventually I realized it was more effective to stay calm and laugh off stupid comments. It took me a few years to learn how to not take people's behaviour and words so seriously. In the beginning I was never good at standing up for myself and dealing with people's ignorance, but I'm far more assertive now.

Something you would find amusing about me is that I am a big homebody. I enjoy nothing more than listening to CBC radio, crocheting and reading. I'm not a big partier at all, although I do enjoy a nice box of wine from time to time.

I would never go to work without perfume, reading material, and a bottle of wine.

The first part of my dancer name has always been my name for a girl. I always thought I would name my daughter that, but now it's tainted so I will probably find another one! I wanted the second part of my name to be wild and fierce, so I put the two together and got my name.

I'm definitely not ashamed of being a dancer, but I never felt genuinely comfortable with my job because I know that most people's ideas about strippers are not positive. It's also difficult to not feel some guilt about dancing as it tends to reflect poorly on your boyfriend. There's always someone who will ask, "How can you let your girlfriend do that for a living?" like I'm his child or something. When I'm ready to go back to work after the baby is born, I worry about what I should put on my resume to fill the gap that is the five years I spent dancing. Should I be honest? This is something I really struggle with.

My advice for new girls coming into this industry is to be smart with your money and don't party your paycheques away. Definitely have some fun with your money, but have a budget, too. Stay single if possible. It'll make your life so much easier and keep more money in your pocket. If you do get a boyfriend, make sure he's employed and isn't going to be sitting on the couch all day while you're at work taking your clothes off for strangers!

I do not regret getting into this business because it was a great life experience overall. I made many great friends in the business, paid off my debt and became a much stronger person, all of which has made dancing worthwhile. It also opened my eyes to the fact that I had quite a sheltered upbringing and that people have backgrounds and experiences far different than my own. This realization has made me a more tolerant and emphatic person.

# Fleur

It all started after I broke up with my boyfriend of four years because he was so controlling. Even though we were broken up, I still wanted to upset him, so I got a job as a waitress in a strip bar. My ex would never have let me work there in a million years! Besides the fact that I knew it would piss my ex off, it was actually a pretty good job. I even met a great guy there and ended up dating him for seven years! We moved to another city, and I went to work at another strip club, this time as a server. Next thing I knew, I was hired by the local dancer agency. I had no doubts about becoming a dancer since my new boyfriend was emotionally supportive with my decision. I also thought that I could make some good money, very quickly.

My mom and two older sisters know what I do for a living. As for my two younger sisters and brother, they think I am a waitress and a promoter. My siblings and I grew up in foster care and we got moved around a lot to different foster homes because my mom wasn't capable of taking care of us. My family are the most important people in my life and despite everything I went through as a child, I had a very happy childhood. Without my sisters and my loving grandparents, it wouldn't have been the same since I am very close to them and all my good memories are when I was with them.

When I was choosing my dancer name, I chose it carefully. I wanted something that would guide me spiritually and help me emotionally. I needed to feel connected to my name so dancing would have more meaning, so that I would be okay doing it... eventually.

I was sent on the road my first week of dancing which was truly terrifying. I was so nervous that I started drinking before I even did my first show. By the time I got on stage I was wasted! To this day, I need to drink in order to do my job. For a few years, I wasn't allowed to go back and work at some of the clubs I worked at because of my excessive drinking. Back then, I would drink a twenty-sixer or more every day.

I hate the fact that I had to drink heavily in order to get on stage and do my job. I never imagined myself doing this kind of work, so I felt ashamed of myself for having to go down this path just to make money and get ahead. For me, it caused a lot of stress in my life, mostly because I didn't want people to judge me. Instead, I was judging myself, so I drank a lot because it kept me from thinking about what I thought about myself... if that makes any sense.

I got to the point where I had to have a drink first thing in the morning because I was hung over from the day before. I needed more drinks, all day and all night until I finally went to sleep. I had a lot of rough mornings where I would call my boyfriend in tears at six in the morning because I wasn't happy doing what I was repeatedly doing with my life. Any normal person would just tell me to quit but it wasn't as simple as that for me. Even though I hated it, I didn't want to quit. I was determined to get my life back on track and work as hard as I could to finally get where I wanted to be.

With drinking came smoking and then I started into drugs. Everything was easy access since it was in my face all the time. It was shocking to find that my paycheque was basically spent at the end of the week because paying for booze, smokes and drugs adds up pretty quickly. If you're not strong enough, you can get caught up in this vicious cycle where you're having a lot of fun, but in the end you're not getting ahead in your life. Since you're always working hard making money, you spend it just as quickly so you can have some fun. When you're having fun, saving is not a priority.

I'm happy to say that I have successfully stopped doing drugs and I don't drink as much as I used to. As a result, I have started to love dancing onstage! I also realized that as long as I love what I do and as long as I can do it without harming my body, then whatever I choose to do (that includes stripping) is good!

I love the people I meet in this industry and I enjoy getting to know them. I've met a lot of really good people who have become my friends. I believe that everyone you meet brings something into your life.

I also love the costumes I get to wear and the freedom I have to make my own schedule. In a way, I'm basically my own boss and I can take any time off I want. If a girl really wants to make more money than just stage dancing, there is five times more to be made selling private dances. That's where the real money is. Tips are good, too, though. The biggest tip I ever got was $900, all in twenty dollar bills! The guy threw it on stage along with a dozen roses.

I've had my share of gifts given to me by regulars over the years. The ones that stand out are the customer who surprised me on my birthday with a certificate for a hot air balloon ride. I haven't had a chance to use it and I still have the certificate. I had a guy surprise me with a real bunny after I told him that I wanted a brown bunny with floppy ears. That same guy also ended up as my hairdresser. The nicest gift a customer gives me is an attentive ear. I appreciate it when someone listens to a concern I have in my life and gives me advice.

One of my embarrassing moments was when I got too drunk and fell down some stairs. I broke my boot heel in half and the management saw it on camera. Of course, I got a fine afterwards.

The one thing that surprised me about the business is that I thought the money would be better. It can be good if you're not spending all your money drinking, smoking, doing drugs, getting fined or losing and replacing pieces of expensive costumes. Some girls even lose their driver's licence and can't drive so they have to hire a driver which can cost up to $250 for the week. Drivers can be a pain. You will be stuck in a minivan with a bunch of other girls. If you're a regular girl who hires this driver all the time, perfect, you'll be the first one dropped off at home and the last one to get picked up in the morning. But if you're the new girl, you'll sit in the van for a couple of hours, being the last to get dropped off and the first to be picked up in the morning.

It's hard to make money. A dancer typically gets 15 shows a week but that's only if no shows are cancelled because the club is slow. She has to pay travel expenses, pay to stay in a hotel, pay a driver, pay for any booze, smokes, drugs, etc. You can end up with a measly $200 at the end of the week if you're not careful.

After dancing for five years on and off, I took two years off and got a regular job. I didn't want to go back to serving in a strip bar, so I got a job selling concert tickets and working for a promotion company. I wasn't making the best money, so I am back to dancing again for a month. At the time of this writing, I'm dancing for one more week and then I'm going to school for health education and medicine. Although I'm starting school, I might come back when there is a break. Never say never!

One thing I wish I knew before getting into this line of work was to be prepared to have a lot of people take advantage of my kindness and to never expect someone to return a favour. If you're too nice and generous, you will be walked all over. I was naïve in the beginning and helped so many dancers with different things. In the end I don't regret helping because I believe we should all help one another and it will all come back to me or whoever needs it the most.

I'm glad to say that I mostly stayed away from all the wrong people and I never went to anyone's house or party I didn't know. I had a supporting boyfriend that I never lied to or cheated on. While I got caught up doing drugs almost every day, I thought I was strong enough to never touch coke, but I have.

I used to feel ashamed about what I did for a living because I was scared to be judged by others without them knowing me first. Before getting in this business, I never judged dancers but I know a lot of people do. I would hear all about it from customers every night working as a waitress at the strip club. Some guys just don't know the full story and they judge dancers like we're basically hookers, drug addicts, alcoholics, useless people, etc. It's wrong of them to assume the worst.

I kept dancing to myself because it's really nobody's business what I do. Like I said, as long as you're not harming your body and others and you love what you do, you should keep your head high and be proud of what you do, no matter what! I only tell close friends or people who are a part of my life that I'm a dancer. If I just meet you for the first time, I won't mention it. You will be told that I work as a promoter at a promotion company.

My advice for new girls getting into this business is this: if you're not mentally strong enough to handle the industry and you doubt yourself, don't get into it. This industry can be emotionally draining and it can bring a lot of unnecessary drama and stress since it's easy to get involved with the wrong people.

I do not regret getting into this business because you learn from everything you do in your life.

# Florida

I snuck into the strip club once when I was 17 and decided then and there I wanted to be a dancer. I admit I liked the attention, but the main reason I got into dancing was for the money.

I was working as a waitress at an upscale trendy restaurant but I hated it. My co-workers always made fun of me, so I quit. I went to see my uncle (who was one of the biggest pimps in our area at the time) and I told him to hook me up with a job as a dancer because his good friend was owner of the strip club. My uncle refused so I told him that if he wasn't going to help me out, I was going to go and be a hooker. He freaked out and reluctantly agreed.

Regarding my family, although my dad was a massive crack head, my mom was great. I told her right away when I started dancing and she was fine with it. What could they she do about it anyways? It wasn't like I was a hooker!

My dad was home one day when I had a friend of mine over that works as a male stripper. Imagine my surprise when my friend said "I know your dad! He was a male dancer for a while!" Boy, was he busted! So he couldn't really be upset about me dancing.

My first time dancing on stage was crazy. It wasn't that I had a problem with getting naked, I just really didn't want to mess up and look awkward. The pressure to do a good job was what made me nervous, not the nudity. I was so nervous I was shaking! Nothing has changed since that first stage show, since I still want to do a good job and put on a good performance. While working in the business, I was always inspired to learn some cool pole tricks.

I was still 17 when I started as a VIP girl and the only person who knew I was underage was the DJ. I'm amazed I didn't quit that first day because I witnessed a guy sitting in front row pull out a huge hunting knife and he stabbed the guy next to him! Another DJ who was hanging out in the bar on his day off ran across the room and tackled the stabber. There was blood everywhere and the cops were called. Thankfully, the guy was okay in the end.

When I first started, I remember not liking some of the older girls who were set in their ways. It seemed as though a small handful of them went out of their way to treat the newer girls like crap. I was a little traumatized by them in the beginning, so I was thankful a few of the nicer girls took me under their wing and looked after me. I felt like a prison bitch!

Sometimes the bar staff made all the difference. Working in this business, I loved the money I made, but I also loved hanging out with the bar staff. I made some great friendships and even joined them after hours for karaoke. It was crazy times back then, smoking joints with friends at 11:00 am every day.

Dancing has provided me with some horror stories though. I refused to go back to work at this one club because I was eaten by bed bugs in my room. I had big red lumps all over my body! They itched like crazy, were very painful and the bites lasted for three weeks. Management wanted me to go on stage and do my show, but I told them to fuck off. I was 'itching' to get out of there so I grabbed my shit and left. I didn't even wait around to collect my pay for the one day I worked since I just wanted out of there. When I got home, I paid $300 to get all my costumes cleaned so that there were no bed bugs in them. Also, one of my girlfriends who worked at that nasty club once had a piece of the ceiling fall down and hit her in the head. We never worked that bar again.

One time, my girlfriend was working and was told by management to dance on top of the bar. While she was naked, some guy came up behind her and poked her in the asshole with his pool cue! She said she had a blue asshole for a week! The staff wouldn't kick him out of the bar and they told her to just suck it up. This is another place we refused to work at after that.

One night I was standing outside the club with a new dancer, Cherry Blossom, when my crazy ex-boyfriend drove up in his truck, he jumped out and yelled at me that he wanted to talk to me. I yelled at him that I didn't, so he jumped back in his truck and drove straight towards us. He drove into the cement barriers that were blocking us and then yelled at me, "Come here and fuckin talk to me!!" I screamed at him to leave, so he took off. From that day forward, Cherry Blossom and I were buddies. Later, we bought about 20 pairs of fake eyelashes and I taught Cherry how to apply them. We had a great time and forgot all about my evil ex.

I remember the time I was doing a VIP dance and my customer started yelling at me for having my lips done. He said it was a stupid thing for me to do, since my original lips were probably nicer looking. I yelled back at him that they WERE my natural lips but I don't think he believed me. Loser.

One afternoon, I was in the dressing room getting ready for my show and I got trapped. I was in my school girl costume and when I was ready to go, I tried to open the door. It was stuck and wouldn't budge, so I called the DJ and he came upstairs and tried opening it from the outside. I wouldn't wait. I didn't want to be late for my show and get a fine, so I crawled out the window onto the roof. Then I went to the window next door, opened it and toppled into the room of another dancer in my schoolgirl costume with my bag in hand, pigtails and high heeled boots. To an outsider, it would have looked pretty crazy!

I was still new to the business when I was doing a VIP dance for a tiny little Asian man. He was so small that I could basically kick a field goal with him. But he wasn't so harmless after all. The hair on the back of my neck stood up when he said to me, "You're so pretty that I want to slit your throat, then choke you and watch you writhe around on the floor until you die." Psycho! I'm amazed I didn't quit right on the spot!

I had only been on the circuit about a year when I had a scary week on the road. It was Monday late at night and I closed and locked the door to my room before I went to bed. The door was pretty heavy and you had to use some muscle to shut it. I went to sleep, only to be woken up around two in the morning by a drunk bald guy in boxer shorts standing beside my bed! Because the door was so heavy, I hadn't shut it properly and he got lost and ended up in the wrong room.

The next day my dancer friend walked upstairs to her room to find a drunk naked man in the hallway! She said she yelled at the naked guy and he yelled back at her. She went into her room, heard a 'bang' and popped out a minute later seeing the naked guy sprawled flat on the floor. The maintenance guy knocked him flat on his ass.

The next two days went by as normal as can be. Then Friday rolled around and we were sitting in the bar relaxing with the staff because the bar was dead. Suddenly a huge girl entered the bar and came running towards us. I jumped up and grabbed the stool I was sitting on, ready to knock her out. She started yelling, "My boyfriend has been in here all week watching you bitches. You got nothing on me!" Then she turned her back to us and gave us the booty shake! We just looked at each other as the doorman ran over to kick her out. She ducked past him and ran back to us. "You bitches got nothing on me!" Again, the doorman pushed her towards the door. She ran back a third time. "You can't handle all this!" she yelled as she snapped her fingers at us and wiggled her neck. That was one weird week!

There were embarrassing moments, too. Once, when I was on my way to the stage to do my 12:30 half show, I stopped at the restroom. I went and did my show like usual but finished off with a legs open type pole move. After my show, I went back upstairs. Just before my next show, I did my usual cookie check and saw pieces of toilet paper speckled on my cookie. Then I remembered the pit stop in the bathroom and realized I forgot to check myself before going on stage. I did my show with pieces of toilet paper stuck to my crotch!

Another time I had major allergies. It was spring time and

very dusty, so my eyes got red and swollen, my sinuses were acting up and I felt awful. I was doing a show and flipped my head upside down. I ended up with two huge snot balls hanging out of my nose!

My dad and my brother like to hang out at the strip club quite often but before they went in, they would call and check with the bar to see if I was working there. If I was, they went elsewhere. One day, I got a call to go replace a girl there last minute. I tried to call my dad to give him the heads up but couldn't reach him. As I was walking towards the stage to do my show, my dad walked into the bar. He saw me, turned around and walked right back out the door, not skipping a beat.

Sometimes I run into people I know, and it can be awkward but I just make the best of it. One of my high school teachers used to tell me that I was a pretty girl. Years later, he came into the strip club where I was working and instead of freaking out, I said to him, "Remember when you said I was pretty? Don't forget to tip me because tipping is sexy!" He didn't know what to do!

Over the years, I have had many gifts given to me by customers. The sweetest gesture was around Christmas when a customer brought in a stuffed Eeyore a couple days after I told him that my aunt was sick and she loved Eeyore. Customers brought me stuffed animals all the time. My favourite gift was a $400 gift certificate to Guess. The weirdest gift was when a customer brought me those weird little Halloween caramel candies that are wrapped in orange paper.

My best customer was a guy I call 'Mr. Good Dick.' I met him while doing my first annual charity event. He tipped me $200 and I sat around with him while he got me drunk. I went to his house and passed out. Later in the night, he gave me a ride back to the bar because I had a show to do. We always seemed to hook up and sleep together when I worked at this bar.

The biggest tip I ever got was when my drug dealer ex-boyfriend came into the bar once and made it rain on stage for me by throwing $800 on stage in fives, tens and twenties. Guess I won't be seeing him for a while since he's in jail now.

Something about me you might not expect is that I like to cross stitch. Three things I can't leave home without are my make-up, baby wipes and money. My stage name is from one of my favourite songs.

I danced for nine years. I quit dancing two years ago because I didn't like some of the new girls and the industry was starting to change. Also, I had quite a few friends who had passed away and it was time for me to do something different with my life. Now I work as a personal trainer and a nanny.

Recently I got a boob job and after I heal I will be going back to dancing so I can make some good money again. I wish I knew how hard it was to get out of this business and stay out. I also wish I knew how much I would miss the people.

My advice for new girls is to shut your mouth and open your eyes. Buy costumes, get promo and don't think you're better than some other girl because she might decide to knock you out!

I will never regret getting into this business. I don't see anything to be ashamed of since I paid my taxes and it was my choice. I made so many awesome friends and I had so many crazy experiences. I was surprised by how nice the girls were and how much different the stripper business actually is from the movies. In one of the Hollywood stripper movies I watched, a dancer kicked a girl down the stairs.

I wouldn't change a thing.

# Forget Me Not

When I turned 19, I worked as a server for almost a year. New management was brought in and some major changes occurred; some of the staff was fired, bad scheduling and stricter rules were put into place. I was told that I talked too much with customers and that made me mad, so I quit and started looking for another serving job. I searched for a month.

I was 20 years old when I got called for an interview for a waitressing job. During this time, my best friend's sister gave me a phone number for a stripper agency. I promised myself that if I didn't get this job, I would call the number. Well, I didn't get hired.

I called and chatted with the agent for almost an hour. He said I would be signed up for an amateur contest the next week but didn't really explain to me what an amateur contest was. I thought it was probably a small audition in front of a few agents. Was I ever wrong! It was a contest for new and upcoming dancers and it was held in a bar that was full of people. To make matters worse, I was the first girl to start off the contest and go on stage. I really didn't have a problem at all with the getting naked part, but I was pretty nervous because I felt awkward and not really sure what to do.

The week after, I was booked for another amateur contest. This time I was prepared and I actually had fun since I felt like I put on a show for the audience. Before I even started in this business, I was at a strip bar on my 19th birthday and I remember thinking, "I could do that!" So I knew I wasn't going to have a big issue with getting naked in front of a bunch of strangers.

I was told by the agency to do a handful of contests, get five costumes together and choose a name. I heard a song years ago where the artist sang about how perfect a girl was by a certain name. I always knew that if I became a dancer, I would use that name. I did everything the agency said and onto the circuit I went!

When I started dancing, I told my older sister what I was up to. I knew she would be upset with my decision, but I didn't realize how mad she would actually get. She was so upset that she told my whole family. I think she was mostly concerned for my safety. My family was just surprised, I think. But, I'm a bit of a different kind of a person so it is not so surprising that I ended up becoming a dancer and my four sisters did not.

I would say that I had a pretty normal childhood. My parents split up when I was about two years old and by the time I was ten, my mom started doing some drugs with her boyfriend. My older sister knew about her doing this and although I was young and I didn't understand what was going on, I knew that something wasn't quite right.

The things I love about this business are the exercise, the dancing and putting on a good show. My favourite comment from customers is, "You made my day." It makes me feel good. I look forward to working at my favourite bars because I have the most fun there and make the most money.

As a dancer, I have received a few gifts from regular customers. My most favourite gift is a bunch of Betty Boop statues which was very thoughtful because I collect everything Betty Boop. I also love it when customers give me hand drawn pictures.

There are some things that I don't like about this industry. I don't like when I'm told by the agency that an owner or manager of a club doesn't like me. It makes me feel bad and I think that the reason why they do this is to try and lower my show price. I refuse to work in a couple bars out of town because of this. Some bars I won't work in because the clientele is really unfriendly.

Another thing that bothers me is when customers (both men and women) sit at gyno row with their arms crossed and look at you like they're bored or not impressed with your show. It's especially rude when people sitting at gyno are busy tapping away and texting on their phone instead of paying attention to your show. Hello! I'm naked up here!

Another thing I don't like about this industry is the creeps. My worst experience in dancing was when I was on the road. One Saturday night, I took a cab back to my hotel. As I was walking in, there was a guy lurking outside and he said that he recognized me from the strip bar. Then he asked me if I wanted to get a room with him and do blow. I told him I definitely didn't and went inside. I hurried to my room, but he followed me. I slid my key card into the door and pushed it open quickly so I could slam it shut behind me. Just before it closed, the guy jammed his arm in the door. I was drunk, so I started to scream and yell. There was a guy staying in the room next to me and I wondered if he was there and if he heard my cries. I wanted to run next door and bang on his door to help me. As I struggled with the creep to try and push him out and shut my door, it got yanked open by the guy next door. He saved the day! He pulled the stranger back and screamed at him to get the hell out of there and leave me alone. The creep took off.

I wish I knew a lot more about this business before I started into it. I love to dance, so I really enjoy my job. But people tend to make assumptions and it can be dangerous. I do love it, though, otherwise. My plan is to travel across Canada and make as much money as possible. I don't intend to do anything else. I plan to dance for as long as possible.

My advice for any girls wanting to get into this business is to be yourself. You'll get other dancers telling you to change things about yourself. Everyone seems to have an opinion and in the end, you should do what feels right for you. Don't get caught up in all the insecurities.

I absolutely do not regret getting into this business. I feel it was the best decision I made in my life. Dancing has helped me with my confidence, is great exercise and has broadened my social network. Since I've become a dancer, I feel more secure with myself and I'm not as shy as I used to be. When I'm asked what I do for a living, I'm not ashamed to say that I am a dancer.

# Ghost Orchid

I grew up as a catholic girl in a very strict family so I moved out of my parent's house when I was 19. I was working at a retail clothing store which wasn't really paying the bills. I needed to make more money. Since I was curious about the ads I kept seeing in the paper about making great cash while dancing, I called the number and went downtown that night to the strip club for an interview. It actually turned out to be an audition in front of customers which I wasn't mentally prepared to do. Since I was pressured to do it, I got on stage which actually used to be a boxing ring. While I was performing, I found myself getting into it and loving the attention as the guys cheered me on. It was such a good feeling!

I worked for a year at this club as a house girl doing VIP dances. It was awesome back then since I didn't have to hustle the customers. They came to me and I was always busy making loads of cash. In the private dance room, there was a couch in the shape of a half circle and when a girl took a customer in there, a security guy would stand at the entrance so there was no need for installing a camera. The customers would sit beside one another while their VIP girl danced in front of them. It really wasn't all that private.

The club was always putting on some crazy boxing and wrestling championships back then. We did ice cream wrestling, pumpkin pie wrestling, Jell-O wrestling and banana split wrestling to name a few. I had a pair of boxing gloves and I was competing every week for prizes. Eventually I was named boxing champion and was even put into a boxing magazine once when they did a feature on our club. Back then, the club was packed every night and everyone made insane amounts of money. Even with my average size boobs I made more money back then, more than I did as a feature girl years later.

A year in, I found out that girls were prostituting there. It was kept very hush-hush and I only found out about it when management approached me to do it! They took me to a hidden room in the back where I witnessed a guy and girl fucking on a couch while two guys sat at a desk watching. I was told that they were security guys making sure nothing got out of hand. I was disgusted and mortified! After seeing my reaction, the manager kept apologizing to me and then he made a move on me and kissed me on the lips! I quit on the spot and hooked up with an agency. That's when I started working the circuit.

I danced the circuit for about eight and a half years but stopped when I got married and had my son. My husband was okay with me dancing until I had our baby. It turned out I had to go back for another five months after our boy was born to make some money, though. As of today, I am out of the industry. I was nineteen when I started and I danced for nine years, ending in 2009.

My family didn't know I was a dancer at first but they found out just before I got married. I was silly and on an impulse I did one of those soft core porn videos. The videographer knew my uncle and one day while they were hanging out together, he said to him, "You gotta check out this video of hot wild chicks at the bar." He started the video and there I was flashing my boobs for the camera. My uncle freaked out and said, "That's my niece!" The guy responded with, "Oh, you know she's a stripper too, right?"

So, I received a call from my uncle out of the blue saying he wanted to get together with me for coffee. Since I hadn't talked to him for two years, I didn't know what it was about. He told me about the video and told me not to worry because he said he wouldn't say a word about it to my parents. I told him I was eventually going to tell them on my own terms because I wanted to clean the slate. I felt bad for lying to my parents all these years. They always thought I was a waitress.

I was proud of myself for being a good girl and not getting roped into the drugs and alcohol and I was also making fantastic money! Unfortunately my uncle broke his promise and told my parents shortly before I was planning to, which was just before my wedding. My parents are very old school people who hated me for it when they first found out. They already loathed me because I moved out of the house without getting married first. I still feel how strained our relationship is today. On the funny side, my parents thought my husband was my pimp for a while!

While growing up, my parents were always very over-protective of me and my older sister. I was never allowed to go out with friends and I was never allowed phone calls. You see, my mom grew up in a household with six sisters and four brothers, all of them being raped by their physically abusive dad.

Because of my mom's awful upbringing, I was always told that men and sex were bad while I was growing up. When I was in high school, I remember the day my parents found out I had a boyfriend. I was taken outside and beaten with a belt and a stick.

In school, I was a band geek. I was the unpopular girl who ate lunch in the bathroom. The tables were turned when some high school friends came into the bar while I was on stage. They didn't recognize me until I said something. They were telling me I was hot and asking me out. It felt so good!

While I was working in the industry, I loved the entertaining, dancing and being on stage, as well as the music, costumes, and getting dolled up because I felt good! The money was abundant and easy to make back then and you always had cash in your purse. I miss it sometimes but I would never go back because I feel that a girl can get a bad reputation from the stereotypes. I'm thankful for dancing though because it opened some doors for me. I was in Playboy and did some modeling, acting and online modeling jobs.

I hated the drama within the industry in regards to the agency and the girls who constantly competed against one another about who had a higher show price. I couldn't stand the cattiness and the constant competition amongst the girls. There always seemed to be two or three girls who hated you because of some jealousy issue.

Another issue I had with dancing was how some customers would get out of control. I was used to the guys who made rude comments, but it was some of the regulars that I didn't like. Just because they gave you money on stage, they thought they had more of a 'relationship' with you and got jealous if you talked to other guys in the room. I guess they expected more from you.

I refused to work out of town because I didn't like going. I didn't like the fact that I didn't know anyone and not knowing if the staff was there for my protection or not. I guess I was still unnerved about the whole prostitution thing at that first bar I worked at. I also found that there were a lot of rules in Alberta and dancers had a quota to do a certain number of private dances by the end of the week which I found quite stressful. Also, you never knew what the bar's standards were. For example, I worked one club where they tried to make me stay in a room that had rat droppings in it! Most of the couches in bars are gross and that is why you will see most dancers lay their blanket down on a chair or couch before they sit down on it.

My embarrassing moment happened in my first year of dancing. I was on stage and wearing a white bodysuit when I got my period. I turned to look at myself in the mirror and was shocked to see a giant blood stain on my crotch area. I was mortified, so I walked off the stage while the DJ told me to get back on and finish my show. Of course I refused and left. Another embarrassing moment was when my tampon string was hanging out while I was on stage.

Once, a girl jumped on stage with me during my show. I'm not sure if it was a good thing or bad thing but I felt like she wanted to attack me. Before I even had a chance to blink, the security guy jumped up and took her down and she got kicked out of the bar.

I was giving a VIP dance to a little Asian guy once. I was only one minute into my first song when he came in his pants. I saw the wet spot and he actually wanted me to keep dancing but I yelled at him, "You're done. Get the hell out of here!" Over the years, I found it quite creepy that I caught a couple guys jerking off while they were sitting at gyno.

A scary story that I will never forget was when a dancer I know overdosed on uppers and downers and I kept her alive in the strip club change room on the floor. She was going in and out of consciousness until the ambulance came. Then she died a few times on the ride over to the hospital. No one else helped. I called 911 and the operator ordered me to lift her from the chair to the floor so she could lie down. I had to keep her awake and constantly check her pulse until the ambulance arrived. She was a mess! She was vomiting and drooling, her eyes were rolling back and she had convulsions. It was crazy! But I wasn't going to let her die because I believe that everyone deserves a chance at life. I have no idea what happened to her after that since I got no thank you. That doesn't bother me since I'm just proud of myself for being the one to step up and save someone's life. It felt good.

My best customer was the guy who gave me a $100 bill on stage once. Over the years I was given gifts such as name brand clothing and designer purses from various customers. The weirdest gift I was given was a fake tiger rug that the guy brought into the club rolled up with a bow on it. The rug is in my son's room now.

Something you would find interesting about me is that I play the drums and the organ because my mom made me take lessons. When I was still in the industry, three things I wouldn't leave home without were my makeup, car keys and wallet. While I was picking my dancer name, I have always liked the first part of my name and then I heard the last part of it in a song. I put the two together and got my stage name.

Before getting into this business, I wish I knew how addicted a girl could get to the money and the attention. It's a glamorous type of lifestyle compared to other women's jobs. Money is always thrown at you so you always have it on hand to buy almost anything you like.

When I got in the business, I was surprised to see the amount of staff, dancers and customers doing drugs in the bars. I didn't know the symptoms until I started doing drugs myself. When I used to see people sniffling, I just thought they had a cold or an allergy since it would never occur to me that they were doing blow.

After I had my son, I had to go back to dancing because my husband got fired from his job and we needed the money. At the time, I was always upset because we were having problems in our marriage and we were constantly fighting. One day, a dancer offered coke to me and I tried it. I ended up doing it regularly for six months. I woke up one day and realized my life was spiralling out of control, so I quit smoking, drinking and drugs cold turkey. I wanted to concentrate on my baby and my other passions which are modeling and acting. I continued to dance for five more months and then I quit.

I do not regret getting into this business because I learned a lot of life lessons from it. I gained confidence and I learned to love myself for who I am. I learned how men work and how to play them, how their minds work and how simple they are and how easy they are to please. I also learned how girls work. Growing up in a sheltered family, I was thrown into a crazy world of nakedness. This whole other world has opened my eyes and I got an understanding how people live and why they go to strip bars. I also learned from other girls as to why they started in this industry in the first place. Am I ashamed of telling people what I did for a living? Most of my friends know but I don't volunteer this information to strangers, so it depends on who I talk to.

Advice I have for new girls getting into this industry is to make sure you don't get caught up in the drugs because they are very addictive. I was strict with myself to be a good girl for many years while seeing it around me all the time. When it was offered to me at a low point in my life, it was easy to fall into. Be strong.

Now that I no longer dance, I miss it and I don't at the same time. These days I am attending school to pursue my passion which is my modeling and acting while I enjoy being a mom to my little boy!

# Ginger

Believe it or not, my rationale for entering the exotic entertainment industry was to help my son. The year was 2005, I had just turned 30 and my son was 7. I was a single mom, sick and tired of struggling to make ends meet. I would spend the majority of my time at odd jobs making shitty money with hardly any time left over to spend with my son.

I saw an ad in the paper looking for exotic dancers. I toyed with the idea for a couple weeks and struggled with my morals for a couple more. Conscious of my nerves, apprehensive because of my age and terrified of people judging me, I finally summoned up the courage. The first night I pulled in $700. End of story.

I was hooked. The money was incredible and the flexibility was ideal. I got to spend the whole day being Mommy. Breakfast, daily drive to and from school, quality time in the evening along with a nice home cooked meal, kid to bed, then off to work. Perfect! The beginning of my career in the dancing world was almost as if a weight had been lifted off my shoulders. I had found a way to find balance in my life and freedom. I had enough flexibility to really focus on being a good mom. I was my own boss, made up my own hours and financially I was finally straight.

After a couple years of freelancing, I got bored, bitter and addicted to the fast cash. I was fed up with the obnoxious men and the rejection I faced on a daily basis freelancing, so I decided to take it to the next level and move onto the stage. The schedule was more demanding, but I wanted more of a challenge and a guaranteed paycheck at the end of the week.

I've always had a passion for dancing and modeling since I was young and I was always very comfortable with my sexuality. So being on the stage and entertaining is something that is exciting for me. However, after a while the demanding lifestyle, scrutiny and schedule really started to take its toll on my sanity and personal life. Ironically, dancing started to take away from the whole reason I got into it in the first place, my son.

It's going on seven years since I started dancing and I believe I'm coming to the end of my adventure in the industry. Mentally, I'm exhausted and the money is not as good as it used to be. It's just not worth everything that you physically, mentally and financially put in. I've been judged and my character has been defined on a daily basis because of what I do for a living. But I can honestly say that dancing has really been my bridge to get me where I'm going. I've established myself financially, met some wonderful women (some fucking twisted ones too) and made some great friends along the way. Being an exotic dancer is something I'll never regret or be ashamed of becoming.

Written by Ginger

*"The ultimate measure of a man is not where he stands in moments of comfort and convenience, but where he stands in times of challenge and controversy."*

-Martin Luther King

# Gladiolus

I started dancing at 15, and I had already seen quite a bit of the business at that time. The first time I got on a plane was when I just turned 17 and I was going with my 18 year old friend to dance in Toronto. I was really nervous and excited but I loved adventure and getting into mischief! My friend was a bit of a bad girl as well. When the plane first took off, I couldn't believe the feeling. I felt free and so happy! I don't know how we did it but we managed to get free drinks on the plane under age (this was a very long time ago). Once we arrived, it was quite late and a maintenance guy came to pick us up and bring us to the girls' house. Back then, we paid $150 for the week to stay in a house with all the other girls that were dancing at the club.

The next morning my friend and I woke up ready to work. We got all pretty and got our best costumes out. Once we got to the club, we were surprised to find that we weren't the features, so we were only getting paid a small amount per day. It was very, very competitive! We had to walk around the club and talk to customers, convincing them to buy dances and pay for our drinks. My friend and I were smashed after a couple of hours but really getting the hang of the job. We were making so much money on stage and off that we were ecstatic!

After a few days, I became friends with the DJ; a gay man who was the same height as me. He was bald, cute and had great style. For some reason, lucky for me, he really liked me and took me under his wing. When I first got there I couldn't do a thing on the pole and I was really nervous but he helped me out so much. He offered to 'show me the ropes' on the pole after the club closed for the night. He taught me my first pole trick; you take a running jump onto the pole, hooking your leg around and spinning as fast as you can! After three days, my leg was so sore and I had a bruise the size of a watermelon. It was worth it though since that became my signature move.

Management told me I couldn't go on stage for a couple days because of the bruising and I also had to cover them on the floor by wearing garters and nylons. So I started spending more time with the customers. The more time I spent, the better I got to know them and the more they liked me. By the end of the week, my friend and I were cleaning house!

Then the trouble began. The girls that had been there for years started getting really jealous. I still don't know why because they were beautiful and amazing. My friend and I would stare at their shows to try to learn from them. We looked up to them. By midweek, my friend was getting close with a certain customer. The veterans didn't like that. Apparently, we were stealing their customers, so the fight was on! One girl told me she was going to smash my head on the shower when I wasn't looking, and that we better watch ourselves or die. Two girls cornered my friend in the bathroom and smacked her across her face so hard it left a mark and a bruise on her eye the next day. Eventually, they made so much trouble for us we had to leave. We were disappointed because we had never seen so much cash in our lives. We learned a lot and felt we were much better dancers. We were ready to take on the world! So off to the next place we went.

Years later, I bumped into the girl that wanted to kill me in a local club. She remembered me first and to my surprise, she was very nice to me. She gave me a skirt that would go with one of my costumes. After that, we were friends every time we saw each other. Funny how our dancer world works!

Written by Gladiolus

# Honeysuckle

I was working at a hardware store when I got a phone call from a friend asking me if I wanted to go with her to Cancun and work at a resort as the entertainment crew. I didn't hesitate; I quit my job and took off.

The resort had a disco and there was a pole on the dance floor. One day, a guest in the resort asked me if we could go up to the disco and dance on the pole. She said that she had taken a couple of lessons in the States and I said I didn't mind, as long as she showed me her moves.

Just by doing one session with that girl, I was hooked and realized I loved pole dancing. Because I was part of the entertainment staff, I asked management if I could add a pole dancing class to the itinerary. They liked the idea and agreed because they were always on the look out for something new and different. So, just from me knowing three little moves, I was now teaching the hotel guests pole moves! After a couple of months in Cancun, I returned home.

When I got home, I went on line and found a pole dancing studio. I enrolled in the class and fell in love with it even more by going to every one of my night classes in the instructor/owner's basement. Four months later she told me she was enrolled in medical school in Belize. Because I was one of her top students, she asked me if I wanted to take over her practice and teach. Since I worked at a gym during the day, I took on the teaching at night.

Then something tragic in my life happened; my dad died. It was too much for me to handle so I quit the gym. Since I loved teaching, I decided to open my own studio. For six months, my students and I had a fantastic time where we even started a burlesque group together. The studio wasn't making enough money to stay open, so I closed its doors and continued classes at the local recreation centre. Another reason why I shut down my studio was that I was not a very good business person. I was too nice and basically gave free lessons since I had a hard time saying no to people when they told me that they had no money. I taught pole dancing at the community centre up until three months ago. This was better than running my own studio because I didn't have to worry about finding students, advertising and collecting money. I just had to show up, teach my class and then take my cheque to the bank. It was really good money!

So, here is the part about me getting into the stripping...

I was about 25 when my friend (a fellow student at the pole dancing studio) and I decided we wanted to try out our pole moves on stage. Together, we contacted the agency and asked if we could do one week out of town to see what the job was like. I educated myself pretty good before I got into this industry and I decided to enter into it slowly. I hung out at a strip bar a lot and became friends with the dancers, so I basically knew what I was getting into._

The agency sent us on the road (I still had the studio open during this time) and we were terrified! The dancer house was a dump and since there was no security, we slept in the same room because we were so scared.

My first time on stage was scary. I remember feeling very awkward and I was flying around on the stage doing every move I could think of. Surprisingly, I felt fine with getting naked in front of people because of the burlesque dancing I had done. There was only one customer in the bar at the time and the staff must've thought I was nuts with my crazy, energetic dance moves! That week, I told friends and family that I was a traveling go-go girl because I wasn't sure how they were going to react. They know that I'm a dancer now.

After that first week, I went back to teaching while my friend continued getting booked and stripping. The reason I didn't continue dancing is because I was pretty freaked out about the sketchiness of the dancer house. That and I basically didn't have enough confidence, especially 'vagina confidence.'

I continued to teach pole dancing at night, and I also found a really, REALLY good job as a dental technician assistant working in the lab making crowns, etc. The people I worked for were fabulous and I learned a lot. They provided medical and dental, which was a great bonus.

Well, it was mandatory for the company to close for two weeks every August for summer vacation. I didn't want to sit around and not make money for two weeks, so I contacted my dancer friend. I was a bit older now and felt like I had more confidence, so I was ready to try dancing again. My friend had now danced for almost a year and didn't want to do it anymore because she felt pretty burnt out, but she went along with me anyways. That first week back to dancing, I actually enjoyed it and had a great time.

After the two weeks, I went back to my dental job. This job was the most awesome, comfortable, supportive job I've ever had. It was so secure. I know this sounds kind of crazy, but I could see myself getting too comfortable with it and coasting along with life, only to find myself not experiencing anything else many years later. So, I quit and they were so upset! I quit the job in order to force myself to go to school in August and that was only five months ago. I plan on dancing until I go to school to become a certified dental technician.

My mom knew that I quit my job, so she called me up and told me to come home and spend Christmas with the family. So, instead of moving right away, I went home for Christmas. Then she convinced me to go to Baja, Mexico with her and her husband. I agreed and we traveled around in a motor home for three months. It was wonderful!

Towards the end of the Baja trip, it was my friend's turn to call me this time. "Want to go dancing again?" she asked. I basically had no job, no apartment and didn't know what else to do, so I agreed. I got home from Baja and had four days to unpack, see my friends, get my financial affairs in order and leave. This was only a couple weeks ago!

I grew up on a farm and had an amazing childhood. We had a trampoline, horses and I even had my own pottery studio. I got along very well with both my parents and my parents waited until after I was done high school to get a divorce. My mom knows what I do for a living and she is supportive. I'm not sure what my step dad thinks and it really doesn't matter. My older brother, on the other hand, is neutral on the subject.

Even though I have only been in this industry for a short amount of time (I have been dancing steady now for four weeks), I have come to love the costumes, music, dancing and the power involved. I wouldn't say that the money is the greatest, but it is nice to receive tips. The biggest tip I ever got was $100. It was during my first week of dancing and as I was walking back to the change room in my blanket, a customer came over to me and was holding out a bill for me. I didn't know the rules or protocol about taking money from customers so I told him I needed to get dressed first. When I came back from the dressing room, he was still there waiting for me. I was surprised when he handed me a $100 bill since I thought he was tipping me a smaller amount than that. If I would've known that it was $100, I would've just grabbed it and thanked him. Never mind the rules!

There is a down side to dancing. Mostly I hate the bad accommodations that are provided for dancers, the black and blues (the bruises) and the stigma that comes with being a dancer since a lot of people think that dancers are not regular people.

There are always horror stories about the different bars from the other girls, but I think I should make my own opinion and try every bar at least once. The only clubs I don't dance at are in my hometown because I don't want to run into any of my dad's old friends or even people I know.

I made the amateur mistake of giving some guy my email once. Although he seemed very nice, he was a lot older than me and he emails me once in a while. I think he just wanted a friend but I ignore his messages anyways. That's as close as I got to a stalker so far.

My embarrassing moment was when I crossed my feet and got my boots laces tangled and caught up in the opposite boot. I was stuck around the pole! I managed to jump around a little and untangle myself. Everyone was laughing, but in a good natured way.

Something you would find interesting about me is that I did stand up comedy in LA. It was an open mike in North Hollywood. I went with a friend and the outcome was horrible; talk about getting your ego crushed! People in the business say that you need to bomb on stage 200 times before you get a laugh.

Two things I won't leave home without is a good black thong (it'll go with anything) and my car. If I forget anything at home while I'm on the road, I just buy it.

One thing I learned about myself is that I am an eye-baller. I enjoy eye contact and joking with the customers. If I see someone texting while sitting at gyno, I don't get upset like a lot of dancers do. I ask who they're texting and strike up a conversation.

I'm not ashamed of what I do for a living, but I am aware of how the world thinks. So, I am careful to pick and choose who I tell about what I do for a living.

My advice for new girls coming into this business is, don't take anything personally!

# Jasmine

I was working part time at a warehouse retail store and was promised full time work but never got the hours. On top of that, I had a quota to sell a certain number of crappy memberships or I would be fired. I found out that a girl I knew from high school was a dancer who claimed to make $10,000 a month by hustling VIP dances. Since I wasn't getting ahead with my payments for my student loan and bills, I called up the girl from high school and asked if I could dance with her. She agreed but had to see if I could handle it. I went shopping with her for some new outfits and she showed me how to apply my makeup. Then she coached me on how to do a VIP dance which I had to do for her boyfriend when he got home from work. All I can say is that it was VERY awkward!

Shortly after, I quit my job and went to the strip club to talk to the manager about hiring me as a VIP dancer. I thought he was going to laugh at me because of my baby face but he said that he would give me a chance and see how it went. I wasn't too nervous about getting naked because I was confident in my looks. I had promised myself that if I couldn't do it sober, I wouldn't do it at all. My first two weeks of dancing, I was completely sober.

My first VIP dance went pretty well. I danced for a hip hop dancer. He was a 30 year old Asian guy who danced for me first and when it was my turn to dance for him, I felt like I needed to impress him and danced my heart out. He was very sweet to say that it was an honour that he was my first customer. I hooked up with the agency shortly after, and went on the circuit. No more freelancing for me!

At this point, I had to choose a stage name. I was originally going to use a native name like Onatha which is based on a princess who was saved by the agency of the sun. For me that would be the agency 'saving me' from having to work as a freelance dancer. The agents didn't like it; they said people might have trouble pronouncing it. I had a friend who used to DJ at three clubs in Florida, so I asked him what I should name myself. He suggested I pick a cute name like Veronica, Betty or Alice and then put something cutesy at the end. My dancer name was born!

There are a lot of reasons why I love my job. I love learning and watching new styles of dance, and finding new music. I love all music, but my favourites are world music (reggae, African, Korean, Bhangara, Latin, and Arabic), hip hop, dance and 80's/90's classics.

I appreciate being told I'm beautiful, making new friends, and losing myself on stage. I love it when new girls watch my show and I know they are impressed by it. I love the exhibitionism, the helpful hints from the more experienced girls, sharing funny stories and the fact that I learn something new every day about everything. I also love knowing that I'll be working with girls that I love or admire because it makes the coming week much more exciting.

I love receiving gifts from customers because it means they think of me. Other than getting joints from customers, one of the nicest gifts I've received was a fuzzy animal print compact mirror (the customer knew that I liked animal print). The weirdest gift I got would be a $5.00 bill wrapped around a small box. In the box was a glow in the dark cock ring. I remember doing a show once and after I was done, a customer walked up to me, handed me a $100 bill and told me it was the best show he had ever seen. That was the biggest tip I got from one guy.

While there is a lot of good in the industry, there are things I hate too. Annoying techno, poor attitudes about crowd response, and girls counting money in front of others or bragging about how much they made. I hate being told what to do while dancing, when customers tell me I'm better or prettier than the next/previous dancer, being told I suck when I did my best, customers who are brought to the club under duress and rude customers.

When a customer is rude, I don't get mad. Instead, I have some witty comebacks. I simply say, "Yeah, your mom!", "You might not like me, but your daddy does", "Wasn't it your big-boned mama that let me in here?" or simply, "Tell someone who cares, I don't!"

Over the years, I have found that dancing can be hard on my body. The injuries that I have acquired over the years are a pulled left rib muscle, dislocated right shoulder (twice!), sprained right foot, sprained thumb and lifted baby toenails.

Working in this industry for the past four years, I have my share of stories. One of my funny stories was when I had to be escorted to the lounge outside the strip club by security because I was too drunk to realize where I was going! I had to be dropped off, picked up for my show, then back to the lounge for more karaoke, then back to the strip club for my last show. (Thank you, A!)

I also remember slipping on the ramp coming off the stage in non-stripper style shoes immediately after yelling to the DJ that my shoes weren't slippery at all! Another time I tried to do a somersault in between the two poles. I banged my head on the pole, and then spun out of control into the back mirror. All that, just because I told the DJ that I was going to put on an exciting show for him! One time I had to call down to the DJ that I needed more time to get ready because I put my shoes on the wrong feet! I was sober too.

Once, I kicked an entire jug of beer on a customer that many people including staff described as a big jerk. It was by accident of course, but I believe it was karma via stripper!

Another one of my crazy episodes occurred when I was the official purse and hoop earring holder while my two girlfriends beat the crap out of five girls downtown. The biker I was with waited with me and we both agreed that if police became involved, we were just innocent bystanders (with all three purses and two sets of earrings being mine, of course).

Some of my embarrassing moments happened because I was new and didn't know any better. My first day, my period leaked through my white costume and I didn't realize it until the end of my show. Did I mention it was a super 'spready' show! I can't believe I'm going to admit this but one time I actually farted just as the music went quiet. I was spread eagle only five feet from the customers!

Another time I was very drunk at work and did a very sloppy lap dance. I fell all over the customer! I was barefoot so my shoes were not an excuse. At this same club, I puked on a customer and was asked to leave work early because I was way too drunk. The manager followed me down the hallway to the dressing room and watched me take forever to put my clothes on and then informed me that I NEED to quit drinking.

One of my scary stories was when I was stalked from work to a bar downtown. It was an old Asian man who propositioned me for $200! As soon as I realized he was there watching me dance with some other dancers from work, I had a bouncer ask him to leave.

Another scary episode was when I was wasted out of my skull while I was walking to the light rail transit after work. I rode all the way home rather than take a cab. I got yelled at by the other dancers the next day because it was a stupid move. I was in a very unsafe area.

The one thing that surprised me about this industry is that it really does matter how you dance. In the beginning, I used to wing it. I soon realized that my dancing should be fluid and smooth. I thought that I was so entertaining back then, but after other dancers told me to slow down and not to take my panties off *like that*, I thought different. I paid attention and watched the other girls' shows in detail to see how I could improve my own dance style.

One thing I wish I knew before getting into this line of work is that people (even other dancers) will try to take advantage of you just because you're a dancer. I find that most girls are pretty naïve when they start out in this business. When I started out, a dancer told me to give her some of my money because she would save it and put it in the bank for me. She ended up taking hundreds of dollars from me but I cut my losses and moved on. Lesson learned – you can't trust anyone.

Something interesting about me is that I get very turned on by belly dancing because I find it very sexy. Three things I won't leave home without are my cell phone, my schedule and heels.

I am always asked about my childhood and if I have any daddy issues. For the hundredth time, I have no daddy issues. My dad and I have a great relationship. He retired early and was always home and always there for me. It's just that I grew up in a very large family, constantly competing for attention so I became a bit of an attention whore. That is why I enjoy my job so much. I love the attention. When I started dancing, I was in a relationship where I was never complimented enough. He wanted me to quit dancing, but I loved getting all the compliments at work. So instead of quitting dancing, I quit him!

My advice to new dancers is to always smile, always follow your heart, always trust your instincts and never let anybody get the best of you. You chose this job so OWN IT! Whether it's 15 minutes or 15 years, embrace only the positive energy and have fun with awkward or embarrassing moments you may encounter. Also, never be afraid to ask questions because if you don't ask, you'll never grow as a dancer or person.

I will never regret getting into this business. Since I've started dancing, I've learned a lot. I've learned how to be independent, how to make friends, how to maintain a good reputation, and how to look in the mirror and not feel ugly. I've transformed from having an addictive personality to having control over my bad habits, like drinking. I've also learned to always be true to myself. I'm a role model to new girls because I teach them to enjoy their youth without damaging their future. During the four years while working in the industry, I always made sure I still made time for friends, family and loved ones.

My plan is to dance for one more year. I would love to get married, work in hospitality and become a mom. When I retire, I know I will always miss my dancer days. I will always be proud to say I was an exotic dancer!

# Jolan

I was going to college and working in retail when I started dating a male dancer. During the four months that we dated, I would go with him to his shows and watch how the women would throw money at him. I didn't have a problem with it and I actually thought it was kind of funny and pretty cool that he made lots of cash. He took me to his agency where I had the chance to meet his agent. Things just didn't work out with us though and so after four months of dating, we broke up.

When I was 24, I decided to make a change in my life. I hated my job at the time because I was making no money, so I called up the agent I had met. He arranged for me to do an amateur contest and I actually found out that the getting naked part really wasn't as big a deal as I thought.

After a few more amateur contests I started working the circuit. My first day on the job, I remember thinking how weird and kind of depressing it was that there were so many guys sitting in a strip bar at noon.

I've met some pretty interesting people in this business. The first one that stands out is The Nudist. When I see him, we end up having very philosophical conversations.

My other unusual customer is the sock guy. He has a serious foot fetish. He buys our old socks for $10 and gives us a new pair. Sometimes he'll throw a chocolate bar into the deal.

Dancing is a great job. I love how liberating it is. My eyes opened when I found out that dancers aren't 'certain kinds of people.' This job has brought me out of my shell. Its fun, the girls are great and I feel that it's an art form. I couldn't believe how physically exhausting it was in the beginning and how bruised your body can get from learning new pole tricks. A bruise on a dancer's body does not mean a boyfriend is beating her!

Although I love dancing, the things I don't like about this industry is the lack of fairness.

I have been dancing now for four and a half years and my family still doesn't know what I do for a living; they think I work in a nightclub. I would like to continue dancing and finish paying off my debt, and then I want to go back to school.

The advice I would give a new girl starting out is to ask the agency to give you $5 more per show right off the bat. You'll always get low balled so with that $5 you have a bit of a buffer.

To this day, I do not regret getting into this business because I learned a lot about myself.

# Kalei

I lived in 11 foster homes before the age of 10. I never knew who my dad was and my mom was an escort and prostitute crack head who worked the streets until I was 15. My mom had me too young, so she was never around when I was growing up. When I was five years old, I remember changing the diapers of one of her friend's babies because my mom and her friends were out partying all night and working so they could keep partying. My grandma had taken me in and looked after me whenever she could until I was twenty one. I consider her my mom. She was my everything.

I was a lost soul growing up and I started to go to the bars with my cousin when I was just 13. She worked with my mom as a prostitute and an escort. When I was 14, I ran away and my cousin found me living downtown. Because I had no other choice but to go home with her, while I was there I was exposed to heroin, crack, coke and weed. I tried it all, and since I was high as a kite, one night I was raped up the ass by a guy my cousin knew. After, he must have felt guilty. He would give me little presents such as perfume and a trinket type of charm for my necklace; he basically paid for my silence. Shortly after, my cousin and I got into a fight over it. I was threatening to call the cops and send her friend to jail for what he had done to me. She said she knew nothing about it and she later told me she had dealt with him.

When I turned 16, I entered a 'Bare as You Dare' contest and by the time I was 17, I had fake ID and started dancing. Three and a half months into the job, I almost got caught. I quit after four months.

Shortly after I quit, I got married, settled down and became a mom. In 2004, my grandma was hit with cancer in her jaw. So, I left my failing marriage (my husband and I were together for two years) and I ran to my grandma's side. She went for surgery to have her jaw bone removed and the doctors made a new jaw for her after removing the back bone from her leg. It was a painful ordeal for her, but she managed to get through it.

Two years later grandma died in a car accident while my grandpa was driving. Her passing was too painful for me to deal with, so I partied for three weeks straight.

My ex was upset with me, so he called the cops on me. The kids were completely removed from my care because of my addiction to drugs and the suicidal thoughts I had at this time (I had tried choking myself with a belt). I'm sad that I missed out on seven years of my kids' lives because of my ex.

I was 24 when I went back to dancing fulltime. I got paid to do an amateur contest and since I was out of shape and really nervous, I got pretty drunk. I remember thinking it was a great escape and it was pretty awesome that I got paid to just get hammered and dance. My cousin came to watch and cheer me on.

I had been experimenting with drugs for a long time and was considered by many to be the cocaine queen. I didn't pay for any of my drugs because I was always hanging out with people who had lots. Because of the large amount of drugs I was taking, at one point I was up for five days straight because I did one and a half ounces of coke. Since I lived and breathed the drug, I started to go crazy and had to take a couple of days off because I thought there were people hiding under my bed.

Three and a half years ago, I was partying at a bar and then left to go to an after-hours bar with a group of people. Someone offered me an orange cooler and the next thing I knew, I was puking and someone was holding my hair. I don't remember leaving the bar and when I woke up, I was in my bed with bruises on my wrists. Money was missing out of my wallet and I knew I had been raped.

At Christmas, my ex was being a dick to me and he wouldn't allow me to see my children. I also owed a lot of money for a bar tab. The combination of stress and loneliness depressed me again, so I took 11 hydromorph pills (44mg) and a line of coke. I felt like hell, realized what I had done and called the ambulance. In total, I have tried over 10 suicide attempts but they have all failed.

I hit rock bottom in January of 2009 and I spent two weeks in the hospital because I was depressed. I missed my kids, my grandma and an ex who committed suicide by hanging himself when I was 18. The hospital wanted to keep me for only seven days but I asked to be held for an extra week because I didn't trust myself. I found a chapel in the hospital and began to pray. It helped me to heal.

For a year after that, I used to drink a twenty-sixer a day. I woke up sick every morning. One day I finally decided that I didn't want to be 'that person' to my kids, so I went to AA and did a nine month sobriety course while staying in a detox place.

My family knows what I do for a living and I don't really care whether they are supportive or not since it sure wouldn't surprise them! My grandfather said he watched my show once and told me that he would come back to watch me again, and that was his way of trying to convince me to quit. I wouldn't put it past him since he has his own crazy issues. My brother and I talk once in a while and I only talk to my mom when I have to. I don't get calls from my family checking in with me or to say hi because they don't really care. The most important thing in this world to me is my daughter and son who are 9 and 10. Other than my kids, I'm alone in this world.

Working in this industry, I love the freedom, the travel and the money. The fact that I can drink and smoke weed at work is a bonus. I love that I have two alter egos. As a dancer, you're always an actress. It's fun to be able to change who you are during every show. It's a fantasy world and I am able to break away from my life and just be someone normal and untainted. I love the power of being able to make the 90 year old man or the geeky guy sitting at the stage think that he is the most important person in the world. Dancing is a world where I make the rules.

While working in this industry, I have come to hate the scandalous girls and ruthless people I have met. It has taught me that I don't know who to trust in this business. There is always a price to buy these people out. A normal person is so naïve, and as a dancer you see everything. I also hate realizing how scummy men are since I have seen guys who won't spend money on their kids but they will spend it on dancers. I also detest some of the crappy agencies that promise you bookings but end up giving them to other girls.

I refuse to work at certain bars because I don't want to run into enemies and certain people that I slept with there. I won't work at places where people remember me as a flaked-out coke head.

One of my creepy stories was when a guy was watching me through binoculars in the bush as I was sitting on the back of a motorcycle. I had no idea until he came by the bar later to tell me what he did. It creeped me out that he was so open about telling me that.

Another guy stalked me on a social networking site and sent me photos of him getting head from some guys as well as some girl with bad hair. I was already grossed out from the pictures of the guys going down on him but I didn't know whether to be grossed out by the girl giving him head or the fact that she had some nasty afro hair! I emailed him back and threatened that I'd have his kneecaps busted out if he sent me any more sick shit like that!

One time, I was doing a show and talking to some guys who were sitting at front row when I looked over and saw some guy with his dick pulled out and he was stroking it. The guy was scruffy looking, wearing a ball cap and had a goatee. He was drinking pop but had snuck beer into the bar and was drinking it from out of his bag. I blasted him in front of everyone in the bar and got him kicked out.

As for regulars, I have a guy that is around 80 and he is the sweetest man I have ever known. He wobbles into the bar on his cane as his nurse (who sometimes hangs out and watches the shows) helps him in. Most of the times she leaves and comes back later to pick him up. He gets shit-faced and I always have to run for Kleenex because his nose runs. He always gave me a 50 cent tip and in return I would give him posters and other free promo. He is such a sweet man. About six months ago, I was dancing there for the week when he gave me a pill bottle full of pennies. He said, "It may not be much, but it's all I have. I just want you to know how appreciated you are." It's a little corny, but I carry that little pill bottle full of pennies everywhere. I consider it my good luck charm and I will save it until the day I die.

The strangest gift I got from a customer was jolly ranchers and homemade beef jerky. The nicest gift came from a guy I consider a creeper. It was a pretty bracelet with tiger-eye beads. There is the scarf guy who brings a bag of pashmina scarves into the strip club and lets his favourite girls pick one. I made such a big deal about how nice they are that I now have eight scarves in all different colors from him. Since money is always a favourite gift for a dancer, the biggest tip I ever got from a customer on stage was $600. There is a stalker that writes love letters to dancers in great detail. It's pretty creepy since he describes his fantasies and what he wants to do to the girls. Most of the letters are very unsettling and many girls have gone to the cops about it.

My most embarrassing moment was when I hadn't slept in two days because I was so high. I was doing my show when I started to sketch out, so I yelled at the DJ to cut my set and get me off the stage. Because I couldn't handle it, I was laughed at.

Another private thing about me is that the three things I won't leave home without are my vibrator, cell phone and bag of costumes.

The one thing that surprised me about this industry was how

false it is. Everybody glorifies it and leaves out the addiction to money and drugs. As a dancer, you don't have a home because you travel all the time. People think that dancers live a rock star life but there is more to it. Dancers are also always being criticized. Girls spread rumours about other girls, some of them try to steal your guy away, are ripping you off or even stealing from you. You don't know who your friends really are and that's sad because you spend so much time with them.

The one thing I wish I knew before getting into this line of work was how much it eats away at your soul. Although girls deny it, but every time you get on stage, you lose a piece of yourself.

I have been dancing steady for seven years. I'm hoping to quit soon and get out by the end of the year although I have quit twice before and came back. There is a saying – a dancer only quits until the money runs out.

The biggest regret in my life is that I have lost many years of being a parent. I also pushed people away when they were actually trying to give me a chance.

Am I ashamed of telling people what I do for a living? Yes and no. Yes, because of the relationships I've had with boyfriends and their families. Also, when I'm ready to leave this industry and I'm ready to apply for a new job, I think about what I should put on my resume explaining the time gap. I have looked after my alcoholic grandfather as a personal care nurse in the past, so I guess I could use that title.

My advice for new girls getting into the business is to take one day at a time. Don't flap your gums to the wrong people and don't act like you know everything. Have fun and enjoy it while you can, but also be careful of who you trust. You can lose everything and everyone in a second, so don't lose sight of who you were when you started off. She's the one that matters the most. She is the one who will still be there when you're done dancing and everyone else is gone.

And no, I am not ashamed of what I do, of who I have

become. In fact, I am proud of it since it is a job which requires a lot of effort. If people don't like it, they can kiss my ass since I do not regret who I am. I have grown a thicker skin and have grown wiser as a person.

# Kalina

The first time I ever set foot in a strip club, I was a 20 year old college student. A friend suggested that I get a job there as a server. I was reluctant to apply because I grew up very Christian and was always told how slutty strippers were and that they were drug addicts with no education. After I got hired, I met a few of the dancers and realized they were normal people. I admired their courage and confidence to go on stage and I wished that I would be able to do that.

After college, I moved to the city where my family is and got a job in the hospital's record department. I worked there for almost a year but ended up quitting because I hated living there. I moved back to the big city and while trying to get another hospital job, I got a gig dancing with a burlesque group. The girls in the group eventually got frustrated with the poor management and quit, so I went on to bartend at various bars around the city while the other girls began dancing.

They told me about the fantastic money they made and we talked about booking with each other. Since there is only one agency in Alberta, I went to them to get my dancing licence. It is mandatory to get a criminal record check at the cop shop, but I had a confrontation with the manager at the record check department and because of a misunderstanding, she smeared my name to the agency claiming I'm a drug addict with a criminal record, which is not true in any way!

Time went on and I found a great nursing program in BC, so I decided to move there and pursue my future plans. I tried getting work but was unable to and was running out of money. I couldn't get a student loan for the nursing program because I was only doing part time classes and to be able to qualify for a student loan, you have to be a BC resident for one year.

So, I found a dancing agency in BC and met with them. They treated me with respect and I felt comfortable booking with them. I've been dancing with them ever since, which was a few months ago at the age of 24.

A few weeks ago, I told my dad that I am a dancer. He's not mad, but he is disappointed. I try to bring it up when we talk, but he changes the subject. My two sisters guessed that I was a dancer because of my travel schedule and the fact that I own a pole. My mom doesn't know because I haven't talked to her in years.

There are six kids in my family. Growing up, my dad made enough money for us to live comfortably in a nice home, and my parents were respected people who weren't drug addicts or alcoholics and they never smoked. We were 'churchy people,' Mormon at one point.

My dad and I were very close and I've always been able to talk to him about anything. My mother, on the other hand has never been very supportive and I've never felt close to her. She left my dad when I was 14, so I consider my oldest sister to be my mom because she basically raised me when it came to girl problems. My oldest brother and sister were already away at school when my mom left my dad with us younger kids (three girls and one boy) all a year and a half apart from each other in age. I feel sorry for my dad having to raise three hormonal teenage girls by himself. I'm probably responsible for most of the grey hair he has.

My first day on the job is a blur. I drank quite a bit of alcohol and I was super scared. I tried to move slowly, but like many new girls I moved too quickly, spinning around the pole. I was scared to get naked but it was also an adrenaline rush! All the girls that week seemed really bitchy, except one. I was already scared and got no support from the other girls since two of them mentioned something about my weight which was hurtful because I struggle with my weight a lot.

One of my most embarrassing moments was on the last night I was drinking. The bar was packed and I was in the middle of a pole trick which is called a butterfly. The pole felt slippery and as I extended the butterfly, my hand slipped and I fell, landing on my hands and knees like a cat. I decided to stop drinking because of this embarrassing episode.

In the short time I've been dancing, two creepy incidents stand out. Once, the owner of one of the clubs I was at for the week got super drunk and coked out. He came into the dancer change room and started yelling at all the girls. I had to go on stage and while I was dancing, he was picking fights with customers. I was scared that I was going to get a bottle or something thrown at me so I barely danced and just lay on my blanket out of the way until my set was over. I won't go to that club again.

The other time occurred while I was dancing at an out of town club. I swear the club was filled with dirty old perverted creepers for the whole week. During one of my shows, there was a dirty man who made licking and finger gestures at me every time I looked at him. He walked over to me after my show and told me in detail how he wanted to eat me out. I was disgusted and got him kicked out of the bar. Just because I'm naked does not give anyone the right to say those things to me or degrade me!

On the bright side, one of my best customers would be the guy that put $100 on stage for me last week!

I hate the stigmatism that comes with being a stripper and there is also not as much money as I thought there would be. I refuse to work at one strip club as I have issues with a DJ who works there. He's rude and very unfriendly and he doesn't do his job. He puts a dancer on stage, starts her CD and then he disappears. Between songs there is a long awkward pause of silence when he's supposed to talk. I was told by another girl that her CD was skipping and he wasn't there to change it.

The one thing that surprised me about this industry was the lack of clubs and work available. I knew the industry was down from what it used to be but it still surprised me with how small the circuit is. I'm lucky to almost always have work, but I know of some girls that don't always have a full booking schedule.

Before getting into this line I work, I wish I knew places and people that sold quality costumes. I've spent money on shitty costumes and I am now paying even more money for better costumes.

With this job, I love the travel. I have no problem living out of a suitcase. When I leave home, three things I can't be without are my cell phone, space heater and a book. People would find it unusual to learn that I'm terrified of girls and I only have a handful of female friends but tonnes of guy friends. I feel comfortable around guys but don't really enjoy being around girls.

When I was in my burlesque dancing group, we had to pick a dancer name. I told the girls that I wasn't sure what my name should be. Someone asked me what I would name my daughter if I had one. Another one of the girls suggested the second part to that name because it sounds nice. So, I use my burlesque dance name as my stripper name.

I'm not ashamed of telling people what I do for a living but I don't brag about it or inform anyone unless they ask. I feel people out before I tell them because dancers have a bad rap. People think that all dancers are drug addicts or alcoholics that are not educated and can't do anything else. Instead, I tell people that I do promo work in bars. I met a guy once and without him even knowing I was a dancer, he told me that all strippers are sluts and whores.

My plan is to dance for at least two more years. I was hired by an Australian agency so I will be going to dance there for a year. They are an international agency and they deal with clubs in Paris, Macau, Hong Kong, New Zealand and the Caribbean which I would like to work at. I might as well make money while seeing the world since school will always be there but being able to travel like this won't.

I have some advice for new dancers coming into this industry. As scary as it is, try not to drink! Once you get into a routine of drinking to do your job, it's hard to stop. When you trip and fall, the customers know that you're drunk and it's definitely not attractive and you feel like an ass. I got in the habit of having to drink to be able to dance. I was eventually consuming half a bottle of gin a night to feel drunk. I was tired of feeling like shit the next morning, so I quit. The calories were unnecessary too.

I do not regret getting into this business because it's given me lots of life experiences and helped me with my body conscious issues.

# Lady Slipper Orchid

This is what I remember from my 11 years of dancing. It's pretty much a blur because I drank every single day. The only way I am able to piece together my story is to look at my posters and the schedules I saved. I am sure there are more stories I could add but I think this is all I want to remember.

When I turned 19, I was working as a waitress at a night club next to a strip bar. That year, my dealer boyfriend bought me a boob job and a brand new convertible Mustang GT!

I wasn't working after I had my operation so I was becoming an alcoholic and craving attention. I had it all; nonexistent money problems and not a care in the world, plus I was just plain reckless. After partying all night with my new rack and hot car, I came home in the morning to find my boyfriend waiting up for me. We had a huge fight and he told me that he was going to stop giving me money to go out with and I would have to pay for my car – $765.00 a month plus gas and insurance. Naturally, I was pissed off and freaked out that he cut me off! I was so young and didn't know what to do, so I started looking in the paper for jobs. Without any education or real job experience, I felt hopeless. Not to mention downright depressed, due to all the alcohol I was drinking.

The next day I was looking through the paper again and started to read through the adult entertainment section. I had seen an ad for exotic entertainers wanted at the strip club, so I called and got a time to come down that night. I grabbed some lingerie and headed down to the interview. They told me if I was ready, I could start right then and there. The bar was really busy so I decided to try it out. The whole time I was thinking, "My boyfriend will be *sooooo* mad! Yes!"

I was a natural at performing and loved the attention. In fact, I loved every minute of it! My first time on stage, I wore black leather pants and a black halter. I danced to AC/DC and

Aerosmith. Everyone loved it! That first night I made $700 in six hours. How easy was that! Management asked if I wanted to come back and I said "HELL YA!" Where else could I make money like that? I ended up going back four more times that week and started to make friends with all the girls. I brought home $3500 in five shifts!!! There were no costs, you just showed up and started hustling (those were the good old days). When I decided to go back, I had to come up with a stage name. I took my friend's name because I liked it and the second part came from a song.

Finally my boyfriend asked me where I was making this kind of money. I hadn't told him anything up to this point because I wanted to drive him nuts. Finally I said, "I'm a STRIPPER and I made $3500 in five shifts! So there!" I waited for him to start freaking out. Instead of being angry, he started to think about it and said, "That's really good money. Do you like it?" I said I did and he showed support. Whatever I wanted I got.

Six months went by and I had made a lot of money but I felt that the bar was taking advantage of me. At that point I had creepy regular customers drop $500-$1000 on me when they came in.

All the girlfriends I had made while dancing started to talk, saying that they were unhappy at the bar. We heard that we could get paid more money working at other bars, so I went to work at a different strip club and started to make even more money as a VIP girl. I brought home $4000-$5000 a week in five shifts (six hours per shift). I also became friends with the feature dancers. I admired their costumes and shows, and I told myself that I would be one of them and so it happened. Be careful what you wish for!

One of the features was a beautiful girl who had a bad cocaine habit. She was the BIGGEST feature in the industry at that time and she had even been in magazines. We looked similar since we were the same height, weight, hair color, boobs, etc. One night she asked me to do her show for her, due to the fact that she was high on coke and felt sick. She even offered me the use of her costumes and music since I would practice dancing on stage in between shows when it was dead in the bar. I was really good at pulling off pole work with ease. She trusted me with her room key and cleared it with the manager. So I wore a green Vegas style costume worth $1000, complete with feather boa, hand beaded bodice and sequined skirt for my show. I had a fantastic response – $200 in tips plus the feature paid me her show price which was $60 at that time. I made $260 in 18 minutes. I was hooked!!!!

So in the next few months, she did more and more drugs. Slowly, she slipped away. I would cover her shows and be her go-to girl if she needed anything. The bar was fine with our arrangement and they were actually happy that I could be her double. They put up with it and then slowly stopped booking her. Meanwhile, I would go work at the bars to cover her ass when she needed it. Finally she went to rehab and quit dancing for good.

After she was gone, I took her place. I found myself working in the best bars in the city, and getting paid top dollar from the very beginning. I had the best custom-made costumes, did the most memorable shows, was an adult film producer/star and exceeded all my clients' expectations. I was trained by the top girls in this business...but at what cost?

It cost me huge. I was at the height of my career, surrounded with unhappy alcoholic/drug addicted people and that was just fuel added to the fire. I had many stresses in my life and then to add to it all, my boyfriend proposed to me after six years. He was a paranoid dealer with no goals, so even though he had proposed I knew we would never set a date. Cops followed us all the time, and I knew I couldn't handle that in the long term. I wanted to escape but just didn't know how. Years went by before I broke up with my fiancé. Then I had another great relationship but unfortunately my path of self destruction ruined that one too.

Work was such a blur. I always got drunk, and I'm talking blackout drunk, five to six days a week. I could drink a forty-pounder by myself in one day. I have no clue how I stayed alive and unharmed, although I would often come home with bruises or something hurt on my body. I started to feel really unhappy in my life and realized that I needed a career change. Even the bars were starting to get pissed off at me for drinking so much, even though they would buy me the drinks.

One day, a co-worker offered me cocaine. She said it would sober me up. It did just that and I could drink more too. Near the end of my career, my boyfriend got a job offer in another province, so we moved there and things got worse. My drinking career was coming to an end, and I had switched my addiction over to cocaine. Some of the DJ's would even have a line waiting for me in the booth before going on stage. I didn't see my boyfriend much and spent many days and late nights alone. I started to hang out with a cokehead stripper and we started to do drugs during the day when my boyfriend was at work for 12-14 hours at a time.

At the end of my career, I went on an eight day bender where one day blended into the next. I was sleeping in my car or on a dealer's couch because I was too fucked up to drive and I didn't want to see my boyfriend because I was so high. After he left the house, I would go home to shower and get ready for work. Finally on the eighth day of this bender, I looked at what I was doing and saw a pattern. Crying in my car at 8:00 am, in a bar parking lot all alone, I had had enough. I wanted to change my life. I started up my car and drove home.

I got home in time to catch my boyfriend before work and I told him what was going on. He had no idea or didn't want to believe how far gone I really was on coke. He asked me why I was doing the things I was doing. I was so upset and told him everything that I was doing behind his back. He couldn't believe how clever I was at hiding my addiction – I would hide in my bathroom in the morning and do lines. After work,

I would hang out in my car or someone's house doing drugs until I went home. Then I would take Ativan, drink a tonne of alcohol and smoke a bunch of pot to finally fall asleep at five in the morning when he would get home from work.

I had it in my mind that it was okay because he was using as well (not coke, but painkillers and pot). He said to me, "I don't understand why you can't stop drinking while you're dancing. Others girls do it all the time." He just didn't get it. I wanted out of the bar life for good!

So that day, I had phoned the bar asking if I could have my first show covered even though it was the busiest day of the week. Of course they said no. I actually threw myself down the stairs so I would injure myself and not be able to work. It didn't work, so I had to go in to do my show – even though I hadn't slept for two days. I had lost 15 pounds from not eating and doing five eight-balls of coke throughout the week. I put my costume on and started to cry. I looked at myself in the mirror and noticed how terrible I looked. I had lost so much weight that my costume was now hanging off me. It was fitted to my body before.

I called the manager in and said, "I will be doing this next show and then I quit. Find another girl to replace me for the five shows that I have left for the rest of the week." In tears for my whole show, I told all the regulars that they would never see me again. Then I packed up my stuff and left without pay. (They won't pay you for the work you do if you walk out. Bullshit!)

At home, I went straight to bed. I woke up and went to my first meeting to quit drinking and drugs (I had tried it before for one and a half years about five years ago, but it didn't work.) This time was really different. I wanted to do this for myself; I wanted to save my own life. I knew I couldn't stay sober and clean in a bar surrounded by sick people.

I broke up with my boyfriend that week (we had been together for two and a half years) and I got my own place which was a beautiful top floor of a house. I didn't have a lot of money so I borrowed some money from a friend for damage deposit. I didn't care how I was going to do it but I needed to make money.

My landlord kept showing up and asking me out for dinner. He was a good looking guy who was my age and I really wanted to get to know him. I told him I was a stripper and I was cleaning up my life. He was intrigued by this. He wanted more and we decided to have him move in with me a few months later. It's funny how love works. He was an alcoholic and decided to quit drinking right after me. We are sober together!

To make ends meet, I talked to the bar owner and begged him to allow me to do some private dances. I told him that I was sober and needed to make money so I could live. I really think he had a spot for me in his heart, and I thank him every day for it. Seriously, you know who you are. Thank you.

I made some good money and I started to save for the first time in my life. I VIP danced for one and a half months and was asked by a friend if I could cover her shows for the first part of the week at the bar I walked out on. I said ok and then I talked to the manager. For some odd reason, they allowed me to cover her shows (a wise dancer knows that you never sell *all* your costumes). Then one of the other girls got sick and I was asked to stay for the rest of the week and I agreed. It was Friday the 13th, almost two months after I quit stage dancing. I was thinking to myself, "God, please help me get out of this job. I really need a way out!" Be careful what you wish for and what kind of thoughts you think.

That same day, Friday the 13th, I had a 12:30 am show and I decided to wear my nurse costume. I was driving home after my show while still dressed in my costume. On my way to grab cigarettes, I was in the left turn lane at a dead stop. Then it happened – I was rear ended by a lady driving a huge van. I couldn't feel my body and I was rushed by ambulance to the hospital. Go figure; wearing my nurse costume, asking "God" for a way out of this career and then I was in an accident that changed my life and stopped my dancing career for good. The crazy thing is that my car didn't even have a scratch on it and her van was fine as well. Wow! Everything was lined up for this accident and I now believe in angels. I believe that my angel was watching over me that day. Today, I am fine with just some muscle soreness that lasted for a few months. At the time my new boyfriend decided he didn't like me stripping anyways and when this accident happened he took care of me. Bless him. He owns his own business and asked me if I would become his assistant.

I have been sober and clean since September 19, 2009. I have a new career, I'm very happy and in love! I read daily. Before, I hadn't picked up a book since I quit school in grade 10. Reading has opened my eyes to success.

Before I became a dancer, I had a bit of a rocky road in life. I was no ordinary girl. I was stuck in the poor me pattern. I was sexually molested at the age of five by a family friend. Amongst other things, I was pushed away from my mom who didn't want to believe the molestation was true. She was raped and I was the outcome. So not knowing who my father is, I had rebelled all my life and I felt I was the black sheep of the family.

This life experience has made me into a loving woman now. I realize that I am responsible for everything I do in my life and I look at life differently now. My mom and I have a wonderful friendship. She knew that I was a dancer and she accepted it. She even gave me ideas for my shows and costumes. Everything happens in our lives by the choices we make. I firmly believe that if you want to change your life, you must change your habits first.

As I grow, I work on dealing with my childhood experiences, mental patterns and the beliefs that I have constructed over the years. I want to make positive changes one day at a time. And if I can stay sober and happy while I do it, others can do it too.

Dancing was a huge part of my life. Of course there were the bad elements like the addictions and the stress, but there were aspects of it that I truly loved. I absolutely loved entertaining on stage and doing my theme sets like blowing fire. I was pretty creative if I wasn't too hammered. I also loved the friendships with the girls, the relationships with the bars and the travel. I danced my way all over Canada, and how many people can say that?

On the other hand, I hated the politics and the backstabbing women. The beautiful pole work that I did has wrecked my body; my shoulder and hip pops out all the time. I also couldn't stand it when the clubs forced the girls to be on the floor to make them money by doing private dances for $30. Out of that $30, the club took $22 and we would be left with a measly $8. At some of the clubs, it was mandatory to do 40 dances for the week; some were as much as 80 or even 90 dances for the week!

There were VIP rooms lined up near the front doors at some clubs and the bar was always there to take the customer's money, making sure they got their cut and that the girls didn't steal a portion of it. With the steady push for girls to do private dances, the customers felt the constant pressure. I would do 20 dances and then call it a day. Sometimes a guy would 'buy out' a girl. This is when the customer has the option to pay a lump sum for the girl's time to party and drink with her while the bar got a percentage of what he paid. It was also mandatory for all the girls to be working during the peak hours of 9:00 pm to 2:00 am.

I've had a lot of interesting experiences. My dealer boyfriend had some shady people working for him, and one of them trained me for counter surveillance and anti-surveillance. I got so good I could pick up on a five car tail. While I was working at one strip club as a VIP girl, I noticed something as I was driving home after work. I was being followed and I picked up on it right away. I was so pissed off! I ended up following him and blocked him at the entrance of a cul-de-sac. Jumping out of my car, I screamed, "Mother fucker! I got your plate number! You're done!" Then I hopped back in my car and sped off. I gave the plate number to some guys I knew but I don't know what happened after that.

The weirdest customer I have encountered was the East Indian guy who would pay me $80 for four songs. While I danced, he wanted me to take my stiletto heal and stomp it in his cock and balls as hard as I could. I would usually be drunk when I did this but if he came in when I wasn't loaded yet, I would tell him, "I can't deal with this right now." He had to wait until I had four shots of vodka.

The creepy underwear guy would come into the bar to buy my thong. He always paid me $100-$150 for it. Before handing me over any money, he would ask me if I wore them all day. The dirtier they were the better, since he would pay me more money if I wore them all day. I was disgusted when he told me he would jerk off to them. I couldn't stand the thought, so one day I yelled at him, "Take your sick fuckin shit out of here and leave me alone!" Then I had another drink.

My girlfriend and I went skiing for the weekend once. One night while we were partying, we got wasted until 5:00 am with some guy who wanted to hang out with us. For some reason we got onto the subject of drinking pee. My friend peed into a beer bottle and the guy drank it while I videotaped it! The weird part of this story is that he was sober.

I have persuaded guys to cattle prod 5000 volts into their balls themselves! I did other crazy shit like having chicken fights on guys' shoulders I didn't know and then doing a lap dance in my panties in the dirt. I would always be the life of the party as I came running at people to give them flying elbows. I also thought it was funny when I would ask cab drivers if I could pee on their car. I'm amazed I didn't end up in jail!

My best customer was the beaver man. He came into the club and gave girls stuffed beavers. On my 25th birthday I was wearing a long black gown and a strap-on and I was doing my usual crazy antics like getting helicopter rides with some of the guys. At one point, I pulled up my dress and yelled at beaver man, "Suck it bitch!" He gave me a full on blow job, complete with deep throat and a head shake at the end!

Something you would find amusing about me is my ice trick. I like to call myself the illusionist. I could make it look like ice cubes and water shoot out of my pussy. First, I would put ice cubes in my mouth and then lay on my back, hoisting my ass up by supporting myself on my shoulders. My pussy would face the crowd and I would shoot the ice and water out of my mouth and it looked like it came out of my crotch. It was an optical illusion and a balancing act I did, but I had to be pretty sober in order for it to work.

I can't say that I had any embarrassing moments since life was one big party all the time. When the music would pause or stop and I farted, I would just laugh. If some guys would laugh in response, I'd say "Ya, you like that? I did it for you!"

When I first got in the business, I was surprised with the amount of drugs and the numbers of girls giving blowjobs in the back or letting guys touch them. It was disgusting when I came across condom wrappers lying in VIP rooms with beds.

Before getting into the business, I wish I knew how addictive my personality was. I also wish that I was taught to save my money because I would be better off today. I don't regret getting into this business, but I wish I would've done things differently. Dancing has made me into who I am and I am one year and seven months sober now! It got me to where I had to deal with my molestation and I'm more respected now too as I hobnob with multi-millionaires in my amazing new career!

I used to talk about my stripper days all the time but because I now have a different career, I pretty much keep it a secret since most people wouldn't understand. Before I trust anyone with my story, I like to build a relationship first. My mortgage broker knows my history and I have support from many of my friends. As for my boyfriend, he wants me to drop it all.

My advice for new girls coming into this business is to save your money and get financial advice. Stay away from drugs and booze. Keep to yourself and don't get involved with bad people because you become the people you hang out with. Plan to get out!

Your thoughts create your future and we are a product of our thoughts. I always wanted to be a Vegas showgirl and the closest thing I got to that was an expert in my field.

Partly written by Lady Slipper Orchid

# Lavender

I got into this industry on a dare. I was a 29 year old aesthetician (I still am by trade) when I started to go to the strip club with a co-worker of mine who was a lesbian. We were a couple of single women and we enjoyed watching the amateur contests every week. Our little group grew over the weeks as more friends joined us. Because we were there all the time, staff told us that we were cute and should enter the contest. That started us talking and some of my friends dared me to try it, so I did!

A week later, I entered the contest while my friends watched and cheered me on. I didn't have a problem getting naked and the only thing that worried me was whether I was going to fall down. Since my friends were there, I was laughing my head off which put a big smile on my face and I won my first contest!

I started dancing but continued to do aesthetics on the side for three years. When I went to work out of town, I told my clients I was going on 'vacation.' After three years of doing both jobs, I packed up the aesthetics and started dancing full time because it was better money. I made three times more dancing than I did at my aesthetics job.

It's not just the money. With dancing, I love the free time and the fact that I get to choose when and where I want to work. I wanted to continue doing both jobs but it was exhausting to dance until 2:00 am and then be up five hours later to start my aesthetics appointments by nine!

My boyfriend is supportive of my dancing but his 12 year old daughter doesn't know what I do for a living. We want to keep it that way for now. As for my own family, I am one out of five siblings; my two younger sisters both know that I am a dancer but my parents, brother and older sister don't know. It wouldn't go well if they found out. Although, I'd rather they found out now instead of when I first started. For all this time, I have been fine, so what complaints could they have? For now, they think I'm still doing aesthetics and working as an extra in film, which explains the traveling. Keeping secrets from my family is something I do not like about this job.

It wasn't easy being one out of five kids. We were poor and didn't have a lot of money. My mom was very busy and when she would get home from work we didn't receive much love from her. As for my dad, he wasn't around a lot. My childhood wasn't super terrible, but it wasn't the best either. I was bullied and teased a lot as a kid because I wore clothes that were not name brand. Now when I run into those bullies later in life, I notice that they are not very attractive while I enjoy knowing that I am!

I love getting paid to perform and entertain on stage, share my energy with the crowd, play dress-up and put on my makeup; everyday is like Halloween to me. The free time in between my shows and the time I am able to take off whenever I want is great. I'm not crazy about the traveling I have to do but I'm thankful that I have seen many new cities and towns while meeting some pretty awesome women in this industry. I have grown stronger and more confident; I have grown a thick skin. I love it when guys tell me I'm hot and how this job keeps me fit. I will always continue to pole dance when I'm done dancing because I really love it.

With the good, comes the bad. I hate the young asshole customers that feel like they are entitled to treat dancers like pieces of meat. The comment I hate hearing the most is, "So, you gonna come and drink with us or what?" I like to respond with, "I'm gonna what." They never get it. I find the question annoying and abusive because the 'or what' raises a red flag. These guys think that dancers have all the time in the world to just hang out and drink with them.

I also can't stand it when dancers are rude and pick on others girls. These are the ones that are catty, competitive and have self-esteem issues.

Another thing I despise is when bars try to short our pay

or cancel our shows (especially when you spend money on traveling to get there). I also get really homesick for my family when I travel out of town. I don't like the long hours, the bad accommodations and travel expenses.

I've worked at an out of town bar twice (to give it a fair chance) but I refuse to work there again. The DJ was creepy, the place has bad energy and the whole building smells terrible. Also, when I was done for the week, I was ready to go home by midnight but I had to hang around until 2:30 am to get paid!

It sucks when you get bumped from a job but it happens, usually because of favouritism between agents and dancers. It can also happen when the bar decides they have too many girls with a similar look (such as having all blondes for example). Sometimes a girl will get bumped because of a past incident such as being fired for bad behaviour (getting super drunk, missing shows, constant lateness, etc).

Scary incidents can happen to dancers as well. One of those times was when a stalker was following two of my dancer friends (Calla Lily and Oleander). I was working at a different club than them one week when I ran into their stalker and he asked me to call the girls on my phone because he wanted to talk to them. Of course I refused and told him I didn't want to get in the middle.

An inconvenient and expensive incident for me was when I was working out of town, and the first night I was there, some asshole kicked in my windshield! I was out over $300 on that one!

A weird story is from when I was a rookie (into my second month of dancing) and I was onstage doing my 11:30 pm show. Two songs had gone by and all of a sudden the DJ got onto the microphone and said, "We've discovered some electrical problems in the building and we are asking everyone to please exit immediately." I wasn't allowed to go to the dressing room to get my purse and keys for home. Once we were outside, we were told that it was actually a bomb threat but management didn't want to tell anyone for fear it would cause panic and chaos. They had to remove everyone from the night club next door and tenants who lived upstairs as well. It was 2:30 am when we were finally let back into the building.

Three and a half years ago I was driving from one booking to the next. Calla Lilly was also driving in the same direction, so we decided to caravan, with her in front. The roads had snow on them and were pretty slippery but we were determined to get to our bookings. We were only five minutes away from our destination when I came around a corner and I noticed her car was stopped on the side of the road. I thought to myself, "Why is she parked on the road like that?"

Then I realized that she had an accident so I pulled over. She had a box filled with 500 posters sitting on her passenger seat and when the window broke, the box flew outside and the highway was scattered with all the posters. I grabbed a couple garbage bags from my car and ran along the icy road stuffing them in the bags. Then we transferred her belongings into my car and I helped her out for the next few days by driving her around so she could deal with her insurance. Most of the posters were saved after we dried them and straightened them back out by setting heavy items on them. Because of that episode, we became really good friends!

The strangest gift I received from a customer was a picture of a guy on a motorcycle. I asked the customer if the photo was of himself and he said, "No, but I want you to have the picture." I hung it up in the dressing room at one of the strip clubs and it's still hanging there all these years later. Another gift I love is weed. I smoke weed every day and it's nice when customers bring me some. Sometimes they'll discreetly put it on stage for me as a tip. The biggest tip I ever got was $500 all in twenties during one of my shows. I believe they were all counterfeit bills, but I took it anyway and bought weed with it.

I'll never forget my most embarrassing moment. Just like every other day, I performed my show and went upstairs.

When I was getting dressed, I looked down and realized that I forgot to insert a tampon. Thank God I didn't find out until after my show because if I would've noticed the blood on stage, I would've ran off and been mortified.

One time while I was on stage, I heard someone yell, "I know her father!" I looked around and didn't recognize anyone. My father still doesn't know that I'm a dancer so either the person is still holding the secret or the guy was faking.

Another time, a guy I worked with at a fast food chain showed up at the club one night and saw me on stage. Also, one of my ex-boyfriends saw me dance once and one of my aesthetic clients saw me do a contest once. It wasn't so bad because he knew I was a dancer but had just never seen my show.

Something that surprised me about this job was discovering that sexual fantasy is so powerful for men. The one thing I wish I knew how to do before getting into this business was to haggle for a higher show price in the beginning. I didn't know anyone when I started out, so I didn't get any advice. It used to bug me in the beginning that I didn't get a higher show price than some of the other girls but now most bars have price caps and it doesn't bug me anymore.

Some personal things about me are that I like to smoke weed, I'm a big recycler and a hippie at heart. I am a very spiritual person; I love animals, meditation, yoga and energy healing. Three things I won't leave home without are my marijuana stash, my phone and my money.

When I was picking a stage name, I wanted something with only one word and I wanted something spiritual and something that reflected my personality. In the beginning I thought of the name Amethyst but I didn't know if anyone would know what that was or even if the DJs would be able to pronounce it.

I know I can't dance forever but I wish I could. I'm not trying to get out of the industry right now because I don't want to waste my time and money going to school until I know what I'm interested in. So, I will continue dancing until I have a hard time getting booked. I travel out to Alberta for work a couple weeks at a time since the money is better there and they book the older girls. When I get home from traveling out of town, I'll book a whole month off.

I have been dancing now for five and a half years and I do not regret getting into this business. I met some really great friends and made some good money even though I've had to dip into my savings from time to time. This job gives me financial peace of mind.

Am I ashamed of telling people what I do for a living? For the most part no, since I use my judgement and feel people out when they ask me what I do for a living.

My boyfriend's daughter plays softball and I won't tell the parents there what I do for work because I don't want it getting back to her. Once, I was out of town and after I finished my shift and got paid, I hopped in my car and drove the nine hours home (with a one hour nap) during the night so that I could catch her softball game the next day. One of the other moms said I looked tired and I told her that I just drove nine hours through the night. She asked me what I did for work and I blurted out, "I was working on a movie set."

My advice for new girls is this: if you feel nervous on stage, act like you've done it 100 times already. Own the stage and be confident. Don't worry about or be intimidated by the poles – or the people. Don't get super drunk at work and always act like a lady!

# Leilani

My girlfriend was a server in a strip club and they were hiring another waitress. I didn't know much about the clientele because I didn't hang out in strip bars, so I was a little uneasy about applying there. Since I had a lot of waitressing experience, I was hired on the spot.

In the year and a half I worked there, my views changed. I used to think that all the dancers were borderline prostitutes and drug addicts, but I found out that a lot of them had boyfriends, were working their way through school and didn't even touch alcohol or drugs.

As I was serving a drink to a guy sitting at the back of the room by himself one day, he told me that his girlfriend was dancing. I was stunned that a dancer actually had a boyfriend who was sitting there watching her. Most of all, he didn't seem to mind that a roomful of guys were watching her, too. Interesting.

I was 24 when I convinced my girlfriend to go with me and try out an amateur contest. A few hours earlier, I was flipping through a gossip magazine. Then I took a sheet of paper and drew a line down the center. On the left side I wrote first names of actresses I liked and on the right side I wrote last names of actors and actresses I liked. Then I put them together to see which ones fit best. The big test was my pretend DJ voice where I would say in a deep tone, "Alright everybody, put your hands together forrrrrr..." It sounded great, so I stuck with it.

The contest was on a Tuesday night and we had to drive to the club which was over an hour away. In the car, I was biting my fingernails to the knuckle because of my nerves. When we got to the bar, it was so busy it made my palms sweat in terror. The DJ could tell that we were nervous and knew it was our first time. He said we looked great and gave us some encouragement saying that we'd do just fine. Then he yelled for the waitress to bring us some shots of tequila. If it wasn't for my girlfriend (and maybe the tequila) I could never have done it.

I remember when he announced my name and I stepped up onto that stage. It's as though something took me over. My body had such an adrenaline surge. I danced my 20 minute set and my girlfriend said that I looked like I had done it before. It was such a rush! I didn't have a problem with getting naked; my nerves came from having so much attention focused on me. For 20 minutes of dancing on stage, you were paid $70 plus any tips you made. That night I made $145. Not bad for only 20 minutes of work, I thought!

We quit our jobs and decided that we would dance for only six months and rake in as much money as we could. This would give us enough time to figure out our next plan, possibly even go back to school. Here I am, still dancing five and a half years later.

Three days before I went to do the amateur contest, I called my parents to let them know what I was doing. It wasn't to ask them for permission. I just didn't want to sneak around behind their back and I didn't want them to hear it from someone else. Although my parents are hippies and they're very open-minded, my dad is still concerned about what people think.

Over the years my mom got more supportive of my job – she's actually driven me to work many times. She has told me that she wishes she had given dancing a try. However, my mom also tells me not to lose sight of who I am. She reminds me that I am selling myself short because I always did well in school. She said that I'm seen as a bimbo and I'm put in the same category as the dumb girls with shitty grades.

Growing up, I was such a girly girl and had a completely normal childhood. If I didn't know someone, I was the shyest little girl you would ever meet. I would hide behind my mom when people would try to talk to me. I was very insecure and self conscious about my body, so I took a modeling course in high school and I think it really helped me come out of my shell. I loved dressing up in costumes when I was little and then choreograph little dance performances with my sister and perform them for our family.

I absolutely love the freedom that comes with my job. Every winter, I take off one month and go on a trip. I don't have to ask anyone for time off work because I book work when I want to. I work very hard during the year and I like to treat myself since my down time is very important to me. Last year I took seven weeks off and I went to Indonesia for one of those months with some girlfriends who are also dancers. I can't imagine being able to afford it if I wasn't a dancer. Also, the chances of finding three other girls that could afford it and take that much time off work would be pretty slim if we weren't all in this industry.

I hate all the preconceived notions and the judgment that dancers get. Also, I can't seem to keep it separate from my personal life. I'm always anxious when I go out with a group of new people. The whole time I dread the question that will come up about what I do for a living. As soon as I tell them I'm a dancer, I can see their mind shifts and they look at me different. The topic of conversation now goes in a different direction and guys think that they can talk to me in a more vulgar way and stare at my tits the whole time.

I also find that my job makes personal relationships a bit more complicated since the jealousy factor is obviously an issue. I travel a lot for work, so it's hard to find someone that will be ok with me being out of town for two to four weeks at a time and trust me while I'm gone.

If I'm going to be working away from home where I'm eating out and not sleeping in my own bed, I will only work in bars that I know I can make a lot more money than I would near home. People don't realize that when we go on the road, we pay for all of our own expenses, including hotels, food, and transportation. I once paid $1200 to fly to a booking for one week. If you subtract that from my total earnings for the week, it has to really be worthwhile.

Sometimes it just takes one person to make your night. It was my first time dancing at a bar where I had never worked before. It was very slow since there were only four customers in the room and one East Indian man sitting by himself at the back of the room. I was on stage and he walked up and set down a $50 bill on the stage for me. When I got off stage, I walked over to thank him and he asked me if he could buy a drink for me. I accepted and we chatted until it was time for me to do my next show. I asked him if he was going to stay for my next show (since I was hoping he would tip me generously again). He said he would but needed to go to the bank machine first.

Throughout my next show, he put a $20 bill down every few seconds. At the end of my show, I scooped up all the money and shoved it in my bag. Then I went to get dressed. I counted the money – it was $800! I came out of the change room to thank him but I didn't see him anywhere. When I asked the waitress where he went, she said that as soon as I got off stage, he paid his bill and left. I didn't get a chance to say thank you and I never saw him again. I still wonder why such a big tip?

Working in this industry, customers are always buying dancers presents, dinner and drinks. Once I mentioned to a regular customer that I had just moved into a new apartment and really wanted to get a barbeque, so he bought me one the next day.

One of my girlfriends that I work with quite often has a regular customer in one of the towns in Alberta where we work quite a bit. He always comes to see her and brings her flowers. One day he brought her a little jewellery box and she could tell that he was nervous to give it to her. She opened it and inside was a bracelet with her stage name on it and on the other side a heart with his name. Now every time we work in that town she brings it with her so she can wear it when she sees him, even though it feels weird for her to wear a fake name on her wrist.

As for embarrassing moments, I've had a few. Once, when I was working out of town I slipped and fell on stage, dislocating my elbow. I had to be rushed to the hospital in the club's limo. When I got to the hospital I was still wearing my pink race car driver costume and thigh high boots. The nurse looked at me and asked, "Were you at a costume party?" She then told me that because my arm was so swollen, my jacket had to be cut off me.

I freaked out and yelled, "Do you have any idea how much this costume cost?" Painfully, I took the jacket off myself so she wouldn't cut it. I was off work for six weeks waiting for the injury to heal and I had to do physiotherapy to be able to bend my arm again.

I can't even count the times when I've been on stage and have recognized a face in the crowd that I wish I didn't. I was on stage once and a young guy called out my real name. I asked him how we knew each other and he said that he had gone to prom with my sister. Another time I was just about to take off my bra on stage when I saw a group of guys walk into the bar. Three of them were really close friends of my dad's and I actually think one of them had changed my diaper at one point when I was a baby. Although it definitely makes me nervous on stage when I know that those people are in the crowd, I've just gotten used to it now and it doesn't really bother me as much as it used to.

Some personal things about me are that I enjoy making costumes for some of the other dancers and myself in my spare time. Three things I can not leave home without are my cell phone (it's pretty much an extension of my arm), my mp3 player (I love to listen to music) and pen and paper (I'm a bit of a compulsive list maker since I'm very forgetful. If I don't write something down, it doesn't get done).

During the summer, I get hired for many special events and functions. I work at luncheons where three or four girls are hired to walk around in bikinis and mingle with the guys. Each girl is paid close to $200 to drink, have lunch and just socialize with the men. I feel like such a geisha!

"What do I want to do with the rest of my life?" This question haunts me every single day. I worry about the resume gap of five years that I have. One day I will want to get out of dancing and get a regular job but I wonder what I should put in my resume during the time I spent dancing?

I wish I knew how hard it was to get out of this business. It's great to make lots of money and have lots of fun but if I would've known how hard it was to get out, I wouldn't have gotten in it in the beginning. I make good money dancing but I have to because I'm used to having it spent on my nails, tanning, nice dinners, etc. You get used to having a certain amount of money all the time and you don't want to go backwards and make less.

For now, I'm not looking to stop dancing because I haven't met my goals yet. So I plan on dancing until something else comes along, I guess. I quit once for a boyfriend because my job was making things difficult for us to get serious. I had no intention of going back, but when things ended between us, I went back to waitressing and had a hard time making less money than I did when I was dancing. I think a relationship will probably be the reason I'll quit for good. This job is definitely a lot easier for a single girl.

I'm not ashamed of being a dancer, but sometimes I wish I could just make up a fake job so that I wouldn't be judged so much and so I could avoid the 20 questions that always come along with telling people what I do for work.

My advice for new girls is to put your money aside and SAVE it! It's really easy to get sucked into making so much money and spending it as quickly as it comes in. I know so many girls that have been dancing for years and have nothing to show for it. I love to hear about girls that have been smart and bought houses or put themselves through school.

# Lilac

I have no tales of abuse or neglect or how I wasn't loved enough, only a series of unfortunate events that led me to life of plastic heels, too-tight metallic mini skirts and fast, easy money. Life throws curve balls, and if you're lucky you catch them. In my case, I got hit so hard by one that when the shock subsided, I was already Alice down the rabbit hole. I was falling. Dancing broke that fall.

There was a 'me' before lap dances. I grew up in an upper-middle class household, with plenty of love and support. My parents divorced in my youth, but together raised me to be the person that I am becoming, which so far, is a pretty rockin chick! I have a degree in Fine Arts and have worked in fields ranging from a white-water canoe guide in Ontario, to bar manager in Australia. Needless to say, dancing was never a destination that I expected my life's path to take me, until a phone call came that flipped my world 180 degrees.

I was in Australia, with no debts, no boyfriend and dreams of jet setting until my body could globe trot no more, when I received the call. My 14 year old brother, my heart and soul, had just attempted suicide. I felt my guts sink like lead. My mother quivered the words, "I can't do this, I need your help." My stepfather, unable to cope, left my mother to 'resolve things' on her own. He left her with the bills and all the worries. To say the least, I'm certainly not his biggest fan. The overwhelming stress and fear got the best of my mum and she suffered a nervous, psychological and emotional breakdown and was hospitalized. I put my credit card to use and booked a flight home. Within three days of hearing the news, I said my goodbyes to my beautiful friends, quit my job, took an 18 hour bus ride to Melbourne and flew 20 hours to get home and start picking up the pieces.

As my mom took time to recover, my older brother (a part-time cook) and me, were given temporary guardianship. We were now in care of our little brother, who needed as much love and support as he could get, and our 15 year old sister, who was also struggling with depression and bulimia. At 23 and 24, it was up to us to play 'parent' and support two teenagers in desperate need of some serious attention and affection. With me unemployed, struggling to land even a minimum wage job and my older brother's measly cook salary, things were looking grim. I spent my days applying to any and all "Help Wanted" signs and job postings I found. Pressure mounted for me to land steady work, but every time I got turned down, my spirits got increasingly bruised. I couldn't land a job because I was so worried about getting one that when it came time for an interview, I fell apart.

One evening, coming home from a day of tirelessly handing out resumes and strapped for cash, I let my thoughts melt into sadness and defeat. How could I ever begin to help my family? I struggled to fight back the tears welling up in my eyes. In that moment I felt very small.

I gave myself a minute to be sad, then heaved myself out of my personal pity party and got practical. I could cry all day long, but that wasn't going to pay for shit-all. I wiped the tears off my cheeks and the snot from my nose, took a few deep breaths and took the long way home. After all, when you just had a public meltdown at 5:00 on a Friday night, smack dab in the middle of the main street, a girl needs time to re-group!

I got home to the 7x10 room my brother was renting and that I was reluctantly crashing in. I needed to expand my net. A friend that I had traveled with years prior suddenly came to mind. She had confided to me that while traveling, she ventured into the world of exotic dancing and used lap dances to pay for her next adventures. My mind stuttered a bit at the thought, but then kept moving onto a million other ways to make some fast cash.

Two more weeks of job hunting went by and I found myself

fighting my mind's tendency to wander back to thoughts of dancing. So I blindly began to search opportunities to do just that. My ignorance of the industry left me fumbling hopelessly through website after website taking me on a joy ride of useless information. Just when I was starting to second-guess my decision, I came across a website that seemed to have all the answers. I navigated my way to a "Work for Us" link. I giggled to myself at the idea of my clumsy self, parading around in seven inch heels and then pressed on. I filled out a superficial form on myself; height, weight, age, experience. Novice! An hour later my phone rang. The man on the other line was from the agency I applied to. To my surprise (I think I was expecting to be answering to a womanizing grizzly bear!) he was extremely patient, kind and sincere, all the while maintaining a no-nonsense attitude that I appreciated. He wanted me to come in for an audition to see if I fit the part.

It took me a week to muster up the courage to set the date for my audition and when the day came to strut my stuff, I quickly realized that I had no clue what I was doing! So, I jumped on the trusty internet and looked up pole dancing. After watching plenty of videos of women bending their bodies in ways I could only imagine, I realized that I wasn't going to be a pro my first go at it. So, I packed a bag with the cutest pair of undies I had (I also had no clue what in the world strippers wore) and a pair of my friend's borrowed high heels, jumped on the light rail transit and choked down my nerves. When I finally reached my destination (after what seemed like the longest 20 minutes of my life), I was greeted by a young guy with a big smile and an even bigger vocabulary. He chatted away my nerves all the way to the audition.

When we got to the spot, I was ushered in to get my music straight with the DJ and go change. I got myself dolled up and ready to go. The DJ called out my stage name, which took me some playing around to come up with, so I could avoid bursting out in laughter every time I heard it. My new name boomed from the speakers, the group of men whose faces I didn't dare to look at, clapped and grumbled. All I could think was, "Don't you dare fall!"

My first show was a blur, too fogged with worries to really remember. All I recall is that I had to keep reminding myself to get naked! Apparently my 15 minutes of fumbling wasn't so bad. The agents thought I fit the part and I was whisked away to start working right away! I told my family I got a job doing freelance work for a bar company, which explained the money and the need to travel. Within a few weeks I was able to pay for a new place for myself and my siblings, for follow-up therapy sessions for my little brother and to register him in football. Life was peachy.

Dancing had re-instilled confidence in me. Not that I was pretty enough, but that I was capable enough. It made me become aware of my resourcefulness, and to me that is very empowering. To this day, dancing has allowed me to better appreciate myself. It helped me to better understand the relationship between *real* men and *real* women, by exposing me to truths about sexuality that I feel are incredibly honest. Above everything, dancing gave me the opportunity to help my mom and my beautiful little brother and sister. I have now hung up the heels, but will always reflect on my experience in the industry as one that has made me an incredibly strong and open-minded human being.

Written by Lilac

# Lily

I moved to Alberta from BC when I was 17 and within the first six months, I was attacked and robbed. One night I was walking to the convenience store around 1:30 am, and I was approached by three crack heads. I got a bad vibe from them so I smiled at them since that's my personal test for people. I figure that if they smile back at me, they're probably harmless. They smiled back but as soon as they passed me, one of them grabbed my purse while the other two pushed my legs, throwing me forward to the pavement. They took off running with my purse.

Shaken from the attack, I stood up and started to walk towards the hotel on the corner of the street. I felt something tickling the back of my leg and as I looked back at my thigh, I saw that I was bleeding. The white boots I was wearing were turning a bright shade of red. The two crack heads who I thought were pushing my legs had actually sliced me with knives! I ended up in the hospital getting 10 stitches on my left leg and 15 on my right.

I believe the more you talk about things that are painful, the less they can hurt you. So, from that moment on, every couple of months I would go to where the attack happened and have drinks at the strip club that was nearby. I became friends with the staff and after months of trying, the bouncer finally convinced me to start doing VIP dances. I was a VIP girl at that club for six months.

I quit VIP dances and started doing amateur contests when I was 19. I liked the guaranteed money while stage dancing, but my first time getting on stage I was super nervous. I thought that the amateur contests would have prepared me but I had no idea what I was doing as I randomly started moving my hips. For a week straight, I was scared to go on stage and had to get drunk just to go through with it. I remember the other new girl who was 28 years old. Her boyfriend was hanging out in the club and they were both high as kites on coke.

My mom raised four kids with two jobs because my dad was in and out of jail. We were always broke because she had to put money aside for rent, food and bills while our clothing came from donations and thrift stores. I was five or six when my parents split up. My family doesn't know that I'm a dancer. They think I'm a waitress in a strip bar.

One of my scariest memories was when I was five and my little brother was two. My dad was a wanted man, so one day the SWAT team kicked in our door, guns pointed straight at us. They handcuffed my dad and his best friend, and hauled them off to jail. To this day I don't know what that was all about.

When I was little, my grandma was a big help to my mom. She was always there to buy gifts for me and my brother when my dad only bought gifts for my other brother and sister since he only seemed to pay attention to them anyways. I always felt that he didn't like me because he told me once that I was supposed to be a boy when I was born. I also got the vibe that grandma and dad hated each other.

When I was eight years old, my grandma died at the age of 50 from a brain aneurism. This may sound a little odd, but at the time, I thought she was playing with me and not really dead. My mom sent my siblings and me to my dad's place the day that grandma passed and he told me that she died. I didn't believe him. When I returned home, my mom told me the same thing and I still didn't believe her. At the funeral, I asked my uncle and big brother who were my idols, when grandma was going to hop out of the casket. They started to weep and this scared me. I finally realized it was true and I lost control, falling to the ground and crying hysterically. My mom had to lead me away. I went to my aunt's house for three days where we ate pizza and chocolate, and watched movies. It was good therapy for me.

My grandma's death had a huge impact on me, because I felt it was my fault. The day before her death, she called my mom to arrange for me to go to her house for a sleepover. I told mom I wanted to go to my best friend's house instead and mom said "No." I was mad and called my grandma on the phone and told her that I hated her. She died the next day.

I ended up seeing a child psychologist named Linda who helped me make sense of grandma's death. She helped me realize that it wasn't my fault and I was able to heal by writing a letter to her with feelings of how I felt about her death.

As a dancer, I have learned to take the good with the bad. For example, I love the girls I work with. There hasn't been a time that I didn't like any of them and I also love all the staff at the bars I work at. Getting into this business, I was surprised with the girls and how great they are! I thought that they would be more catty but there is always a girl to help you out if you need it. On the other hand, I hate the travelling because I'm a homebody. I try to stay home as much as possible!

The rude customers I encounter in the bars, I can do without. I would say that the rudest guy I met was when I was only into my second week of dancing on the circuit. I was filling in for a girl who didn't show up. I went on stage and did a trick at the pole where there was a guy eating chicken wings. He threw his wings to the side and yelled, "I just lost my fuckin appetite!" Real nice, huh?

I try not to refuse working at any of the clubs because it's money that I could be making. I did blacklist one strip club because it feels like you're just a background dancer. Nobody pays any attention to the dancers as it's more of a night club atmosphere. One time, a guy threw a toonie at my head, so I chucked it back at him. After that, I chose not to work there anymore.

There have never been any stalkers in my dancing career so far, but there is a guy who buys my socks for $10, then gives me a new pair.

A scary situation for me was when I got drugged. I don't know how it happened but I think it was this creepy Latin guy who kept following me around or the millionaire guy with the lesbians. I was doing a VIP and I felt the drug hit me. I swung open the curtains and stumbled out of the room and called for the other VIP girl who was walking by. I don't remember anything after that but I was told that I was puking blood and foam all night.

In this industry, a girl is bound to have an embarrassing moment. Mine was when I was done doing a private dance. I asked the guy if he enjoyed it and he said he did. Then he asked me if it was my time of the month. I said it wasn't and then he told me to have a good night. I wondered what he meant about the question until I went to my room and noticed I had toilet paper stuck on my crotch!

My other embarrassing moment was when I was working on the circuit. After my show, I went to my room and looked in the mirror and noticed my black blanket left black fuzzies on my crotch!

My best customer is an Asian guy that frequents one particular club. I notice that he doesn't tip any of the other girls, but he always tips me $40-$60 during my shows.

Many people would find it shocking to know that I'm shy and a complete nerd; a total dork. My idea of a good night is a hot bath, a good book and a cup of tea. Another personal thing about me is that three things I won't leave home without are my cell phone, wallet and lap top. Also, before I was a dancer, I was a waitress in a family restaurant.

I was 21 when I got into the business and have been dancing now for five months. My cut-off age to finish dancing is 26. For now I just want to get by and make money to pay my bills. My plan is to go back to school and take a psychology course and become a child services counsellor. Linda changed my life and I want to help other kids by doing the same.

When I was picking my stage name, I picked a porn star with a name I like for the first part and I also think her name is dark and mysterious. The second part to my name is sexy.

I do not regret getting into this business. I actually love it; the good, the bad and the ugly on a daily basis.

My advice for new girls coming into this business is to smile all the time! Although I'm not happy with my teeth, a customer once said to me, "Your smile brightens up the room!" Also, if you already have problems with drinking and drugs, don't bother getting into this line of work because your addiction will only get worse. You'll need it to go on stage because you get caught up in all the drinks the guys will want to buy you. You'll want to drink and have a good time because everyone around you is doing it. When you're drunk, you're more loose and flirty so you'll make more money in VIP dances. I was constantly drunk for the first few months of dancing.

# Marigold

I bounced around from job to job for a while, but I always felt there was something better out there for me rather than a quiet work environment. I was working as a receptionist and going to school when I first thought about dancing. I took dance classes when I was young and I loved to go clubbing with my girlfriends, so I figured that I would enjoy being a dancer. I had just met my boyfriend and we talked openly about me dancing and he was very supportive. Although I was scared to try this new venture, I was even more scared to do it alone.

It was close to Christmas and I had one more paycheque coming to me before the holidays. I was low on cash to buy Christmas gifts and because of school, I had to quit my job in order to receive a grant from the government (they would cut you off if they felt you made too much money). So, I was basically stuck. I looked at it this way; I could either buy some crappy little Christmas gifts or I could take that paycheque and buy some gear for dancing and go make some fantastic money. I obviously picked the latter; I bought shoes, a dress, a bag, perfume and other little incidentals I needed for my new job.

It was a Friday when I strolled into the club while my boyfriend waited around the corner for me because I was scared to go by myself. I met the manager and he obviously liked me because he was showing me around the club and where the change room was. I had no agent at this time since I basically walked in off the street knowing nothing about this uncharted territory. Back then, I was a bit of a thicker girl so that night as I dolled myself up in the dressing room, I felt overwhelmed and intimidated around the other dancers.

When I was ready, I walked out of the change room onto the floor. I was scared stiff so I just stood there shaking in my high heeled shoes, hanging onto a pillar so I wouldn't fall down. I called my boyfriend and asked him to sit in the audience for moral support. Being raised catholic, I had feelings of guilt wash over me as I thought about my mom and how she drilled into my head that I should not be showing off my naked body.

There were 15-20 girls that worked in the club doing VIP dances, so I had to really hustle the customers to make some money. I found that most of the girls were catty and had diva attitudes, so I felt like I was thrown into the shark tank. I was the new girl but nobody offered me any advice or helped me out. That first night, I made $150. It may seem great, but $50 of it went to the house and $50 was spent on a cab ride home, so I went home with $50. That was okay because the next night was Saturday and I had my hustle ready. That night I made $750! The weekend after that, I made $1100. $700 of it came from one guy who fell in love with me.

I was good at my job. The problem was that the other girls got jealous and mad. Since my boyfriend hung out at the club most of the time, some of the girls lied and told the manager he was a pimp, so I got fired. I figured that I would work at another strip bar down the street, but when they heard my name, they wouldn't hire me. I found out I was blacklisted, so I went across town.

It wasn't long before I got work at another club as their solo VIP girl. I met a lot of people who became my friends and I was comfortable there. I didn't make as much money as I did in the first bar, but at least I enjoyed working there. I worked there for six months until I decided it was time to try stage dancing. I had been watching and studying the other girls the whole time, so I felt ready.

I was with an agency at this point and they sent me to do an amateur contest on a Friday and Saturday. I ran into another dancer who was a girl I knew from high school. We didn't like each other, so she had all the dancers that week gang up on me. She started yelling at me and said that I was a thief since her pants were found in my bag (which someone had obviously planted there). That worried me because I didn't need these girls going through my things because I had almost $100 hidden in my bag and I didn't want them to steal it from me. I called the agency and explained what happened. They said that they believed me because this girl was a skinny little thing and I was thicker. The tiny pants wouldn't even fit me, so why would I go to the trouble of stealing them?

The week after, I was working at a different strip club. At this time, my mom and step dad had just got a divorce. He was very verbally abusive and sometimes a physically abusive man. We couldn't stand each other. A server at this club who knows my parents, had called my stepdad (she told me that she ran into him at the liquor store) and she told him I was working as a stripper! He called my mom right away and told her. This was not the time for her to find out that I was a dancer, especially from him since she was under too much stress from the divorce and being mentally screwed up from him. So, I got a call from my mom on a Sunday afternoon as my boyfriend and I just got off a rollercoaster at the amusement park. My mom asked me, "Are you a stripper?! Are you prostituting yourself?" It wasn't how I wanted her to find out, especially not from my piece of shit stepdad, thanks to some idiot server.

I said to her, "Mom, I'm not whoring around at clubs and my boyfriend isn't pimping me out. Dancing is a legal job where dancers have to pay taxes and customers aren't allowed to touch us." She still freaked out but eventually we had a long talk about it and she has now grown to accept it and supports me. My mom knows what I do for a living and she is 100 percent supportive now since she understands and knows why I dance for a living.

My childhood was normal and there was never any sexual abuse. My parents split up and divorced when I was seven years old and shortly after, my stepdad came into the picture. He is the reason that I moved out when I was 16.

I was 24 when I started dancing and have been at it now for a year. I was surprised with the amount of girls that criticize rookies because the freshness and newness to these older girls has worn off. It's not about how good you are or how good of a dancer you are. I think that guys like the rawness and newness of a girl so that is the reason why new girls rake in the tips.

Before I got into this line of work, I thought that all strippers were whores or single moms needing to make some money. I was totally stereotyping them. I didn't understand the time, effort and money women have to invest in this job. I respect dancers for having the patience to deal with the stupid comments from some of the idiots who they deal with on a daily basis.

I appreciate some of the relationships with the girls in this industry since I have never had many close friends growing up. Girls like Sunflower are nice to give me advice or help if I ask for it. Then there are girls like Lavender who stick up for me and tell the story straight when the 'stealing of the pants' episode comes up.

This job builds your confidence and changes your body. It's great to be able to stay in shape just from your job. I find that there are two kinds of girls – I like to make as much money as I can while some girls concentrate on partying and having fun. I also like to make as many connections as I can because I think they can help me out later in life. In this economy, a girl should profit from this business as long as she can and it would be wise to invest this money one day. One day I would love to open up a facility for youth, as well as my own lingerie store.

One of my regular customers reminds me of a grown-up child. His mom was a 'B' actress in the 1950s and when she passed away, she left him a fair bit of money. He's had no relationships with women and he has a hard time interacting with women, and people in general. With me, he thrives on trying too hard to please me. He calls me in the morning to ask me what I would like for breakfast and then personally delivers it. He also takes me shopping, opens my car door and won't even touch me because I think he's too scared. He even comes by the club and pays for my lunch. He likes to talk about his cat like it's a person, commenting to me that the cat was too playful today and it wanted its wet food but it has to wait until exactly 6:00 to get fed. When he was at the club once, he got a dance from a girl that I didn't get along with. He knew that we didn't like each other and he knew I was pissed off. Feeling guilty, he pulled out $100 from the ATM machine and gave it to me while he cried his eyes out! He always buys me lavish gifts and will spend up to $2000 a week to sit with me in the bar. He always spends a lot of money on me, but the largest tip I got on stage was not from him. It was from some guy I had never seen before – he just plopped down $100!

Another time while I was dancing out of town, my boyfriend sat in the audience and had a very unattractive woman buying him drinks all night. I didn't have a problem with it because I figured that if she wanted to spend her money on his drinks, I didn't have to! Well, my friend Pink Lily saw this woman make a pass at my boyfriend and she freaked out. I told her not to worry about it since he would handle the situation, but my friend bolted across the room anyways and shoved the woman back. The woman's girlfriends came running over in tiaras and fairy wings (it was a stagette) and we all started to yell and fight, so the bouncer kicked us all out of the bar. My boyfriend and I dropped off Pink Lily at her room and as we were on our way to our hotel, we ran into the fairy squad again. They were trying to get at me as my boyfriend tried to get in the middle by pushing them back. Suddenly we heard, "Hey!" behind us; it was a team of cops. I started to explain the incident we had at the bar with these women when another fight erupted with a different crew of guys down the street and the cops took off. We took off running too.

One time, a guy had just paid for his friend to have a private dance for his birthday. I found out the guy was someone who teased me in high school and during the private dance he was drooling and kept saying to me, "You look so awesome!" It was a pretty good feeling.

There are some things I hate about my job. What I hate are the rude and bitchy attitudes of some of the other dancers. It sucks when you have to work for a full week with girls that you don't get along with. I refuse to work at certain clubs because of the dirtiness and the fact that girls are doing more than just private dances.

I also hate when costumes go missing. I have had a girl comment on one of my cute costumes and shortly after, the skirt went missing. I have also had a brand new bra and panty set disappear into thin air.

Some girls have been around for a long time and it's mostly these girls that have a chip on their shoulder. Because of this job, they're used to guys kissing their feet and it ends up getting to their heads. This industry is a catty world of women; a high school drama where you add men and money, and the girls are all competing against one another.

When I leave for the day, three things I won't leave home without is weed, my phone and fake eye lashes.

I haven't had any embarrassing moments but I do have an embarrassing story that belongs to another dancer. She got her period on stage and her flow was very heavy. Two guys saw her dripping blood while she called me over to ask me to get her some paper towels. She wiped herself and the blood off the stage, then threw the paper towel to the side.

When I was picking my dancer name, people always told me I look like a famous singer and actress combined. I used that first name and then researched the internet until I found the second part to my name.

Am I ashamed of telling people what I do for a living? Hell no! I couldn't care less what square people think. Get over it because it's not prostitution. It's the art of dance and the beautiful naked body. I plan on profiting in this industry for as long as I can and one day be a feature dancer. I do not regret getting into this business since it's a very empowering job that I love. I am always in control of the way I dance, dress and look.

It feels great to be complimented and worshiped by others.

My advice for new dancers coming into this industry...keep your eyes on the prize and let the little shit slide!

# Morning Glory — ME!!!
## (I'm Not!)

When I was four years old, I remember thinking to myself that I wanted to be a stripper. Of course, my older sister wanted to be a lawyer. She was the honour student at university, and she had the good boyfriend. I was the complete opposite.

My mom had my sister at 18 and then me at 20. She named me after a lady who owned a thrift store. I was about three or four years old when my mom met my stepdad who was a hideous alcoholic. Growing up, I had to deal with a lot of mental abuse from him when he didn't like some of the decisions I made such as the friends I chose or the type of clothing I wore. When I was in kindergarten, I remember looking at my stepdad's motorcycle magazines (which had topless women posing on motorcycles) and my mom questioned him whether it was appropriate for me to look at that.

His reply: "What's the big deal?" From that day forward I adopted his 'what's the big deal' attitude. In all honesty, I really didn't understand what the big deal was. I went with him to the cigar store and looked at the nudie magazines there (back then they were kept out in the open). An older gentleman in the store looked down at me and said, "Those aren't for little girls." I almost crawled inside myself like a turtle from embarrassment, but I still didn't understand why it was so wrong.

When I turned 14, I had a bit of an identity crisis and on new years day, I moved in with my birth dad and his soon to be wife. She was a wonderful woman who ended up passing away a couple years ago.

Within two years, I got a job as a supervisor in a fast food chicken place. When my future ex came in at the end of the night, he asked me for the last chicken sandwich and I asked him for his phone number.

I had dropped out of high school for most of the year but when I returned, I am proud to say that at the age of 18, I had graduated with honours in the automotive program! Shortly after, I was approved for half a mortgage on an 1800 square foot rancher with my future ex. The home was situated on half an acre and was called 'The Ranch.' It was known to everyone as the party house, though. It was a dirty place with red shag carpet, dark and dingy inside because of all the wood and had a brutal mouse and beer fly infestation problem. There were five of us living in the house and another guy who lived in a trailer in my yard.

When I turned 22, my man proposed and we were married a year later. We took off on a Cancun honeymoon. It was an ongoing thing for him to tell me that all he wanted from me was three things: not to sell my 4x4 truck, not to quit my job at the parts warehouse (I could drive a forklift better than most of the boys!) and not to be a stripper (because he knew that I would be good at it). We both knew I was ready years before I even got into the industry since I was skilled and passionate about the private strip tease shows I performed for him in the living room. I had an enormous stock of costumes in the making (I guess I was preparing myself for dancing in the future without even knowing it). Although he loved it, he didn't want to share me with anyone else. We were together for 10 years and our marriage only lasted for three. The day I told him it was over was when we had flown out to the south western part of the USA to visit my grandparents. He mentioned that something had to change in our relationship and he wanted me to see a counsellor and try to work it out. I refused and said I was moving out once we got home. I felt bad because I know it was a cruel way to end it and break his heart. The next three days were very awkward since we were stuck with one another before we left for home. Then we had to deal with our long flight home together.

During Christmas of 2004, my sister bought me a set of pole dancing classes. I was running for exercise and going to counselling because I was stressed out from being alone in my life. It was the final ammunition for me to get on stage.

I decided to go do an amateur contest and my dad was there in front row to cheer me on! Many people find this strange but we didn't think it was a problem because I grew up with porn in our household being normal and not taboo or dirty.

When I did my first contest, I was a little scared but I still felt confident and it was actually quite exhilarating! Although I had practiced on a pole I had in my living room, I wasn't sure if I could take my underwear off. It turned out that I was actually fine with it since I got caught up in the moment and realized that I almost forgot to take them off. It was actually a big blur. I remember that everyone didn't believe I was an amateur. Because of this, it took close to half a dozen times before I actually won my first amateur contest which was a little frustrating.

What helped me finally win my first contest was a college student that recognized my dad from my other amateur contests. Dad told the guy that I had to win a contest or else I couldn't be put onto the circuit. So, that kid ran around the bar yelling that I had to win because they wanted to see me on the circuit. I guess that helped because I finally won that night!

I was put onto the circuit and was dancing part time when I started dating a psychopath. He was my gateway to the dark side of dancing – drugs, drinking and hard core partying. I got repair done to my flapjacks in August 2006, and he wanted to pay for it but I refused. After the surgery, I continued to work the two jobs. Two to three months later, the psychopath started to get super psycho crazy. He was constantly buying me insane amounts of gifts (but always held it over my head). I had to kick him out of my life. Around this time, I had met a man who was from the women's victim's service and after I told him about the psycho, he gave me some important information on how to get him out of my life. I was to give back every single gift he bought me to clean myself of him. When I sent all the gifts back, I said to him, "If I would've let you pay for my boobs, you would want those back too, right?" His response was, "Probably." Psycho was finally out of my life!

Although people always knew me as the fun, party girl, I took it a step further and gave myself completely to the drugs and alcohol. Not knowing what was happening and how to stop, I was about to lose my job at the warehouse. I put dancing on hold and told my boss about everything from start to finish. I told him that I didn't want to be the person I had become and I wanted my old self back. I was working two jobs, but I was broke. I just didn't know how to quit. He was very sympathetic and because he knew I was an asset to his company, he agreed to send me to a treatment centre of my choice. I went away for 42 days and he even paid the $19,000 bill as well as all my aftercare! I was so lucky to have such a great boss. After the rehab I went back to my job and slowly started back into dancing again. It was tough. Although I had to work late nights, I wanted to dance because I loved it!

The company I worked for got shut down by the corporation in November 2008, so I decided to go on the road for a month and try dancing full time. I realized I loved it and continue to this day. On June 11, 2009 I had my boobs refurbished (a lift) and I needed to take eight weeks off to heal. During this healing time, one of my first ever regulars who I have known for a very long time flew out from Saskatchewan to visit me in BC. We had so much fun hanging out together. We drove all over BC and I showed him around.

While growing up, I had a loving and close nurturing relationship with my mom which is probably why I'm more affectionate with my women. When my step dad was more pleased with me, the way he showed his love and rewarded me was with material items, and it's still like that. Today, my relationships with my girls are more introverted and with my guys it's extroverted. Oddly enough, I meet lots of cuddly men.

As a dancer, I love that my job keeps me in shape. Also, I have never had a job where I could travel as much as I do now and I find that my road trips get longer because I enjoy them. The energy and excitement in the bar is what I thrive on, especially the chaos. I love to focus my attention on a girl who sits in front row with her arms crossed and a pissed off look on her face. I'll turn the tables from myself being the star of the show to paying her a compliment and give her attention in a positive way.

I dislike the clichés of dancers and the fact that many of them burn their bridges without making amends and think they'll be welcomed back to a club with open arms. I am proud to say that I hold my own. I have regulars who like me and it is because of me that they come into the bar and spend their money. Many dancers (me included) find it frustrating that until only recently, most clubs went to seven day bookings, meaning that we get no day off during the week.

Here's a weird one. Most clubs make it mandatory for every girl to get walked out to her vehicle, especially late at night. I was finished work for the week and went out to my car. It was a warm night so I had my driver's side and passenger windows rolled down half way. I lit a smoke and leaned my head back against the head rest when I noticed two guys on my passenger side and a guy on my driver's side walk up beside my car from behind. I realized that the doorman hadn't seen me go out to my car and I froze as they stepped up to the open windows. The guy on the driver's side peered inside to look at me and asked, "How's it going?" I thought I was going to freak out, but I tried to stay calm. I responded with, "Good," as my heart pounded out of my chest and I looked at him with wide eyes. "That's not her," one of the guys on my right said as he stared at me and looked me over. "Ok, see you later," said the guy on my left. (I sure as hell hope not!!) I think back to that episode and wonder why they were looking for 'that girl' and what they would have done to her if they found her. It still gives me shivers when I think about that night! From that day onward, I always grab the doorman and demand that he escort me when I go out to my car. I also lock my doors and only open my windows a crack, if at all.

Because I have a strong personality, stalkers don't usually bother with me. But there was this one fellow (I'll call him Creepy) who claimed that he had a friend that designed a pair of shorts that I happened to wear in a photo shoot for one of my posters. I don't know how he got a hold of my number, but he called me up one day. He told me he wanted me to model a new product design for him – crotchless shorts. Although I told him I wasn't interested, he always managed to track me down at every club I was at and asked me to reconsider. During another one of his phone calls, he told me that he wanted to pay me $2000 to be the guest of honour at a private party. I wondered what he expected of me, so I questioned him. Since his story was inconsistent, I challenged him on it by asking him why he would pay me money like that unless he expected me to turn tricks. He said that there would be other beautiful girls at the party to take care of that for his clients. I told him that I was not a hooker and I had enough work. Then I told him to get lost.

Shortly after, I was kicking an addiction to percocets (I was taking 20 percs a day). I drove to eastern Canada to work and I used the three day drive to detox myself. As I struggled to release this addiction, I was going through hideous physical withdrawal where I couldn't sleep or even talk, and I was crawling in my own skin. While the painkillers were fun to be on, the withdrawal was unbearably awful! During this drive, Creepy called me again and I was very agitated with him and asked him what he wanted. He said that all he really wanted was to meet me. I freaked out on him pretty good and I haven't heard from him since.

One time, I was working the 2:30 pm show on Sunday when my dad and a lifelong lady friend of his came into the bar. Those two were the only two customers sitting in the bar and they got absolutely shitfaced. They started arguing and fighting with each other, and by the time I came back down to the bar after getting dressed, they had thrown a temper tantrum, got cut off and then were kicked out of the bar.

As for an embarrassing moment, here it is! I was working at a strip bar by an airport where they play loonie games for promo. I was using my underwear as a trampoline (they were pulled down just above my knees) so guys could throw loonies and if the coin landed on my underwear, that guy got a prize and my panties. It was a slow Tuesday night and there were only about twelve people in the bar with five of them sitting at the stage. I rolled onto my back to pull the panties up before rolling them down to my knees. I had my feet above my head just as my song stopped. Silence... and all of a sudden the only sound heard was a loud quack! I had farted. I moved my body into the crash position for two minutes and all I wanted to do was crawl off the stage and hide under a rock.

Over the years, I have been given many gifts by customers. The overwhelming gifts that stand out are a Harley Davidson diamond necklace and matching earrings that a regular gave me. I also collect t-shirts from different cities and I have a regular who is super attentive and really knows my size because he picks up t-shirts for me that look great and fit me perfect! I also had one of my stage blankets stolen once by a customer and another customer went out and bought a new one for me. I still use it today. I like to incorporate the gifts into my photo shoots, such as a pink corset, cowboy boots and jewellery, just to name a few.

The biggest tip I ever got was $800 which came from a guy who invested in shares that went from $.03 to $.89. I remember what he said as he did it; "Honey, I want to give you a tip you deserve!"

On a weird note, I have had my psychopath ex-boyfriend send me 75 long stemmed roses and a watermelon to my parts warehouse job once. He wanted to do something different other than send a fruit basket. But really, a watermelon?

On the other hand, I like to give gifts as well, especially

to my steady regulars. I text them when I'm coming to their town, and since they treat me so well, I like to return the favour and show them my appreciation by giving them lots of up to date promo and attention. I want them to feel special, so last Christmas I shipped out a Christmas poster with a Christmas card to them. They had no idea it was coming so it was a nice surprise.

Things the reader would find amusing about me are that my first car used to be a 1973 Gremlin. I also own my second Harley and I used to four-wheel a 1982 Chevy one-tonne that was snorkelled, locked and lifted eight inches. I used to do dog agility with my golden retriever and I ran 30 half-marathons in a three year time span. I also like to bake cookies; "Batter is a vehicle to hold chips" is what I like to say. When I gorge on sugar, the crash is similar to someone coming off a hard drug.

Four things I won't leave home without are my own pillows, yahtzee, crib, and Bob (my vibrator with a stock of AA batteries). Bob doesn't cuddle or snore and he doesn't want breakfast.

With my old dancer name, people spelt it wrong all the time so I changed it to something I felt was more marketable and catchy. I also wanted a single name instead of two.

The one thing that surprised me about this industry was you didn't get a week off when you menstruated. Also, I didn't realize that the girls and customers would find it so easy to talk to me and use me as their personal therapist.

The one thing I wish I knew before getting into this business was that when you're on top of your game, every day is tiring. Also, I wish I had a better filing system to organize my tax papers.

I just turned 28 when I started dancing part time for the first three years. I'm dancing into my sixth year now (I'm 34), but I plan to keep dancing until I don't love it anymore or if I have to do too much maintenance to keep myself looking like I'm in my 20's, whichever comes first.

I'm not ashamed of telling people what I do for a living but

I need to be smarter about who I tell because not everyone is as open minded as me. I look at it this way: you come into my club to watch me, so what am I ashamed of? In the end, I do not regret getting into this business, but I do regret not getting into it sooner since I was living by other people's boundaries. I should have just been honest with myself about what I wanted to do a long time ago.

My advice for new girls coming into this business is to stay on top of your promo and have lots of variety to give away to customers – and be generous. Don't just use cheap lingerie. Have some custom-made costumes and dress in lots of layers so you are always taking something off. If you're dealing with a catty dancer, kill her with kindness. Also, build a good name for yourself and be professional. Learn to dance and detach yourself from your problems on stage because you're an entertainer. Remember that you're not the only one with problems such as fighting with a boyfriend, your dog dying or getting evicted. Remember to stick to your bookings and don't lie. You're a performer so always remember that if you don't have the smiles, whistles and winks in the front row, you don't have a job!

# Oleander

At age 11, I caught a glimpse of Demi Moore in *Striptease*. At age 26, I have a weird obsession with Annie Lenox's song *Little Bird*. I don't think that seeing one movie is to blame, but it most definitely opened my eyes to it. I can't fully explain why I'm a dancer.

I came from a household where nudity was not a shameful thing, which is probably why I'm comfortable with that aspect of dancing. I was in gymnastics as a child and became a cheerleader in high school – I am definitely a sexual person by nature. I think a combination of things led me down this path.

At 18, I took myself down to a strip club and applied to be a dancer. The first few years were awkward because I was finding my style and discovering what worked for and against me. I was surrounded by magazine worthy women who had been in this job for years and knew how to play the game. I slowly developed the skills of hair, makeup and figuring out which costumes suited me best. It has taken eight years but I have finally achieved the perfect 'me!'

The things I have learned from this job could never be replaced. I have discovered things about my body and myself that made me more comfortable as a person. I have made amazing friends that have helped me throughout the years. If there is a reason for everything, then the friends I've met were the reason for me dancing.

Over the years, I have had many customers take me by surprise. I have been spoiled! I've had purses, trips and a vehicle bought for me. But with the good, sometimes comes bad. I've had customers cross boundaries and invade my personal space. Not cool since I am a private person and am entitled to that privacy!

If I had any advice to new girls, it would be to SAVE your money! If I had been smart, I would own several houses by now and would have a lot more in RRSPs. Keep your head on straight too! I've seen beautiful, smart, wealthy dancers lose everything to drugs and alcohol. Your goal is to better yourself with this job, not to use it as a party. That being said, I may not have made all the right choices, but they were mine with no regrets.

Written by Oleander

# Orchid

I always knew there was money to be made in the bar industry. That's why I started out at the age of 16 as a coat check girl in a nightclub. I had fake ID made up and got my foot in the door.

When I turned 19, I moved to a bigger city and got a job as a cocktail waitress in a downtown nightclub. After working only two shifts, I was immediately promoted to 'bottle service.' The other servers were upset and didn't understand why I got this position (and to this day, I'm not even sure myself).

My job was to wander around the bar and sell bottles of liquor that ranged from $400-$2000. Legally, the customer is not allowed to pour the alcohol, so I would stand there as their personal VIP bartender and pour the alcohol while they added their mix of choice. People will pay big money for bottle service because they like the personal service and they don't have to stand in line to buy a drink. They also feel like royalty and get to play the big shot. It was an awesome job that I did for almost two years. I made insane tips, too, usually $600-$1100 each shift. The only downfall was that it was only Friday and Saturday nights. The rest of the week I had to work at an upscale restaurant where I only made a measly $100 in tips.

One night while I was working bottle service, I served an exotic dancer. She was stunning; I couldn't take my eyes off her. She told me that I should come out and see the club. She also mentioned that I should look into getting a job there. I thought about it and out of curiosity went to check it out.

I got hired as a VIP girl but soon realized that to make money, I had to hustle the customers and persuade them to buy my private dances. To really make money as a VIP dancer, you have to have regulars. Just sit with the guys and get to know them. Then they return to the club to visit and buy VIP dances from you. But I was so nervous, I was working against myself. I felt I didn't have a chance against the other dancers.

They were like tigers, constantly pouncing on the prey before I had a chance to.

When I started dancing at 22, I was working for one of the pickiest managers I have ever dealt with. Before a shift, we had to get her approval on our appearance. We had to show her our fingernails (no polish allowed; only clean white French tips). Our hair had to be clean and well styled, and we weren't allowed to color it without their permission. If she thought a g-string didn't look good, it had to go. As for the dress code, we wore only white, and had to cover any tattoos completely. It was tough on the brain to work there, but you could really make money. We made $600 after the club charged the customer a booking fee (about $100-$150 at the time). I worked there for four months, then left and returned to work for another two months.

My mom and dad know what I do for a living and they are really supportive. My mom even helps make my costumes. They are happy that I'm proud of what I do, that I make great money and that I have never touched drugs.

I love entertaining and really wanted to dance on stage, so I left the strict club and went to work for another local club where I could do stage shows. I didn't stick around for too long; only two shifts as a matter of fact. As soon as I found out girls weren't paid for stage dancing, I was out of there. Also, the club was a rip-off. When you did a private show, you only got paid $300 and the club kept $100 of it. Compared to the money I made at my first club it didn't seem fair, so I left.

I went home and researched one of the local agencies. After talking to the agent, I was sent to do an amateur contest. From that point on, I worked through the agency and entered the circuit.

What I love about the industry is that you have full control of when and where you want to be. The attention is great, too! What I hate about this business is that it makes you doubt yourself. In the beginning I had a lot of confidence. As time goes on, I feel more and more inadequate.

Everyone seems to have an embarrassing moment. Mine is not too bad. I was naked on stage and lost my footing, falling in front of the whole bar.

At the first bar I worked at, I met my first stalker. We'll call him Mr. T. He was at the club every single day, all day. He followed me from club to club for seven months and brought me random gifts all the time.

Private dances are expensive. Usually a girl will charge $40 a song ($10 of it goes to the house). The price didn't bother Mr. T. He would spend hundreds of dollars at one time on private dances. At first, he didn't seem to have a problem when I sat with my other customers to have a drink or give them a private dance. However, many of my other customers told me that Mr. T would stare at them and make them uncomfortable.

Things got even more intense with Mr. T after that. He even asked for my email address. I would never give out my real one, but I decided to create a separate email account for him and my other regulars. I figured as long as it was separate from my personal life, it should be okay. After all, if regulars could keep in touch with me and find out where I was working on certain weeks, they might visit and buy dances. Then Mr. T asked for my personal phone number and wanted to hang out with me during my time off. I refused. He was going too far. He was starting to smother me at this point, so I decided my New Year's Resolution was to get rid of him. One day when he came to the club, I snapped at him and told him that I didn't want him coming around so much. He showed up a few more times at some of the other clubs and I yelled at him to get away from me. I haven't seen him since, thank goodness.

I don't have a favourite customer story but all my regulars are very sweet men. Some are lonely people who are happy if I sit and talk with them or have a drink. Many of them don't really want private dances, but will still hand me $50 or $100 because I always have time for them and am nice to them.

Something funny about me being a dancer is that I don't have the drive or ability to rob these guys of all their money. I have told men who get private dances from me when they have spent too much money and it's getting too expensive. I know there are girls that would take advantage of these poor guys, but that's not me. If you aren't a good person, it'll age you and rob you of a lot in life.

The one thing I wish I knew before getting into this business is how addictive the money can be. There is no other job out there that has the freedom and the great money. It's very hard to quit. So far, I have been dancing for seven months and I plan on dancing for another year. The money is too good.

Something I didn't know before I started out as a dancer is how helpful some of the veteran girls like Calla Lily are. People think the girls are nothing but catty but it is the opposite. These women have their shit together and they help anyone who asks them.

Another shocking thing about being in this business is the cost! Photo shoots and promo are definitely not cheap. You also spend a lot of money on shoes and big stage costumes. I see it as an investment, because dancing is a business to make money. I am a true professional at heart. My goal is to make money for the bars because I want them to rebook me in the future. If they make money, I make money.

My favourite club to work at is like a home away from home. I make a good paycheck and I usually double it within a couple of days by doing private dances. Also, the staff is great. Again, the bar makes money, I make money!

My advice for new girls is that this business is all about teamwork. It's not about you, it's about working as a team with the other dancers. I believe that you should all work the room and help to keep the customers from leaving. By keeping customers in the room and showing them a good time, not only do the dancers make money, but everyone else does too, including the bartenders and servers. Also, have an exit plan!

# Peony

I was laid off at my assistant manager job at a recruitment agency two years ago when the recession hit. I took the summer off and bought a car with the money I had saved. When my money ran out, I thought about stripping. When I called up the agency and talked to the agent, he asked me why I wanted to get into dancing. My response was, "I like dancing and taking my clothes off. I like getting naked." Pure and simple. I figured that since I was at a popular nudist beach pretty much every day, I might as well get paid for it! My first day on the job, I was so excited to take my clothes off at the amateur contest that I took them off before I was even supposed to. I didn't win that night, but I got put onto the circuit right away.

Before I hit the circuit, I had to come up with a name. I chose mine because it signifies exotic vixens, the dangerous, the unknown, the seductive and the alluring.

I realized that I entered a very unusual world my first week on the circuit, when I stepped into the dressing room to find a girl bent over, spreading her ass cheeks at the mirror and using baby wipes to clean herself. I asked her what she was doing because she looked like she was cleaning very vigorously. Turns out it's a necessity so you are clean as a whistle for stage shows.

I found out quickly that wearing regular boots with a stiletto heel killed my calves. Normally, I'm a sandals and running shoe kind of girl. I also ended up with bruises all over my arms and legs from doing pole work. The only reason I would ever regret getting into this line of work is because of the damage to my body. I have worse back problems now than when I first started, and all the bruising. I had so many bruises that my boyfriend of five years thought that someone was beating me. He supports me in what I do, but he's happy that I'm planning on getting out and going to school because we're now planning on marriage and kids in the future.

My mom has never seen me dance. She's not upset about the fact that I'm a dancer but she's not thrilled about it either. My aunt was a dancer for 10 years, first in Toronto and then California. She said that back then, the costumes were elaborate and the shows were very fancy and Vegas style. My 81 year old grandma understands the industry since she was exposed to it through my aunt. Grandma drove me to work one day and said, "Don't forget to sell private dances and make some money!" She has even told me that I need to put on more makeup so customers can see me on stage better and asks me to try on my costumes and model them for her. She likes it because she knows I have fun and enjoy it. I love hanging out with my family in my spare time, but it's hard because I'm on the road so much in this job. I miss my family a lot when I travel.

As for my dad, he left my mom when I was born. When I was 16, I contacted his family and wrote him a letter. He wrote me back, so I flew out to see him. When my mom and dad got together again after all those years, they ended up in bed the next morning! They stayed together for two years and broke up again because my dad is an irresponsible alcoholic. In a way, I regret contacting him because I starting drinking and doing drugs. I guess I was rebelling against him and used him as an excuse to drink and get high all the time.

Since my aunt was a dancer, I already knew a lot about the industry before getting started so there were few surprises for me. The one thing that did surprise me however was how quickly I got into shape dancing. When I started in this business, I was 150 pounds and two months later I was 20 pounds lighter. I never had muscles in my life and I do now because of the dancing and pole work. I love that I am in the best shape of my life. I also enjoy learning new pole tricks, traveling, meeting new girls and hanging out with all the staff at the different bars. I even had friends come visit me at the bar. I had stopped talking to a bunch of guy friends from school. When I posted on a social networking site that I started dancing, every single one of them came to the strip club to watch me dance.

The one thing I wish I knew before getting into this business was that the pay isn't as good as it used to be twenty years ago when my aunt danced. She told me about the crazy amounts of money she used to make. I had high hopes of paying off my bills quickly and saving some money. I was definitely expecting a lot more money. My aunt told me that getting naked for the money I make now is not worth it and she wouldn't do it.

I hate the pay structures at some of the bars since they are not always honest. I find that some bars skim money off the top of my cheque for random fees. I was at one club a few weeks ago and when I was checking into my room, I found screws on the bed and wood chips on the floor, so I asked for another room. At the end of the week, I found that I was charged for both rooms and they even charged me for the keys I returned.

Another thing I can't stand is when dirty old men tell me what to do on stage. For example, once I was dancing at the far pole when a guy yelled at me from the other side of the stage, "Hey, there's nobody over there!" And then he took his $20 off the stage!

My most embarrassing moment was when I fell right off the stage. I wasn't even drunk. I had my top off and I stumbled because I miscalculated my step. I ended up on the floor with my boobs out and since my boyfriend was sitting there, he saw the whole thing.

When I first started dancing, I rarely did private dances and I still don't hustle customers for them. One night after work, I was sitting in my street clothes at the bar having a few drinks. It was after 1:30 am and a guy came over and asked me for a private dance. Although I was a little tipsy, I still went into the private dance room with him. When I was naked, I bent over and shook my ass at him. As I bent over further to look upside down and back at him through my legs, I was horrified to see my tampon string hanging out! I forgot I had put in a new tampon after my last show and since I was done work for the night, I didn't cut the string. He wasn't even bothered by it! He said, "Wanna go have some drinks and do some coke? It's my friend's birthday." I thanked him for the (ridiculous) offer but refused. All I wanted to do was crawl out of the room in embarrassment.

Another uncomfortable thing that happens to me once in a while is that I get aroused at work. It's unintentional. I know it's natural but it is something that should be for my boyfriend and me.

There have been some scary moments. Once, as I was giving an old Asian man a private dance, he got very close to my pussy and even tried to put his fingers inside me. Then he pulled some money out and wanted to push it up inside me! He asked me how much I wanted for him to take me home and I refused. He offered me $500 and I declined again. Then he upped it to $1000 and I still said no. I couldn't believe it when he said that he would give me $2000 if he could just lick my pussy! He grabbed me and pulled me close to him and I screamed. He got kicked out of the bar and I was told that he had tried this on other girls.

There is one club I refuse to work at because the greasy owner is a womanizer and I also find that the dancer house is very creepy and unsecure. I've heard the horror stories!

The weirdest customer I've encountered is the sock guy. Usually, I just wear one pair of socks in my work boots for the week. Sock guy loves that. He says that my socks are the best because I give them to him wet with sweat!

My favourite customer is a very sweet man. He has bought me gift cards, a bathing suit, dinners and he tips me hundreds of dollars. It's all very innocent, he just wants company. He loves beautiful women! Another one of my favourite customers pays me $500 for a VIP dance because he loves my, shall we say, private area. He always tells me how beautiful it is. I don't care as long as he doesn't touch. He's about 45 years old and we smoke weed together sometimes. I think he gets welfare or a disability cheque and blows it all on me.

The most common gifts I receive from customers are clothes and money. The weirdest gift I received is the pair of socks from the sock guy along with $10 when I give him my old pair. The biggest tip I got was $500 all in hundred dollar bills on stage once. The guy crammed the fifth bill in his mouth and wanted me to get it. I told him to spit it out already, and he did.

Something you would find interesting about me is that I am an artist and I like to draw. I also know everything about computers. I guess you could say I'm a hacker. I'm also an adrenaline junky. I love things like bungee jumping and sky diving. I'm also more of a tomboy than anything else, other than the way I dress and the fact that bugs freak me out. I love football, camping, beer, and drinking shot for shot with my guy friends. For the record, all my guy friends are just friends and I have never slept with any one of them.

Things I will not leave home without are my pillow, blanket, slippers and vibrator.

I was 25 when I started in this industry and I have been dancing now for two years. I'm quitting dancing in September to go to school since I'm upgrading and then taking a whole bunch of courses like computer, video game design, sound engineering and forensics. I figure that I might as well learn a whole bunch of material and see what interests me.

I'm not ashamed of telling people what I do for a living since I have told strangers who ask. Some people take it in a weird way and others don't. I find that most people don't believe it because they respond with, "You don't even look like a dancer!" That comment is confusing to me since I wonder what a typical dancer looks like. It's not like we wear our costumes out in the street or anything.

My advice for new girls coming into this business is to make sure to condition your body beforehand because the bruising sucks big-time. Also, don't let the agents push you around and make you work in places you don't want to. I was once told that they were sending me to Alaska although I didn't want to go. My plane landed in a forest up north and it didn't get dark until midnight. I was not very comfortable there. You will be told that places are glamorous when in fact they are not. They will lie to get what they want, so be on guard.

I do not regret getting into this business because I love it. I enjoy dancing.

# Petunia

When I was 22 years old, I tried dancing for a day at the strip club. Back then, dancers only got paid for VIP dances they sold and since this business was new to me, I wasn't sure what I was supposed to do. I had only sold one dance, so I only made a measly $30.

Fast forward almost six years. I was managing a couple of my mom's clothing stores. When the recession hit and my mom's business partner screwed her, the stores were closed and she filed for bankruptcy. I left the small town we lived in and moved to the big city. I had a hard time finding a job (even the coffee shop wouldn't hire me!). I eventually got a job selling shoes. While working in retail, I had a hard time getting by with the small amount of money I made.

Then I saw a job ad calling for dancers for an amateur contest. It said a girl could make $50 just for dancing to three songs. I went down to the club with a bottle of Jagermeister and sat in the bathroom by myself and got shitfaced since I was too scared to talk to anyone. A girl came into the bathroom and asked me if I was doing the contest. I told her I was and she invited me to sit with her. I was so nervous because I had no idea what to do or even what to expect. I wasn't even properly prepared since I didn't bring any music or proper heels. I had brought kitten heels. Shit, I was so green! I was terrified that the other girls would be beautiful Barbie dolls with fake tits but it actually wasn't that bad, probably because I was drunk enough!

During the day, I worked my retail job selling shoes and then I would go in the evenings to do amateur contests because I needed the extra money. Since I was always around doing the contests, the agents had asked me when I was planning on working for them full time. They said that I would have to quit my job because of the travel out of town and the hours. I took the plunge, quit my job and joined the circuit.

When I revealed to my mom that I was a dancer, I was glad that she took it well. My sister on the other hand, is a polar opposite of me who was very upset when she found out. I don't talk to my dad.

I grew up in a big house on the same street as a very well known wealthy BC businessman. Although I went to a private school and was spoiled, it wasn't a happy childhood since my dad was an abusive alcoholic. Maybe I do have some daddy issues. It took a fair bit of convincing from me, but my mom divorced my dad when I was 15. He was really not a nice man.

My first week of dancing, I was sent to a strip club out of town and I hated it with a passion! I found the customers really rude and most of my shows were cancelled. I only did seven shows all week! The apartment where the dancers stayed had mice and I found a used condom on my bed and even puke on the wall! I mentioned this to the manager and he had the nerve to say, "Well, excuse me Diva!" I couldn't believe it. I just wanted a clean and safe place to stay. I didn't think I was being unreasonable!

That experience left a bad taste in my mouth, so I quit dancing after that hellish week and tried to find another job. I couldn't find anything so I went on EI for a couple of months just so I could get by. Then I started doing amateur contests again because I knew what to expect and I was comfortable doing them. I also liked the fact that I wasn't travelling out of town. I told a few of the girls about my bad experience that first week and they all said that it normally isn't that bad. I met a girl at the contest and we became friends. We decided to get back onto the circuit together.

We traveled all over together. One night, the club we were working at held a wet t-shirt contest and customers were allowed to bring in their super soakers. While I was walking through the bar in my heels trying to hustle the guys for private dances, I wasn't prepared for how drenched the floor was and

I fell and broke my wrist. I needed surgery and had a plate and bolts implanted in my wrist. I'm thankful that I was covered by workers comp, but because it was such a bad break, I was off work for three and a half months.

I refuse to work at certain bars especially if the pay is bad. I hate the way some bar owners treat dancers. There is no guaranteed show count and it sucks when shows are cancelled especially when it costs you money to travel out of town. By the end of the week, you're lucky if you break even after getting paid. I also despise some of the douchebag customers and some of the shitty work conditions. Sometimes the bar has no security and I don't feel safe.

I was doing my last show of the week when some guy tried to 'bottle' me (I was naked and he tried to cram a beer bottle into my vag!). After it happened, the DJ told the guy on the mike, "Do not touch the dancers." The servers kept serving the guy drinks and he didn't even get kicked out! I refuse to work there again. I heard that another girl had some guy try cramming a pool cue into her rear-end and there was blue chalk on her asshole as evidence.

My best customer is an older gentleman who owns a big house on the lake and he invited me to stay with him. He was a complete gentleman and didn't try anything with me. He even drove me all the way back home at the end of the week so I didn't have to bus it. He also gave me a big bag of weed and tipped me hundreds of dollars. I wish all customers were like this!

The weirdest gift I received was of a pencil/charcoal sketch of me that was not very good (it was actually quite creepy looking). My favourite thing to get from customers is weed and cash money! The biggest tip I ever got was $1000 thrown on stage in $100 bills.

Something people would find shocking about me is that I was a heroin addict and lived on the streets for five years between the ages of 16-21. I shacked up with people when I could and squatted or lived in tents. I would basically steal to survive, so my mom wouldn't allow me to come home because I would steal from her. I was at a point in my life where I didn't care if I were to live or die. I would go downtown, get a balloon or baggie of heroin and bang it for days. I've woken up in different cities and not known how I got there!

I went to drug and alcoholic treatment centres seven times. I would usually run away after about 30 days. When I was 21, I was sent to a pig farm in Alaska. It was during the winter and I couldn't run away so I ended up sticking it out. I was clean and sober for four and a half years after that. I went to university for a year and was active in AA for years, talking to kids at churches and youth groups. The kids could relate to me because of my age. All I can say is that I never want to be homeless again!

Another private thing about me is that I won't leave home without my make-up, heels and stuffy.

I'm not ashamed of telling people what I do for a living because I see nothing wrong with what I do. I do get some negative reactions from some family members but I see them as ignorant and small minded. I have met many different types of people over the years and I would never judge or look down on them or what they do. Now that I understand this business, I really respect strippers.

When I first got into this industry, I found that everything about it was surprising. You're not sure what is expected of you so you're totally unprepared for work. I didn't even know that I was supposed to bring my own music since I assumed the DJ had it covered.

It would have been nice to know the details of this job right from the beginning. You find out who you have to avoid, who to suck up to, etc, pretty quick. I have a history of partying and dealing with all types of people, so I pretty much fit in. I worry about the younger girls who are so naïve and new to the business since you definitely need street smarts to do this work or you're going to be taken advantage of pretty quick. It's a sink or swim kind of thing.

I was 31 years old when I started dancing. Since I'm older than most of the girls and I'm pretty new into the business, I'm just enjoying it right now. I plan on dancing for a couple more years but I know that I need a plan because I'm not a spring chicken. You can't make too many plans, though. You know the saying – when you make plans, God laughs!

My advice for new girls getting into this industry is to not get into it unless you're emotionally, mentally and physically ready to handle it. Some young girls don't take this job seriously and are here to party most of the time. 10 years ago, I would've been a mess and wouldn't be able to handle this job, but since I'm 32 years old now, I have matured. Also, don't burn your bridges.

Despite all the craziness, I love this business. There are not too many other jobs where you're allowed to have a drink. It's a party type atmosphere where a girl can meet guys and interesting people. I'm an exhibitionist and not shy, so this job works well for me. I do not regret getting into this business because it's a learning experience and something I can check off to try on my bucket list!

# Pink Lily

It all started when I lost my job at the coffee shop. I dropped off my resume at a strip club and was hired as a food server. While I worked, I always admired the beautiful dancers with their gorgeous costumes. After six months in the job, I needed a change and wanted to make better money. I called the local agency and they gave me a shot. They sent me out to do two amateur contests so I could try the job out and then I was put on the circuit right away.

The first day that I got on stage, I was so scared! I barely remember it, other than the fact that I drank six shots of tequila to give me liquid courage. I never expected that I would be dancing naked for a living.

I was 20 when I started dancing and I've been at it now for a little over a year. My family knows what I do for a living and they don't really care. They didn't care much about me anyways as I have been from foster home to group home since I was a kid. I got addicted to drugs at a group home and ended up living in a crack shack. When my mom found out, she freaked out and (kind of) saved me by coming to take me home. I was 13 years old and addicted to crystal meth at this point. It took me two years to finally quit. Although I was living back home with my mom, I ended up getting addicted to coke when I was 17.

My mom actually picked my new stage name for me. I changed my dancer name because something bad happened at another club and I didn't want that incident associated with me anymore. She loved the first part of my name and wanted to name me that when I was born but my dad hated it. She also suggested the second part to my name too because it fit together nice.

I have a wonderful boyfriend who's good for me and treats me well. He doesn't drink or do drugs and he helped to reconnect me with my religion. It's nice because I'm starting to pray again.

Something you may find amusing about me is that when I see the color yellow, it makes me happy and puts me in the best mood. I like to have a couple of the tips on my nails painted yellow so that when I'm sad I can look at them and my mood is instantly changed to positive!

Before I started dancing, I wish I knew how crazy this business was. You're on the road and travel all the time, rushing around nonstop. You also get addicted to the money so you feel stuck in this business. You think you can't make this kind of money doing something else. I think I'm addicted to stripping.

While dancing, I have come to appreciate and love the freedom, time off, the hours and the attention. I'm always in control of how much I work and I feel good about myself. The customers can be really sweet, too. This past Christmas I received one of the nicest gifts from a customer. A young guy who has a crush on me likes to go into the strip club with his dad. He gave me a pretty pair of earrings.

The down side of this job is that we are getting hit hard in the current economy. Also, with the drinking and driving laws tightening up, it seems like people aren't coming into the bars like they used to. It's hard for a dancer to make good money now.

Other things that I dislike are when women come into the bar and watch. It feels as though they are judging me for taking my clothing off for a living. Also, I didn't realize how hard and painful the pole work is as you crawl around on the stage, destroying your knees.

I have a scary story that involved a friend of mine who drugged me. He popped up out of nowhere one day to visit me and we ended up going back to his hotel where I spent the night puking. I tried to leave but I was so out of it I didn't know where I was. I ended up falling asleep and when I woke up, I dug around in my purse to pull out my stash of coke. I took some of that and it actually made me coherent enough to get out of there.

There is only one club I refuse to work at because they allow girls to perform 'actions' to degrade themselves. I have heard of girls making a quick $200 for fucking a guy in the back room. There's definitely a very fine line between stripping and prostitution.

All that aside, the only major thing I hate about my job is when I end up getting zits on my bum from the dirty stage!

I have some advice for new girls coming into the business. Keep your nose clean. Keep your eyes open. Take what you want, and get out as soon as you can. This business is hard work and can be hard on your body, as well as mentally draining. It's hard to worry about what people think of you all the time. Also, never date anyone you meet in the bar. In the beginning the guy will love the fact he's dating a stripper but eventually that will wear off and it turns to jealousy.

I definitely do not regret getting into this industry because I have experienced some cool things and met the most amazing people. My plan is to be out of this business within one year and go back to school to become a child psychologist so I can help young people.

# Poppy

My mom told me, "If I ever catch your boney ass on stage, I'm gonna break your legs!" Because I was of age and I could do what I want, AND to piss her off, I started dancing!

Growing up, my mom was a dancer so I was always hanging around the agency and going with her to work. When I was 13, I remember my grandpa calling her 'Jezebel.' He said that she takes her clothes off for a living and I wasn't sure what that meant; I thought she was probably a porn star.

Mom would get photo shoots done and she would cut a little picture out for me from her contact sheet. It would be some sexy shot of herself with her titties hanging out. I would take the tiny little photo to school and would show it off to all the boys and my friends. The response was always, "Your mom is hot!" I told everyone that she was an actress.

I was at the club with her one day and one of the agents said to me, "If you ever want to start dancing, give me a call. Here's my card." As he held the business card out to me, my mom flew across the bar like Superwoman and ripped the card away.

I was almost 20 when I started dancing. After I told her, she responded with, "Well, I guess you are of age and I can't do anything about it now."

When I did my first amateur contest, I was really nervous before getting on stage. I was told to picture myself at the club next door dancing, but just naked! All my friends came to the club that night, sat at gyno and cheered for me like crazy.

Although my mom danced for years, I never knew how much money she made. As funny as it sounds, I didn't get into dancing because of the money. Before I started dancing, I was going to cosmetology school.

Working in this industry, I love meeting different people from all over the world and from different walks of life. Many customers live through the dancers since we are their soap opera. The industry is what you make of it and everyone has different views. Some girls are focused on making lots of money and others are focused on partying and not saving any.

I don't like some people's opinions about the industry, thinking that all dancers are alcoholics or partiers. Also, I have found that if a girl is not favoured by a club, she doesn't get booked by that club; agents are responsible for this as well. I don't necessarily refuse to work at any bars. But if I do, it's usually because of the clientele, staff or even the type of bar it is.

The weirdest gift I got from a customer once was a coupon for a subway sandwich. My weirdest customer would have to be a 65 year old guy who showed up at all the clubs I danced at. He was a very well dressed, sleek, Italian-type guy who looked like he had lots of money. He would call the bar every morning and ask for my show times. When he would arrive, he would tell staff that he was my husband. The bar would call upstairs to me and say, "Your husband is here." When I came down to join him, he would pull out his comb and start combing his hair and grooming himself as I walked towards him. At the beginning of his visits, he would get mad and yell at any guys who would interrupt us to ask me for a private dance. I would tell him not to be rude to them because I am there to make money.

Shortly after that, he said to me, "Ok. I know you're at work to make money and when you sit here talking to me, you're not making any. So, I will pay you to sit here and talk with me." After that, he would slide $20 over to me every 10-15 minutes. I haven't seen him in years now. He probably died.

I encountered my rudest customer when I was dancing in a club one week and he called me a racial name. A fight erupted in the bar and the guy got his ass kicked. After the beating, he was told to get out and if he ever wanted to come back then his attitude better be changed. I didn't even hear the comment in the first place. The way I see it, it was his opinion and if I would get upset and feed into it, it would just give him more power anyways. In the end, he's the one that ends up looking like the fool.

My best customer was a fisherman who owned a company with a bunch of fishing boats and he gave me $600 once. He started by giving me a $100 bill and because he was drinking pretty heavily, I asked him, "Do you know how much you gave me?"

He replied, "Ya. I know I gave you a hundred bucks." Then he put $50 on stage, then another $100 and pretty soon it all added up to $600!

A few years later, I ran into him again and this time he was sitting at the back of the room with his workers. He was buying private dances for them. He paid the waitress $20 every time she was asked to bring me a tip (every tip consisted of fifties and hundreds). Just from him that day alone, he gave me $1500. This was the biggest tip I got from one customer at once.

This embarrassing story belongs to a customer at the bar one night. He was sitting at gyno and I saw his hand moving around under the stage. Every time I took a piece of clothing off, his hand would move faster. I got the bouncer's attention and told him, "I think that guy is playing with himself but I'm not completely sure. I don't want to embarrass him if he isn't." So, the bouncer went over to the guy and asked him to stand up. He said he needed to look under his chair for something that someone may have lost there earlier in the night. He refused to get up, so the bouncer grabbed him under the armpits and pulled him out of his chair. The guy's pants and underwear fell to the floor and he tried grabbing them with one hand while the other hand was holding onto his cock. It was a priceless sight to see a grown man hanging onto his penis and trying to pull his pants up while he was being dragged outside and thrown into the street.

I have to mention a weird incident that belongs to one of the dancers I know. She had a customer keep track of her period cycle and bring her chocolate bars during those times!

Some personal things about me are that I won't leave home without my purse, my psp (portable play station; music) and my phone. I don't smoke, drink or do drugs, ever.

I like to do hair extensions and make costumes on the side, so if I ever get a big enough clientele, I may cut down on dancing. I don't mind dancing though. I'm used to the dancing lifestyle. Besides, if I'm stuck at home, I'm just sitting around watching tv and eating all the time anyways.

I have been dancing now for 14 years and I plan on dancing until I decide I have had enough. When that is, I don't know because I still enjoy my job and I'm taking it as it comes.

When I meet a guy, I let him know what I do for a living right away because it gives him a choice to back out if he wants to.

When I was picking my dancer name, I fell in love with the name of a park. My boyfriend at the time lived in that city and I decided that if I ever became a dancer, that would be my stage name.

Nothing surprised me about this industry when I got into it because I was never left in the dark. I was always asking my mom about anything I needed to know.

My advice for new girls coming into this business is to try and save as much of your money as you can. Also, it's good to be cautious of other dancers at first, since dancers can take advantage of you. If they know that you are not a pushover, you won't be messed with.

I do not regret getting into this business because I enjoy my job and I have fun doing what I do. I am not ashamed to tell people what I do for a living. I tell everyone that I'm a dancer and when I'm asked what kind of dancer, I respond with, "a stripper dancer."

# Rhododendron

I've been hanging around strip bars since I was 16 because I was sleeping with one of the DJs that worked there. When I turned 19, I begged for a waitressing job in his bar and was hired. I loved playing around on the pole and I definitely wasn't shy, so when I turned 20, I started in the business. At first, I did ring-girl competitions and amateur contests. My first day on the job, I remember that I didn't want to fall because I've never took dance lessons in my life!

People always ask me how I chose my dancer name. It went like this: I was going through a fast food drive-thru with five friends and we were all crammed in the smallest car imaginable. After waiting over an hour in the drive-thru (no joke) we had a discussion about nicknames and my friends were trying to think of one for me. One came up with my name because I reminded her of a character from a movie. I was a good girl that just broke out of my shell and went a little crazy by stripping!

This industry is not that bad. I love the costumes, the attention and the work out. It's a treat to work at my favourite bar because the magpies and the staff are a lot of fun. As for the dancers, I have never had any major issues with any of them and I get along fine with everyone. I have been asked if I had any dirt or stories on dancer fights but my lips are sealed!

Looking back, I've been around some pretty greasy managers. These characters tried convincing me to sleep with them by promising me extra shows, buying me drinks and giving me money. Back in those days, this was nothing out of the ordinary. I remember people hiding out in the back of bars doing cocaine and other drugs.

This job has taught me a lot. I had to learn to stand up for myself, and to be aggressive when it came to the pay and the bookings. Also, there are more rules than I thought, and you have to make sure the customers don't pressure you into breaking them. I learned to have great stamina. If I had to use one word to describe a working week for me, it is *long.*

My pet peeve is when customers don't tip. I don't ask for much, but that one really bothers me. Nobody likes to be treated like dirt.

The other thing I worry about is seeing someone I know, but it happens. I was a nerd in school, so imagine how I felt when my high school bully showed up at the bar I was working at. My stomach jumped when I saw him but I felt better when his jaw dropped in awe and he couldn't talk.

I meet my share of weird people in this job. One of my crazy stories is when I was at work standing outside chatting with some guys. We watched a drunk guy drive across the parking lot, barely missing a fire hydrant and pole and bottoming out his vehicle. Creepy thing is that there was a baby seat in the back.

I also have a creepy stalker story. This geeky guy with glasses would follow me to every bar I worked at and he would bring me stuffed toys and presents. He told me that he loved me and asked me to marry him. When I turned him down, he said his life was over and he cried. He wasn't a bad guy, just weird.

Some personal things about me are that I love to travel and during my time off I love to relax. My hobbies are snowboarding, music and anything outdoors. Something most people don't know about me is that I played classical piano for 12 years and my passion is music. When I leave for the day, three things that I would never leave home without are my make-up, laptop and extra shoes.

Dancing makes your personal life interesting, to say the least. My take on dating guys I meet at work is simple. When you work six or seven days a week in a bar, it's hard not to, but kick them to the curb quick if they aren't right for you.

My family knows what I do for a living. They are mostly concerned with my safety.

My advice for dancers coming into the business – don't act like a snob. Fight for what you want. Do your best and be true to yourself, friends and staff. Have a plan for after you retire from dancing.

I'm in the process of seeing an employment counselor to figure out what I want to do with the rest of my life. It's hard to get out of this industry.

I can honestly say that I will never regret getting into this business!

# Rose

I was 18 years old the first time I went to a strip club. My girlfriend and I were on ecstasy one night and decided to go because we had nothing to do. As we watched the dancers, I thought, "I could do that." I needed money at the time so I phoned the local agency and the agent hooked me up with some amateur contests. After that, I was booked on the circuit.

My first day on the job was kind of surreal. My best friend came with me for support, and helped me stay calm. It was ultimately a positive experience because I won the contest. I remember getting ready in a tiny disgusting closet, but it didn't bother me too much because I always make the best of bad situations. I'm a very easy going person.

When I told my parents that I was a dancer, they couldn't believe it. My mom was ok with me dancing after I told her what I was making. My parents were very supportive after that. They always said that I was going to be a stripper one day anyways because when I was a baby, I would always strip my clothes off and run around naked.

As for my childhood in general, it was awesome! There was no sexual abuse or anything like that. We went camping a lot when I was a kid and had a good family unit.

I danced for five and a half years. I quit and I am waitressing in a pub now. I loved the travelling, dancing, music, costumes and meeting tons of new people. After I quit dancing, I travelled like a gypsy to Montreal and back in a van.

One part of dancing I hated was that it changed me as a person. My new boyfriend doesn't understand my openness towards nudity; to me it's no big deal. I also hate the fact that I didn't save any money.

When I was a dancer, I wouldn't dance in my hometown in case people I knew would show up and see me there. I also refused to dance at one of the local strip bars until it got renovated.

I had a weird customer who wrote me a poem that was pretty creepy. He started the poem off by comparing me to the sun and then it went into 'doing lines' and then blowjobs. It ended with a flower reference. He was not a great poet, to say the least.

My best customer was Mike the book guy. He is super polite and we used to go out and smoke a joint together. He bought me drinks and we had some nice conversations. Another time, I wanted a stripper pole for my house, so a customer took me to the store and bought me one for my birthday. The biggest tip I ever got was $300!

My embarrassing moment was at the beginning of my career. I was learning to walk in heels and I was given a used pair of hand-me-down, falling apart stripper shoes. One time while I was on stage, my foot slipped into the moat and I almost fell down. That was pretty embarrassing.

Another uncomfortable incident was when my uncle who is a regular at one of the clubs I was dancing at came in wearing a 'support your local pole dancers' t-shirt. I was wearing a naughty nurse costume when he came into the bar. He sat in the corner and didn't watch when I danced.

The drugs in this industry really surprised me. If you look for it, cocaine is always available. I got addicted to it for four years. I had never done it or even seen it before I got into dancing. One thing I wish I knew before getting into this line of work was to save my money and not spend it all on partying.

Something you would find interesting about me is that I went to a bible college and majored in music because my parents were bad asses (they were hippies/bikers who smoked dope). So in order to rebel, I wanted to be good! When I was born, I weighed four pounds and my parents brought me home in a motorcycle helmet! One thing I would not leave home without was my pillow.

Just before I got in the business, I was working at a fast food restaurant. On one of my shifts, I was talking with my friends about stripper names. We all agreed that names with the letter "V" were hot. In reference to some tattoos on my body, that is how I came up with my stage name. I picked the name Rose to use for this book because that is my middle name!

My only piece of advice for new girls coming into this business is to save your money! Enjoy your job because one day it'll be gone. When I danced, I didn't have a problem with telling people that I was a dancer. Now that I'm retired, I don't tell people for a long time. Now, it comes out slowly.

I do not regret getting into this business because it was an amazing period in my life. It has made me adaptable, outgoing, and more confident. I grew stronger as a person.

# Saffron

I started doing amateur contests at my hometown bar. I didn't have a problem with getting naked, so I thought I would at least try it. I ended up winning the $1000 grand prize! There was an agent in the bar watching that night and he told me I had the right look for this industry. He seemed like a really nice guy. There were also some veteran girls drinking in the bar and they told me that if I can make it work, I would find dancing very rewarding. I called the agent the very next week. We chatted for a bit and he told me that he wanted me to work some weekends first before I started full time. I was fine with that; I wanted to ease myself into this business slowly as I still wasn't sure if this was for me.

It was on a Sunday, when I did my first amateur contest. I drove the 10 minutes from my house to the bar and took my time getting ready. I was rooming with a girl who is my best friend now (she won the amateur contest the year before). I like to say that we are 'two of a kind' as we are both born on the same day and basically look the same. I worked a couple of Sundays and then started to work the back half; Thursday, Friday, Saturday and Sunday. I still wasn't sure I could do it. I used to be a lifeguard, so I was in great shape and I figured I should be able to do it without too much trouble, but it was a big step.

My parents know what I do for a living and they are supportive. They don't have a problem with the nudity, but they hate the reputation that dancers have of being drug addicts and alcoholics. The funny thing is that once I became a dancer, I completely stopped hanging out in bars and drinking. I don't really enjoy partying anymore because I spend so much of my time working in bars.

It can be hard to make money in this industry. When we travel around from job to job, we have to pay for our gas, plane tickets, ferry rides and room rental out of our own pocket. It adds up quick! It's all the little things like remembering your tweezers and eyelashes, so you don't have to buy them again when you're out of town. I love how challenging my job is. It seems like every tour I take, I become more independent and I learn more.

Some private things about me that people would find amusing is that I'm a boring nerd. I played the violin for 18 years! Before I started dancing, I was a dishwasher, a baker, a lifeguard and an insurance saleswoman. Three things I won't leave home without are my track suits, soap and wipes.

My most embarrassing moment was falling off the stage, just yesterday! I also ended up getting my period in a white costume once.

I only refuse to work at the bars that are dirty and unsafe.

At my hometown bar, there is a regular that shows up at every single one of my shows and tips me every time. He's my best customer.

Gifts that customers like to give me are Hello Kitty stuffed animals (I collect Hello Kitty stuff), other stuffed toys and flowers. I wish guys would just give me $5 instead.

I was almost 21 when I got into this business. I started dancing part time while going to school full time for business. I'm interested in marketing and advertising for commercials but since school is on strike, I'm dancing full time at the moment.

I've been dancing and going to school now for one and a half years. I'm planning on dancing for three more years or longer so I can bank some money. I would like to go to Alberta and dance in the high-end clubs and do Miss Canada pageants. I'm still looking forward to finishing up school and getting my degree.

Before getting into this industry, I wish I knew how much my body would be damaged from the constant dancing and pole moves. I also didn't realize the number of times I would be changing my clothes. It can be as much as 18 changes of clothes for only six shows. This includes your robe, costumes and street clothes. There are also the non-stop days of working. You can work six or seven days a week, every week, for months.

The one thing that surprised me about this industry was how much hard work dancing is. I thought that I would be doing one show a day and the rest of the time I would be sitting around in my glamorous room. I was wrong about that, especially the glamorous room part!

My advice for new girls coming into this business is to not take anything personally. The first time you get a "boooooo!!" from a customer is the worst! You have to realize that the guy is just a drunk stranger, so get over it and move on. As strange as it seems, it really has nothing to do with you. Also, train your body hard and get into shape!

I do not regret getting into this industry since it has taught me so much about myself, other people and the industry. I have a bird's eye view of how the world works.

# Snowdrop

In my teenage years I never had a legitimate job. I left home when I was 16, and I had nothing, so I bought a quarter ounce of weed, rolled it into joints and sold them for five bucks each at the market. I made $100, so I bought a larger amount of weed, did the same thing and made more money. This was my pattern to make more money with every turnaround.

I smoked a lot of weed back then and always hung around the drug dealers I bought my supply off of (others would consider these people 'ballers'). The tables were turned a year later and these same people were buying 'e' from me and working for me.

I had nothing to lose; I was a drug dealer. I made 20 times more money then I do now dancing. I remember being at one of the biggest raves in the city. That night, there were about 7,000 people there. They had security at the doors but it was easy to get almost anything 'illegal' inside without getting caught. I gave 20 people 20 caps each and they would run off to sell it, then come back to get more from me a short time later. That night I made more than $5000.

Shortly after, I got pregnant with my daughter so I had to get a legitimate job. I couldn't justify the risk of getting caught anymore. What would happen to my daughter if I went to jail? With the large amounts of dealing I was doing, I would have been locked up for sure – and for quite a while. I was lucky that I was never caught and charged. A few years ago I was pulled over by a cop for not wearing a seatbelt and he made a comment about me selling drugs and that freaked me out pretty good. I obviously stuck out and was still in the system.

Getting an ordinary job wasn't the answer because I needed more money than the average person. I couldn't go from dealing and making crazy amounts to a minimum wage-type job.

I thought about dancing even though I have never been in a strip club before because I was sure the girls made some pretty decent money. I was 21 when my daughter was born, and I started as a VIP dancer shortly after. I would leave her with the babysitter after I put her to bed and then go to work. It was great to have a job with a schedule so convenient for a mother with a baby.

My first day on the job, I was nervous because dancing for 20 minutes seemed like forever to me at the time. I wasn't even sure what I was doing on stage, so I definitely liked half shows better back then. In the beginning I was very sensitive and would get upset if some of the girls or customers didn't like me. Now I just don't care so it doesn't bother me anymore.

Over time, my daughter started spending a lot more time with her dad which is great because it helps cut down on childcare costs. I am planning on working as much as possible so I can bank some money because I would like to go to school. I haven't decided on what yet, but after dancing for four years, I've realized that I can't dance forever.

My childhood was full of a lot of negativity. I was a straight A student who got in shit if I got a B and I remember getting accused of smoking weed when I had never even touched it at the time. It's a long story and I pretty much blocked out my childhood anyways.

My only family left now is my daughter and my girlfriends. My parents and younger sister passed away in the last six years. My dad was hit by a car a day after my 19th birthday and my mom ended up addicted to drugs and living on the streets. I heard she ended up with AIDS and died. As for my sister who is a year younger than me, eight days after her 22nd birthday, someone murdered her. Her body was found stuffed in a fridge downtown.

I love my job and I go stir crazy after a couple of days of not working. I love the attention, being on stage and feeling like a Barbie. I mingle with customers between my shows and find that I can make better tips than some of the girls that do not socialize although they do great pole work.

Because of the economy, the only thing I hate is that the show prices aren't as good anymore and you feel it when shows are cut. I'm lucky that I still do quite well with the tips.

In regards to customers, I have had them buy me all kinds of gifts over the years. Mostly the usual stuff that girls always seem to get, such as clothes, shoes, diamonds, gold and flowers. The biggest tip I ever got was $350 which was thrown on stage.

The only people that have shown up at my work unexpectedly are people that knew me as 'their boss' in my teenage drug dealer days which is quite awkward for me. I never imagined they would see me naked.

Something personal about me is that I love music – it's my life.

Also, most people would find it shocking to know that I've had a slave and a bitch. A slave is a person who thrives on humiliation. I love power and control so I love someone submissive. I made my slave dress in women's lingerie and high heels, then tell him to crawl around on his hands and knees and bark like a dog. When I had a dirty ashtray, I would make him lick the ashtray clean. If I ended up with gum on the bottom of my shoe, I would demand he take the gum off with his teeth and then chew it. If he drove me anywhere, I made him wear high heels. I would even make him get out and open my car door for me.

I've had a bitch for three years. This 36 year old guy was making his car payments, paying his mortgage, his food and his parents even sent him $1000 a month. I took all his money and his car and made him take the bus to work. I did really mean things like call him at work and make him leave so he would meet me, only to fill the car up with gas. I made him work seven days a week and I didn't allow him to drink any alcohol because he used to get wasted and fall on his face. I made him go out to buy my groceries and made him set them on the step outside my door. He had to leave them on the step since I never allowed him inside my home. I made him buy my boobs which he never saw, and I wouldn't allow him into strip clubs. I was mean to him and controlled his mind and his whole world. Because I made him work hard and he wasn't allowed to drink, he actually got three raises during the three years he was mine. During our second year together, he texted me one day with the message, "I want out." I brushed it off and things went back to normal. In the end, I could no longer stand his voice or even stomach the sight of him, so I let him go. He wasn't strong enough to end it, so it had to be me to cut ties.

A couple weeks later I met a guy at the club. I asked him if he wanted a private dance and he said no but I still sat down and talked with him. The next day he showed up at the club with a bouquet of roses, two bags of good weed, and a CD. He dedicated three beautiful songs to me. We dated for about a year and he spoiled me the whole time. While we were together, he spent close to $20,000 on jewellery and gifts for me. He was a drug dealer so he could afford to take me out to high end restaurants all the time, spending $300-$500 on our dinners out every time. Then a terrible thing happened. He was murdered at the side of his house. One day I had lots of money and lived like a queen. The next I was learning to cook, buy my own groceries, pay my own bills, etc. Dancing has made me feel stronger and more independent. Even so, I feel I still struggle with money, even though I make more than the average person.

I had started as a VIP dancer with no real stage name. Back then, I knew of certain girls that would go home with guys for money after the club closed for the night. One day while I was sitting in my car smoking a joint with a bunch of girls, one of them (she was known to go home with guys after the club closed) said to me, "You should start your own agency and we'll work for you!" She was laughing, but I was serious. "You better be serious because I will invest the money in this!" I said. I ended up getting a business licence, a huge website and started advertising in every major newspaper. It was an escort agency and I had about six girls working for me and I took $100 on every call they did. When it came time to hit the circuit, I used my agency name as my stage name.

My advice for new girls coming into this business is to have confidence in yourself and when you're doing a show, have fun with it. Act like you're the hottest girl in the world and forget any flaws you have. Guys will love your confidence!

I do not regret getting into this business because I love my job and I'm not ashamed of what I do.

# Sunflower

On my 18<sup>th</sup> birthday, my girlfriend surprised me by taking me on a train trip. 12 hours later, we got into a cab in Quebec and the cabbie dropped us off at a strip club. Inside, I was shocked to see a naked girl on stage sitting on a blanket. I wanted to run out the door but my friend stopped me. She told me that this was where she had been hiding out for weeks on end. Dumbfounded, I sat down and watched the dancers while drinking champagne her boss had bought me. I got on stage that day and haven't stopped since!

For two weeks, I stayed in the dancer house. I hustled my ass and made $200 every night by doing $5.00 private dances. That was 23 years ago! Nowadays, private dances cost $40. I worked at the club for two weeks, then went home for two weeks; that was my routine for a year until I went to Toronto for two years. Eventually, I moved to BC.

Up until the age of 17, I worked with my parents. I worked at a hardware store as a checkout girl and my mom was the manager. I also worked with my dad as a carpenter's helper until the age of 18. When I started dancing and travelling, my parents thought I was modeling. When my mom found out I was dancing, she cried and said, "Just be smart with your money." My dad suspected something was up so he called me when I was out of town and in the middle of our conversation he asked me what street I was on. I made up some name. I think he wanted to see what I was going to say. He said, "You better not be taking your clothes off for money!" I told him I wasn't as calmly as I could.

I was an only child and I lived in the country surrounded by animals. My dad did not believe in laziness so he always had me up at 6:00 am on the weekends, as well as school holidays to work in his carpenter shop with him. All I can say about my mom is that she is an angel. My parents are amazing people and they always taught me to be kind to my elders and to be a good person.

My incredible boyfriend of 18 years is very supportive of what I do. When we met, I was terrified to tell him that I was a dancer. It took me two weeks to have the guts to finally tell him and his response blew me away! He told me he was honoured and proud for me to be his girl. I knew he was a keeper for life.

I hate when customers proposition me at work. I refuse to work at a certain strip club because the energy there is too overwhelming for me to handle. I also don't like hearing about some of the mean things that some dancers do like convincing new girls that they should sew sequins onto their tampon string and let it hang out.

There is a lot more to love than hate in this business. I adore my agents because they treat me so great. I love the freedom and performing on stage. I also find all the girls I work with every week and the staff at all the different bars absolutely amazing.

In this business, I have been fortunate to do a lot of traveling. I have worked coast to coast from Newfoundland to the Yukon. Internationally, I have traveled to Macau, China (six times), Japan (eight times), Portugal (six times) and Iceland once. Back in those days, seven girls would travel together internationally with an agent acting as a chaperone. When we went to China, we had bodyguards with us and I remember some of the girls making $50,000 in two months! The agency used to book overseas work and help us girls get visas but they don't book international work anymore because it's too dangerous.

The owner of the Tokyo strip bars would come to our city to interview and choose the girls he wanted to dance in his clubs. When I was in Tokyo, I worked from 10:00 pm to 12:00 am on a rooftop balcony and all I did was three topless shows. The shows were choreographed and got great reviews.

When traveling to Macau, we were told to grow out our pubic hair because that is what the men like. I was blessed to live and work in Sendai, Japan for two months. The people there were so very kind with beautiful souls and have such great respect.

While working overseas, we were always well taken care of on all our amazing work adventures. We had drivers, maids, even chefs cooking our meals and professional kick boxers as our chaperones. I even got to experience living in a country farmhouse while we were in Portugal. It was so surreal and amazing being around all this beauty and experiencing the different cultures. I'm so blessed.

Over all these years, I have been privileged to travel around the world entertaining and make stupid amounts of money. The most amount of money I made a night is $1200 and that was by doing clean private dances. Because of my time working in this industry, I was able to purchase three homes. When I returned from China, I put a down payment on a penthouse and six years later I bought a five acre ranch. Eight years later I bought a 320 acre ranch. My dream as a little girl was to have a dog rescue and because of dancing I was able to realize that dream. It is non-profit since I use all my own money and I am now at my maximum of 11 dogs.

Dancers receive gifts from customers now and then. One of the strangest gifts given to me was a ceramic statue of an angel that a customer gave to all the dancers working that week. In Japan, customers give dancers chocolates, flowers and money after their show. Once, I got an ugly purple Chanel purse that was worth $1200 from a Japanese customer. It was a sweet gesture.

The biggest tip I ever got was from one of my regulars. He was very wealthy and always shared information with me about stocks and making money. He gave me $14,000 to put towards my dream ranch! Customers don't know this, but all the tips I receive from them on stage are saved and go towards my dog rescue operation.

With the good comes the bad. I have my share of scary stories too. I was in Portugal and getting ready to leave the club for the night. All the girls were standing at the exit with the manager and there was an enormous box of roses on a nearby table. All of a sudden he screamed at us to hit the floor. We fell to the ground and he reached into the box of roses and pulled out a machine gun. It was like a scene from an action movie! He kicked open the front door and started shooting the ear-splitting machine gun into the street! Thankfully, nobody got killed. I found out that one of the dancers got into an argument with a customer earlier on in the night and he left to get his gang. They were waiting outside when we were closing down for the evening. We hung out and waited in the club until very, very late and then our driver took us home. The next day our chaperone made us pack our bags and we took off to the airport. Before we left, the owner of the club begged us not to leave. He said he was going to get killed. At the airport, we were being circled by six mafia guys. It was truly terrifying!

While working in Macau, we often went to this local pub to let off some steam. One night we left just before closing time. The next day we found out that the bar was targeted and a spike bomb was thrown into the club just after we had left.

Another time while working in Tokyo, shortly after leaving the restaurant we always liked to hang out in, a few men entered with machine guns and absolutely destroyed the place. I can't believe how close I was to being hurt and how lucky I was to escape it all unharmed.

One of the creepiest episodes I have encountered involved my acupuncturist who kept asking me very personal questions during my appointments. One night I saw him in the club while I was on stage. I was really shocked but kept my cool. When I got off stage, he greeted me and told me that I had an amazing body and that he wanted to take me to his truck and get naked with me. Before I had a chance to react, he grabbed me and tried to stick his tongue down my throat! Sickened by his behaviour, I ran to a bouncer and got him kicked out of the club immediately. I ended up reporting his actions. His boss was appalled and he lost his licence as a result. I was later told that they had had many complaints from younger women.

One of the weirdest customers I have met would be the sock guy. He gives the girls $10 and a new pair of socks in exchange for our dirty ones.

An awkward moment for me would be when the land surveyors knocked at my door to have me sign some papers. The guy asked me what kind of dancer I was and I responded by saying that I was a ballet dancer. I guess it showed on all his papers that I was a dancer of some sort.

Another uncomfortable episode for me would be when I went to pick up my truck downtown one afternoon and my mechanic asked me, "So, do you take all your clothes off?" I was shocked by his question and didn't know what to say or do, so I just walked away and got my boyfriend to go pick my truck up for me.

One of my darkest moments was when I woke up one morning with a herniated disc and could not move! The MRI showed that I only had twenty percent left on my L5 disc. It took me seven months to recuperate and I couldn't walk or stand straight for three months. I was terrified that I might not be able to dance again.

There was one strip club I worked at that was an experience in itself. I can't begin to tell you how many celebrities I met there over the years. There was a famous basketball player, a famous male model/actor, a couple of very famous actors just to name a few. Oh, the stories I could tell!

Some things you might find interesting about me are that I was scouted for Penthouse magazine and was voted 'Miss Nude Environment' which is a dancer that supports animal rights. Also, I have done many photo shoots with my amazing photographer and he put me in numerous calendars over the years. You can probably still find one or two around.

I was one of the first girls to work in a landmark BC strip club when it opened and I worked there for three years. That was a long time ago. People are always shocked when they find out my age. I've been in this industry a long time, and it's changed a lot. When I started, dancers used to keep all their music on cassette tapes. Now the girls use CDs, ipods, smart phones and memory sticks. It used to be a bigger business – there used to be 57 strip clubs in BC. Now there are about 12.

About me, personally, I'm Dutch, but I don't speak the language. I do speak French. Another interesting fact about me is that I did the lead role in a local movie. When I leave for the day, three things I can't leave home without are my pit stick, lipstick and perfume.

Four years ago, I traded in my stilettos and mini skirts for rubber boots and overalls and I lived 'off the grid' for three years. My boyfriend and I lived on solar power, used an outhouse and cookhouse, and we lived in an 800 square foot military tent for the summer until we built our cabin. Then we took in troubled teenagers and put them through a boot camp program where we helped them find the right path in life. This whole lifestyle was a very humbling experience. During this time, I had a face to face encounter with a cougar. Jessica-Lynn (one of my rescues) saved the day. If she would not have been with me that day, well, let's just say that she's my hero! It was the most surreal experience of my life.

We are planning on operating an 'adventure ranch' on our property when we move there fulltime in the future. Also, we will be holding outdoor festivals at the ranch starting this summer and all proceeds will be going towards my non profit dog rescue.

When I was picking a stage name, my agent told me that I looked like a certain actress but I told him that I didn't want a name from an actress or model. He blurted out my stage name off the top of his head and said, "Well, what about that?" It was two unique names he threw together and I just loved it.

The one thing that surprised me about this industry was the tampon issue. Before getting into the industry, I always wondered what a girl did with the tampon string. Now I know.

I have been dancing now for 23 years with my head held high. I plan on dancing as long as I can. I told my agent that he will have to rip me from the pole at the age of 50 because I love my job so much. I'm not trying to get out of this industry, but I enjoy investing in stocks and real estate.

A year ago a special friend of mine asked me, "What do you want to be when you grow up?" It got me thinking and I want to do care aid for people. My mom is very sick and I'm touched when I see the special care she receives from these amazing people. I'm also planning on taking animal massage therapy or I might just retire, become a mom and pursue my dog rescue. I will never regret getting into this business because I truly love what I do.

My advice for new girls coming into this business is to have a five year plan. I have a vision board with pictures and all my dreams on it. Visualizing is important and if you do this, your dreams will become reality. It worked for me.

Also, get yourself insured (God forbid you hurt yourself and you can't work for weeks or even months). Be kind to your body and get an MRI every 10 years to see how your back looks. ALWAYS have money saved for a rainy day. Be proud of what you do and be as classy as you can. Don't get caught up in the craziness of it all. We all have the power to be anything we want to be in life.

My last words are to remember to smile, life is beautiful. And please rescue your next pet!

Love and light to you all!

# Tiger Lily

While growing up, my parents were very open about having adopted me. They told me I arrived when I was two weeks old. We had a middle class lifestyle; a nice house and car, 2.5 kids and a cat. It was the typical kind of life for a kid that anyone would be lucky to have.

As a teenager I was very independent and I did what I wanted, when I wanted. My parents were wonderful people and while they tried to get me to follow rules, my need for independence had me run away a couple of times between the ages of 11-13. I ended up living with friends and I would sometimes experiment with drugs. I started dating older guys, and I learned how to manipulate them to get what I wanted. It was great because I never had to pay for my own drugs. I lost my virginity when I was 12 years old to a guy that was 22 (he thought I was 18). Throughout all this craziness, I still kept up in school because my parents had always drilled into my head how important education was.

Finally, my parents had had enough. They gave me an ultimatum to live by the house rules or leave the house. I left. Because my friends were all older (around 17-26) they all had jobs and cars and lived on their own, so I went to stay with one of them. My parents were worried and didn't know where I was, so they called the cops. The cops found me and brought me home three different times.

Staying home was too hard. Plus, the advice from my older friends was to just leave again. They told me if my parents forced me to stay by physically restraining me, it was abuse. So every time the cops brought me home, I would just turn around and run out the door again.

I hung out with some bad people who introduced me to meth and coke, and soon I became addicted. I remember waking up in a dirty and disgusting house where people were freebasing meth. I barely slept that night because I was freezing cold even with three layers of clothes on. Something in the back of my mind said, "This is not right! This isn't my life and I shouldn't be doing this." I thought of my parents and realized that I had hit rock bottom (even though I was still going to school at this point). I picked up the phone in the house and called my counselor. He asked me where I was and I told him I had no idea. I was told to walk outside and find a street sign. Then he came and picked me up. I didn't want my parents to find out where I was because I was such a private person by this point. My counselor put me in a youth treatment program for three and a half weeks. I was pretty much shell shocked at this point and my mind was pretty foggy; I wasn't even sure where I was half the time.

After the treatment, I returned home and stayed for one and a half weeks before I left again and moved in with a girlfriend (yup, I was still going to school). I thought I was an adult but I was very angry at the world and I resented being controlled. Looking back, I think I was pushing my parents away to see if they really loved me. A lot of it had to do with me being adopted. The big question was 'why.' Why was I given away and why was I so unwanted? I definitely had some abandonment issues.

When I was 13 years old, I went into the bar for the first time. Since I was a tomboy, my friends had fun dressing me up and doing my makeup (my mom never taught me because I was too young). It was my first taste of the bar scene.

I decided I needed to get a job, so I got hired at a fast food restaurant where I worked in the early mornings and evenings so I could go to school during the day. I got my own place because an older friend pretended to be my parent and co-signed for me. I always had the same social circle of friends and I never told them I was 13, 14 or 15 years old as they always assumed I was 18 or older.

To get to work everyday, I walked past the strip club. I was intrigued by the posters of the girls in the windows. I was sober since my treatment, so I wasn't doing drugs. I was doing my best to keep up with school, work and bills but it was stressing me out. I was exhausted.

I started to wonder if I could handle working as a dancer. I talked to a girlfriend who dolled me up and then I walked right into the strip club. I was only 15 (almost 16) and nervous as hell! The club only served non-alcoholic drinks, but the dancers still had to be of legal age (18). The girl who interviewed me didn't ID me as she was just filling in for the manager who was on holidays. I was told to bring in a pair of heels for the audition class on Sunday.

My first audition/dance class was uncomfortable to say the least. It was weird to learn how to move like a woman at the age of 15, but I felt very liberated in my short shorts and tiny t-shirt so I went for it. It was all about showing sexuality and selling a fantasy. The club liked me and hired me to start the next day. I was still attending school but I didn't have to take a bus home anymore because I made enough money that I was able to catch a cab.

At the club, you were expected to sit with customers and convince them to buy you a $7.50 drink (non-alcoholic of course). You had to sell 12 drinks per shift or pay the house fee of $120. Many of the regulars knew about the quota. The odd guy would just pay it up front so you could stay with him and not have to worry about hustling other guys. He could now spend much more time with you. Once an hour, you would do a stage show to promote yourself. It was usually just one song and you didn't get paid for it.

Although I wasn't embarrassed, uncomfortable or ashamed of my body, the first time I got on stage I felt kind of freaked out, maybe because I was stone-cold sober. I knew exactly what I was doing and it wasn't my last resort. I never thought I was better looking or more exciting than anyone else since I've always been humble. I stumbled into this business because I was curious. I was always trying to figure out who I was sexually. After I got naked in front of strangers the first time, everything else was easy. I found that guys under the age of 30 didn't want anything to do with me, but the older guys loved me. I was told that as I got older, I exuded a confidence and self assuredness that many guys are intimidated by.

The bar used to be really busy and a girl could make a lot of money back then. When the girls did their VIP dances, the customer sat on a couch while she danced no closer than six inches away. The girls usually followed this rule and you didn't see any contact with the customers back then because cops were known to come into the club and take a walk around.

It was all about fantasy and customers were known to buy girls gifts. Gifts that guys bought me over the years was a lot of candy, socks, bras, panties and strange outfits they wanted you to wear on stage. I had a guy who used to bring me a new bottle of perfume every time he came into town and another time I had a guy buy me a living room set. Someone drew a sketch of me once (it totally looks like me), so I framed it and I still have it to this day. It was kind of like having a sugar daddy relationship where sex was not expected, since most of the guys had a wife and kids anyways.

I found that most of them just craved company and comfort in an emotional way and I was like a personal psychologist. I guess it was a lot cheaper than going to the real thing. Some of our conversations were geared towards getting advice on making their marriages better! Or sometimes they would just vent or talk about their wives and their lives. I was expected to just sit and listen. I was never judgemental and I learned pretty quick what a guy wanted to hear. I also noticed that guys wanted to give money to the girls because it made them feel good. Working at the club, I felt like I was wanted and it was a place where I belonged. I felt like I was accepted in a social group (the dancers) which was very liberating.

I was making close to $1000 some nights and I never walked out of the club with less than $300-$400 a night. I was still going to school since somewhere in the back of my mind school was still expected of me. My schedule was tight. I was in school from nine in the morning until two thirty in the afternoon, then I would study for two and a half hours and off to work I would go until three in the morning. I was never an A or B student but I always seemed to maintain my C plus average.

One night a bunch of guys came into the club and one of the girls said to me, "They're the agents; the stripper circuit agents. Don't bother to try to sell them dances." I also found out that they would recruit girls for amateur contests. I said hello and then left them alone as I was only 16 at the time. The agents came into the club on and off for a year. The girl who I was working with was underage as well and she tried to convince me to do an amateur contest with her. I told her that I had no fake ID and she said that no one cared anyways. We went and watched our first amateur contest and I noticed that the girls danced very quickly to very fast music (like they were on coke) as opposed to how we danced which was very slow and seductive.

The week after, I called the agency to get myself booked for the next amateur contest. I don't even remember if I won the contest that night but the agency booked me to work the week after. I was sent to work the circuit and I was done at my old club as a VIP girl.

After talking to the agent and some of the other girls, I learned that the dancers working the circuit were highly paid professionals. At first, I felt very inferior to these confident and self-assured women who wore head pieces and boas with flare. On the circuit, the dancers sparkled; they had tons of bling and sequins all over their bodies while performing Las Vegas-type shows. It was a totally different world for me. At my club, we only wore nighties, negligees and corsets. These girls were amazing – they wore $1000 costumes and performed theme shows with fire.

My first week of work on the circuit I was terrified! The

agent said that he tried to pair me with a veteran to lean on but they had to book girls according to the club's budget, and a big feature wasn't in that week's budget. Starting out, I made $30-32 a show. I had promo made up, got my nails done and started to acquire some costumes. I knew I had to spend money to make money but I wanted to stay grounded and not change into someone else overnight. I learned that I had to treat it like my own business and just figure it out for myself. I also figured that the less contact with the agents the better for me because I was still underage and I didn't want to get caught and fired. I dropped out of school when I was in grade ten because I had to travel when I started working the circuit. I was making so much money! When you give a 17 year old $2000 a week ($1000 in wages and $1000 in tips), she grows up pretty quick!

I told my parents I was a waitress. I had limited contact with my family because I had some emotional crap I was dealing with when moving out. One day while I was onstage naked for my last song, my dad walked in with a bunch of men he was entertaining from work. He usually didn't frequent strip bars but he was entertaining clients from out of town that day. Our eyes locked and he quickly turned and walked out. My body started to shake and I couldn't stand up. I had to get off the stage right away because I was starting to have a panic attack. I did the throat slash motion to the DJ and yelled at him to get me off stage. Then I ran upstairs, caught my breath and grabbed my smokes.

When I got outside, I found my dad waiting for me. He basically said, "I don't have a daughter anymore and I prefer your mother didn't know." He left and I cried. I was a mess and felt so ashamed and so angry – mostly because he didn't ask me why I did it. It completely broke my heart. To this day, we have never talked about it.

Another time while I was working a two week gig in the Yukon, I walked out of my hotel room and I ran into my uncle (my dad's brother). His band was playing in the same hotel I was working at that week and I had to explain to him why I was there as I was only 18 at the time. Although he was shocked, he actually took it quite well. He told me he wouldn't come into the bar when I would be on stage and we've never talked about it since.

The biggest tip I got was on New Year's Eve when I was 17. I didn't usually drink, but that night I had a few too many while celebrating the new year. The guys felt sorry for me and threw down $500 while I was crawling around onstage in my drunkenness. The first thing I bought with the money was my tattoo and my mom had a heart attack because I showed it off at a family function. It's kind of funny because both my parents got a tattoo in Hawaii last year!

I was working out of town when I met my twin sons' dad. I fell in love! He was one year older than me and the first guy who really floated my boat. I went home, packed my stuff and moved there the next week. For the seven months we dated, I quit dancing and got a job as a waitress in a bar and in the summer I ran a go-cart track. I turned 19 and I said it was my 24th birthday as a joke! I soon realized that he wasn't the man for me so I left him, came back home and started dancing again.

He came by to visit me on his way to Australia and we slept together. Although I was on the pill and he wore a condom, I still got pregnant! I was out of town working when I did the pregnancy test. I was so upset that I called my mom. I told her my two secrets, that I was a dancer and that I was pregnant. How else could I explain to her why I was in a different city? I was tired of lying to her. She dropped everything and flew out right away to be with me. I will never forget that. It let me know that everything was going to be okay and we would figure it out. At 19, I felt like a little kid again and realized I still needed her. She was always going to be there for me whether I pushed her away or not. (I found out later that my biological mom still lives in that town and I was even born there!)

When I was three months pregnant, I called my ex while he

was still in Australia (he was there for five months). He was shocked when I told him about the pregnancy but he didn't seem to care. He asked me to have an abortion and I said no, even though I had thought about it. Abortion is a choice, but it's not my choice. I figured that if I was old enough to make this child, I was old enough to look after it and I don't regret it to this day.

I tried to ignore the fact that I was pregnant and at four and a half months, I had to change agencies because they wouldn't book me anymore. At five and a half months, I finally went to see my doctor and he told me to go get an ultrasound. Since I didn't have anyone to go with me, I went by myself. The woman doing the ultrasound said, "They're both doing great!" I freaked out. She assumed that I knew I was having twins, but it was news to me!

Right after the ultrasound, my ex came back from his trip and I gave him three choices: a) he could pretend it didn't happen, go home and continue on with his life, b) he could be in the kids' lives but not mine, or c) we could try to make our relationship work. He moved in with me.

I sucked my stomach in and continued dancing so I could save some money. At night before bed, I would bind my belly. I was working at a super busy club one week and while I was on my back during my show, I felt the babies move. It was the most horrifying, most uncomfortable moment I ever had because I was so hormonal. I danced until I was six months pregnant and finally had to quit because I couldn't suck in my stomach anymore. I had a bit of a rough pregnancy; I didn't eat a lot so I was still thin and because I threw up all the time from morning sickness and I had dark circles under my eyes, the other girls thought I was a heroin addict. When I quit, I finally let the agency know I was pregnant and they were shocked because I had kept it a secret this whole time from them.

At seven months, I started to piece together my relationship with my parents and I also met my biological parents. My dad got a phone call from a lady claiming she was my biological mom. Because I was 19, the adoption files were now open and she had tracked me down. I called her and didn't say anything but "hello" before I broke down crying. Then she started to cry. We cried for almost 15 minutes before we even said anything. We exchanged addresses and exchanged letters. I got medical information from her and she filled in the blanks on the whys.

I was eight months pregnant when we met for the first time and I wanted my parents to meet her because I felt that my biological mom deserved to see who raised me. During the meeting, it was very emotional and there were a lot of 'thank yous' and tears. I met my biological dad a couple weeks later and we did it all over again. My biological mom was 100 percent accepting and understanding of it all. Today we have a positive adult friendship. We are very good friends and we talk every second day, but I don't call her mom. I could never replace my mom and dad who raised me. Meeting her has helped me understand who I am as a person. I feel complete.

So, I had my babies and the father of my boys supported me while I went back to school. I got home from school early one day and found him cheating on me in our bed while my kids were sitting in their car seats beside the bed. She was naked and I grabbed her by her hair and dragged her out of the house. "It's not what it looks like!" he yelled at me. Looking back I know that I was all wrapped up in my schooling and looking after the kids, as well as being emotionally vacant while struggling with postpartum depression. I wish he would've just told me that he was done with us and wanted to move on instead of playing around with someone behind my back (they are actually now married to one another).

When we broke up, I demanded that he was going to move me and pay my damage deposit as well as a few other things. He did as I asked at first and then the custody fights began. Fortunately I had a best friend from school I could lean on. We filled an emotional need for each other at the time, but it was nothing sexual. It was a rough time. I went on income assistance for a short period because I couldn't be away from my babies and I tried to date my ex again while he was still seeing that girl on the side. We realized it wouldn't work, so we split again, for the last time.

I was now seeing my guy friend from school and I shared my kids with my ex on a week on/week off schedule. I went back to dancing on the weeks I didn't have the boys. It was funny. I would have baby puke on me one week and be strutting around on stage in sequins the next. It wasn't easy being alone. I wondered what man would want me with two kids.

It didn't help that I was still struggling with depression, my finances and my personal life. To make a long story short, my friend and I got married because he was going to be kicked out of the country. We did love each other and he took my emotional problems as his own. I had to spend $20,000 in court to get custody of my kids and he helped me out financially. Before we started our life together, we didn't talk about raising kids, our goals, retirement or what we wanted out of life. At one point we realized we didn't want the same things, so we decided to end it before the kids got any further involved in his life. We celebrated our one year anniversary and got divorced six months later.

I continued to dance even though there was less money and the industry was tanking because of the internet and webcam stuff getting big. This was when the industry started to change and I was making an average of $40-$50 a show.

I met my spouse in a bar and we have now been together for eight years. At the time, I wasn't even looking for a relationship. It was Feb 16 – two days after Valentines Day. I was feeling lonely and sorry for myself and wanted someone to play around with. I asked the shooter girl about the cute guy and sent him a shooter. He was the complete opposite of the big buff gorilla man I am usually attracted to. We started dating that week (I only wanted a one night stand) and he wouldn't sleep with me which pissed me off. He was definitely a challenge. I started dating him every second week when I didn't have the kids. Instead of telling him that I had kids, I told him I was working out of town when it was my week to have them. He came to the bars I worked at to visit and have dinner with me.

After two months, I decided it was time to tell him about my boys. He was shocked. I explained to him that I wasn't looking for a dad for them as they already had one and then I told him to take a couple days to think about it. He called me that night and said he was fine with it. The kids were about three or four when he came to visit me at my place during the night while they were asleep. Before they woke up in the morning, he would go out to his truck and make it look like he just drove up. Eventually he moved in. Shortly after, I got pregnant again. This time I got pregnant despite the fact that I was using an IUD *and* condoms. I swear that I'm a walking billboard that birth control doesn't work!

I took a year maternity leave and then went back to dancing part time. I was doing amateur contests occasionally on Sundays while the kids were away. It made me feel as if I still 'had it' and could compete with the 19 year olds. I am now 33! Dancing is my little confidence booster.

Last year I finished my grade 12 at the adult education center and got all my credits. I also took some courses in psychology. Three years ago I let go of anti depressants and I am happy with me and my life. I wanted to be present for my kids and I realized that I can't work six days a week and still be there for field trips, parent teacher interviews and extracurricular activities as I need to be and as they deserve. For me, the money wasn't enough and I had never, ever taken money for sex to boost my paycheques. I could never lower myself to that level. I am now waitressing and only dance once in a blue moon.

Dancing makes me feel powerful and expressive. I have never been a very creative person so with dance I can be free and let go. I block out life and in that moment, I am someone else; I describe it like losing myself in a character of a book. I am able to act and play dress up, and by becoming this other persona I can forget about my life. I rarely drank because I didn't like the feeling of losing control. Being on drugs, I felt like I was in control, powerful and empowered (in reality, you probably aren't).

Sometimes it's hard to get past the negative comments since people are quick to forget that even though I'm on stage, I'm a person with feelings and emotions. They say really hurtful things like "her butt is too big", "she's ugly" or "we've seen better." When you're sober, you don't have the drugs to fall back on and you start to question whether you really do need bigger boobs, a straighter nose or a smaller butt. Your self esteem breaks down and you start to lose your dignity and self respect. You need to grow a thick skin because men will say anything to make themselves feel cool in front of their friends. It's already bad enough that you are always comparing yourself to the other girls because you spend so much time together in the change room.

Society has a view on what dancing itself is and movies have glorified the industry and what it represents. There are intelligent women in the industry but no one sees it. People only hear and see the bad things like gangs, drugs, drinking, etc. Fair enough, there are some dancers that get caught up in this life and need drugs to survive. But the majority are great girls just working a job to get ahead. People make you feel ashamed and it's not fair because we were all born naked, so where does this modesty come from? It was ingrained in us that nudity is naughty and wrong. Dancers aren't hurting anyone and we pay taxes as well.

I have been dancing for almost five years full time and four years off and on. I told the agency to let me know when I am too old and when I am embarrassing myself. I don't want to be that girl who thinks she can still do it but in reality everyone is laughing behind her back.

Over the years I have met some crazy people. One night after the doorman escorted me to my car, I drove out of the parking lot and turned the corner. I realized I was being followed, so I called 911 on my cell. The attitude I got from the dispatcher was that it was my fault and it was to be expected because of my profession. They sent someone out anyways and they pulled him and me over. He was over the legal limit, arrested and taken away.

Another time I was bent over on stage while naked and some guy tried to grab my crotch! He almost touched me when my heel nailed him in the face and I broke his nose. He tried to sue me but he lost because he was drunk. I got $4000 which covered my legal costs. He considered it assault, I considered it self defence!

My most embarrassing moment was when I got my period on stage (it happens to all of us at least once). The most common question asked by guys and girls is if I have to take time off of work because of it. The answer is no, you just cut the string! It's also embarrassing when I would get rug burn on my tailbone from a crazy night, and when I end up with bruises on my body from doing pole work. The pole pinches your skin and it leaves bruises. People automatically think you are being abused.

Some personal things about me are that when I go out of town, I won't leave home without my own pillow and sheets, a kettle (you can use it to make noodles, tea, hot chocolate, etc) and rice cooker (used to make pasta, stir fry, etc). When I work in town I can't leave home without a book and tweezers.

Other personal tidbits about me; I own lots of animals (two bearded dragons, two cats, a dog and fish) and I figure skated for 10 years. Also, I'm so normal looking outside of work you wouldn't even recognize me. I like to keep my private life very separate from my work, so I am very strong and vocal about my boundaries. So, if you see me in public, don't approach me! I could be with my parents or my kids and for you to call me a strange name (my stage name), it will only confuse them.

When I was picking my dancer name, I picked a name I wanted to be named as a little girl. It was a one word name but not very creative. When I entered the circuit, I added a second name and it referred to something private.

I knew next to nothing about this industry in the beginning because I was so young. Being a 15 year old girl in this business, everything was shocking to me – people's vulgar language, the constant nudity, the girl shooting ping pong balls out of her hoochie, the girl giving a 'ride for five.' When I was 16, I saw my first porno downstairs at the first club I worked at. It was my first sexual vision of bestiality involving a woman and a horse. I found it extremely shocking and disturbing, but I couldn't show that I was offended and appalled because everyone else in the room thought it was funny and not a big deal.

When I started in this industry, I wish I had the maturity to market myself as a product and consider this job a business. I admire Calla Lily because she is sophisticated, she has her shit together and she runs herself as a business. She is very classy and seductive, and she always makes money. She knows what she is doing with every look and every movement. That is why she is very successful. On top of all that, she is never late, never drunk, gets along with everyone and never causes problems.

I do not regret getting into the industry because I've learned a lot about my sexuality and I am more comfortable with my body and who I am. Because of it, I have a very satisfying sexual relationship. I am well educated on drug use and I will be much more understanding with my kids when they hit those years. Being open and understanding, I will be able to relate to my kids.

Am I ashamed of telling people what I do for a living? Well, it depends on the people since my parents still refuse to talk about it. They do not know I still dance occasionally! My mom thinks it was a passing phase. Outside my family, I find that when I tell people, they almost always become judgemental and change their perspective of me. They think I am flawed or defective somehow. As for telling my kids...when the time comes to tell them, it'll be from me. I hope I'll know when the time is right.

My advice for new girls coming into this industry is to avoid this job unless you really want to dance. Be smart with your money. Do your research, talk to the other girls and most of all, treat it like a business. Remember that dancing is very hard on your body. I have feet problems now from dancing around in stilettos for years, as well as severe lower back pain.

It's not a big party and it's not all about getting wasted. Times are different now; the show prices are not as high and guys don't tip like they used to. Publicize yourself and make money by doing private dances, selling promo and travelling.

It's not glamorous like a TV show. Make sure it's what you really want.

# Tulip

I started dancing almost five years ago when I was 19. I was living back home in a small town in Ontario, and still in school. I was actually studying to be a police officer. My best friend and I lived together in an apartment and she had spent all her tuition money from her parents on partying. We had crappy jobs working in a clothing retail store making minimum wage.

One day she said to me, "I got it! I figured out how we can make some money. We can become strippers!" I laughed and didn't think too much about it until she came into my bedroom a few days later. She had researched some clubs, called the owner of one of them and he told her that we should come down that night and try it out. So we combined my last $300 and her last $20 and went shopping for two pairs of shoes and two bikinis. Now we were completely broke.

I was scared out of my mind when we went to the club that night. The bartender bought us a few drinks to give us some liquid courage. In the club you had to go on stage and dance for free to advertise yourself and if customers liked you, they would buy private dances from you.

My girlfriend said she would go on stage first because I was practically having a panic attack. I was terrified of taking my clothes off! I made it through my stage show (it's actually kind of a blur to me) and for the rest of the night my girlfriend and I did double dances; the two of us would approach a table and offer dances together because we were scared to do them on our own. We couldn't believe the money we went home with that night... almost $700 each. We quit our crappy retail jobs the next day.

We decided that since we were still going to school, we would only dance on the weekends. Also, because we were worried about our boyfriends, friends, classmates and parents finding out, we went to dance at a club that was located one and a half hours out of town.

My boyfriend of two years knew that something was going on because we kept disappearing every weekend and we stopped hanging out with our friends. Soon we bought new cars and we always had money on us even though as far as he knew, we had quit our jobs. We kept our new part time jobs a secret for almost two months until one night my boyfriend followed us. When he walked into the bar and realized what we were up to, he totally flipped out. He did the slice across the throat motion with his hand and yelled, "We're done!" That was the last time I saw him. He told all our mutual friends and classmates. I was mortified and decided to switch schools and move back home while my girlfriend continued to stay in the apartment.

She came home one weekend to visit her family. Before she went to see them, she put her stripper stuff into my car so her parents wouldn't find out her secret. I didn't think it would be a problem. Well, this plan actually backfired and caused a very big problem for me. One morning, my mom decided to surprise me and clean my car. I was in the shower at the time and I heard her screaming at me to get out of the bathroom. I came out and she dragged me to my bedroom where I was horrified to find all of my friend's stripper clothes and shoes laid out on my bed. I tried explaining to her that this stuff belonged to my girlfriend who went home to visit her parents but she didn't believe me.

I was on hardcore lockdown. My mom didn't trust me. I wasn't allowed to drive out of town (she actually counted the kilometres on my car) or even go out for a few drinks with friends. I wasn't even allowed to go out for coffee! I was 21 years old and felt like I was a child. For a full semester (which is about four months), I lived off the money my mom gave me for food and gas. I did as she told me and I finally gained her trust back. I told her I wanted to transfer back to my old school and move back into my old apartment with my girlfriend. She had no reason not to trust me after the last four months, so she let me go.

Back at my old apartment, my girlfriend and I decided we didn't care who knew. We said 'fuck 'em all!' and went at it full time.

We decided to visit BC for a week. Of course we visited the local strip club and asked a few questions. Turns out that in BC girls had agents to get them work and actually got paid to dance on stage. It seems like a pretty glamorous lifestyle. The girls wore beautiful costumes and put on amazing shows.

After we returned home, I had thoughts about moving to BC. I put it off for a year or so, but it was always in the back of my mind. Eventually, my girlfriend met a new guy, they moved in together and she quit dancing. When she started her new life, I took the plunge and took off to BC by myself.

My family didn't know what I did for a living until I moved out to BC. How my mom found out was that she got my phone bill and called me to find out why the statement had calls from all over BC. I admitted I was dancing and she responded with, "I knew it! I knew it all along!"

My mom is supportive now that she has gotten used to the idea. As for my dad, he is not happy about my decision. I think they are both a little disappointed that I took this road and not the police route.

On my very first night dancing, the DJ had asked me what my stage name was. I told him I didn't have one, so he gave me the first part of my name because of my hair. Out East the girls usually only have one name. In BC, I found that most of the dancers have first and last names. So when I got to BC, I called him up and asked his advice. He gave me the second part to my name, and it was perfect. I think he has named a lot of new girls. We ended up being great friends, and still keep in touch.

Dancing is a great job. I love the freedom to travel and to take time off when I want to. It's nice to know that if I wanted to move somewhere, I have a job right away.

There are some quirks to the job. Back home, I had a regular who was kind of weird. He was a harmless guy who owned his own business. He liked to take out a handful of girls and would pay you $150 to have lunch with him at a restaurant of your choice. Then he would give you a shopping allowance of $200 a week. He had a few rules that you had to follow, though. We weren't allowed to wear a bra during the lunch date and we couldn't use our cell phones. After lunch he gave you his bank card and pin number so you could go shopping. There are also rules for the shopping trip and if you break them, he'd say, "That's $50 less for you to spend!" We weren't supposed to talk or even look at him, just pretend he's not even there. He just liked to follow us around and watch us shop.

Sometimes, he paid my girlfriend $500 plus bonus money if she went to visit him. He wanted her to walk around in his store after hours in white bootie shorts. One time he paid her to just sit around and read a magazine while she was naked, and he watched her.

Another weird person was the guy with the foot fetish. He would pay my girlfriend and me to massage our feet. He also paid us $300 to be foot models for his website. All he wanted was to take photos of our feet. It only took about 20 minutes! He seemed to get pretty horny as he told us to scrunch up our feet and told us that he loved the lines and grooves it made on our soles. He asked my friend if he could put her foot in his mouth while I took pictures. It was a strange way to spend 20 minutes, but by the end of it we were $300 richer.

Before getting into this line of work, I wish I knew how it would affect my personal relationships with my family and boyfriends. I have found that most guys don't want to get serious with me because I'm a dancer. The one thing that surprised me about dancing is that the money is worse than I thought.

My advice for new girls getting into the business is don't bother getting into it. Save yourself now because you get used to the money and it's very difficult to make a change and downgrade.

I do not have any regrets about getting into dancing and I know that I would take the same route if I had to do it all over again.

# Violet

I was 21 when I rented an old boxing gym and my boyfriend helped me turn it into a gourmet pizza restaurant and venue, open from noon until 3:00 am. I wanted to make some extra money for advertising.

Once or twice a week I liked to go to the strip club to have a drink and watch the girls that were so beautiful and had so much confidence. I became friends with a dancer I met at the club and she gave me the contact information for the agency. When I was 23, I started dancing on the side to make the extra money I needed to run my restaurant.

My relationship with my boyfriend was mentally abusive and he was also stealing from me. He stole a total of $50,000 from me and my business. I moved out of the city to get away from him and closed up my business. The owner of the bar across the street was interested in buying my restaurant but because it was my baby, I would rather shut it down than have somebody else own and run it. When I closed it, my other neighbour opened the same restaurant and idea in my location under a different name. I should have sold it after all.

My first day on the job, I arrived to find the club locked. I didn't know what to do other than sit in the car and wait. Finally, someone noticed I was outside and they came to open the door for me. At that bar, you had to go up and down five flights of stairs in heels 16 times a day! There's been times when a girl gets all dressed up for her show, walks down those five flights of stairs only to be told that her show is cancelled because there are not enough customers in the room. Then she has to walk all the way back up to the dressing room again. The room was a dump and the other dancers were scary (I was with a different agency at the time). Looking back, I know I was taken advantage of and they ripped me off. The place was a real dive; thank God it's been renovated and became more professional.

The week after, I went to a different club and was entered in a three day competition with 17 other girls. On the day of the finals, I won! I got $1000, flowers and the spot to dance there for the rest of the week. After that, I was instantly accepted and started work as a dancer.

The only things I hate about this industry are the politics involved. Other than that, I love the fact that I get a workout everyday and I'm constantly meeting new people; it's great for networking. It's also like having Halloween five times a day because I get to dress up in costumes. The best part is that people give me money for getting naked! I get to travel and I love to dance to my own music. I've met some of my best friends through the industry. I get to work when I want, where and how often I want. I train dogs, so when my business slows down in the winter, I book more dancing weeks. In the summer, I do more dog training.

I love dancing but I don't overdo it. I like to keep balance in my life. A lot of girls get caught up in the money, attention and the status. There is a lot of competition over who has the fanciest costumes and who the agents love most. You always have to remember that the stripper life is a total fantasy world.

My family knows what I do for a living. My mom and older brother would prefer I do something else but they don't pressure me to stop. My dad has never said anything so I don't think it bothers him. I'm very open about my job with my family.

I was adopted and I know my birth mom and half brother. I am very lucky that I have the parents I have. Growing up with nothing, my parents worked very hard in life to get to where they are now. They didn't just hand money over to me and my brother; we were given an allowance and had to learn to respect money. Something that I will always be grateful for is that my parents took us on three vacations a year. We went to places like Scotland, Cuba or Africa. We had a really good life with good family friends and a close relationship. I have never been sexually abused or raped.

When I was in grade seven, my parents sat me and my brother down one day and told us that my dad got a new position at his job. They wanted to know how we felt about possibly moving. If we were against it, dad wouldn't take the position. It was very thoughtful in the way they approached us with it.

I've met a lot of interesting people in this line of work. One of my best customers is a guy who owns an oil company in Alberta. For three weeks, he hung around watching my shows and kept asking me if I wanted to go shopping with him. I'm always concerned about my safety, so I met him at the mall on my day off. We went for lunch and he ended up buying me a laptop, boots, leather jacket, and some new clothes. He even called me the day after I flew home and asked me if I needed any money. He said if I ever needed any money, he would send it. He was a young dorky kind of guy who inherited his father's business. He was nice but just socially awkward. I told my boyfriend about the shopping spree and he said he felt uncomfortable about it because he wasn't able to do this for me himself. I promised him I'd never do it again if it bothered him. The dorky guy started calling me a little too often, so I changed my phone number; I was moving anyways.

This next story just happened to me this week. I had three guys sitting at the stage and they were cramming $20 bills into their empty beer bottles and then setting the bottles on the stage. I was doing a show but I walked away from them and the DJ told them to remove their bottles from the stage. They pulled the bills out and set them in the mouths of the bottles. So, I went back over, but when I sat in front of them, one of the guys grabbed my boob and then giggled like a girl! His friends were horrified and I was stunned because I've never had a customer grab my boob before. It was actually kind of funny because of the way he was giggling. The guys grabbed their giggler friend and they took off. But they left me $80.

Another time, a man paid me for six private dances and after I did a few, he asked me to sit down on the couch so he could dance for me! He paid me to sit there naked while he danced with his clothes on.

One of my weirdest customers was a really drunk man with a wedding ring on his finger. He was sitting at gyno by himself and he put almost $700 on stage. I was concerned and said, "I'm sorry, but I can't accept that. You've been drinking quite a bit and I can see that you have a wife." I guess he got embarrassed that I didn't take his money so he started to freak out and yell at me. I should've just taken the money.

I refuse to work at a bar when it is unprofessional. I worked at a place once that I ended up quitting at and left because I thought it was unprofessional and inappropriate that the owner would sit down and watch my show. I also had a feeling that he thought it was funny to watch me leave the bar, go get ready for my next show and then inform me that it was cancelled. One girl had already quit and left and the other girl working that week was pretending to be sick. There was nobody left to work for him. When he saw that I was packed up and demanding my pay, he started to grovel, "You don't have to leave!" I told him my boyfriend was on the way to pick me up. That was the last time I was there.

I went to work in my hometown for one week (it's a one girl gig so I was alone). Just before doing my show, I had made plans with a few guys that I would join them for a drink afterwards.

During my show, I was in my white bra and panties and all of a sudden I had blood pouring down my legs like the Mississippi! I still had two songs left and didn't know what else to do, so I finished up my show doing exactly what I usually do; spreading my legs and smiling. Everyone clapped and the audience acted like it was no big deal. I walked off stage and went to clean up and change. The way I see it, shit happens. Women have periods; it's nothing new. So, I came back to that group of guys and the first thing I said to them is, "So, how'd you like the blood sports?" They laughed, bought me drinks and nobody brought it up. If I would've panicked and ran from the stage crying, I'm sure everyone would've turned it into a big deal.

I'd like to share some interesting information about the business side of this industry that most people don't know. The agency will take 15 percent as well as the GST off your paycheque at the end of the week. Dancing is considered self-employment or contract work, so that the bars are not responsible for us if we are injured etc.

When girls get posters and other promo material made up (like lighters, magnets, etc.), it costs them a lot of money. A photo shoot can cost up to $2000, or more. Hair, makeup, nails and outfits need to be done; it all costs money. The chosen photo from the shoot has to be made into a poster and additional work such as graphics and touch ups are done, which costs more money on top of the shoot. A finished poster can cost a girl anywhere from $.80 or even more than $1.00. It can drive a girl crazy when guys yell at her, "Hey! It's my birthday! Do I get a free poster or what?" It always seems like female customers want free promo too, just for being in the club! Girls will never have a problem with giving away a poster if $5 or more is placed on the stage. There's a reason why a girl is on that stage and that is because she just wants to make some damn money. Dancing is a business, not a party.

When I started dancing, it would have been nice to start with a friend so we could go through everything together. It was a bit scary at first getting used to it all. Everything surprised me about this business because it's an alternate reality. It can really mess with your head if you let it.

For the first couple years in the industry, I didn't let anyone buy me a drink because I didn't want to feel like I owed them something. It was just easier to buy my own drink and when I wanted to get up and leave, I did.

I like to pick and choose places where I work now so I don't waste my time. I only work at bars that I know I will make some good money and enjoy the work environment. Life's too short for crappy gigs. I'm looking into going to New Zealand to work with another dancer. To start out, you are expected to work there for at least one month and you can do up to three months. I'm excited about it because there is absolutely no contact with customers there, which is the only way I'll work.

Three things I won't leave home without are a mirror (for the cookie check; to make sure I have no toilet paper stuck on me), soap and my laptop. I was always a very busy person. Most people find it interesting to know that I used to raise and show cats. I also did web design on the side.

I always try to stay as professional as possible. Five minutes before going on stage one day, I got a phone call informing me that my mom had cancer. I had no choice but to put my emotions aside, put a big smile on my face and do my job.

You will find a lot of dancers who give more attention to the older men who they call grandpa than the younger ones. The dancer will smile at him, give him more eye contact and spend more time where he sits at the stage than the other guys. You want to know why? Well, grandpa claps and tips her on stage. He is polite, respectful and thoroughly enjoys her show. I find that the majority of young guys are rude and they expect everything for nothing, so why should I spend my time dealing with their crap?

I have had guys put $20 and $50 bills on stage for me. I like to take the bills right away because I find that if I leave the money sitting on the stage until the end of my show, some of them will take it back before I have a chance to collect it! When guys are rude to me and put money on the stage, I won't take it. I'll just walk away from it.

For my stage name, I picked the name of someone I knew that passed away. I had something tattooed on my body that signified that 'special someone.' I had it done just before they passed so that they could see it and know how much I loved them.

I was 23 when I started out in this business and have been

dancing now for five years (I took two years off). I've always only danced part time. I'm not leaving yet because I really enjoy it so I will continue, even if it's only for three weeks out of the year. If I feel like visiting friends out of town, I go work there for the week because I get to visit and make money at the same time.

I am not ashamed to tell people what I do for a living however I have to feel out the situation. Most times I tell people that I am an exotic dancer but there have been times when I have told them that I am a dog trainer. My grandma does not know that I'm a dancer as my mother prefers it that way.

My advice for new girls is if you can't say no to the drugs, alcohol and partying, it'll destroy your life. A smart girl will save her money and not blow it all at once each week. I would suggest to any girl that she should bank half her money because she can't do this job forever. I see the strip bar industry on a bit of a decline as there are now price caps at a lot of bars and quite a few strip clubs have closed down. Also, be careful of the people you meet as not everyone is who they seem.

Even though there were some shitty times, I don't regret getting into this business. It is all about learning and moving on. I wouldn't be the person I am today without those experiences. Working in this business, I have learned confidence and independence. When I dance, I feel liberated and powerful!

# Zinnia

I was 23 when I started dancing, and I danced for 11 years. I have now retired from dancing completely, but still have the memories. This is my story.

When I was 21, I was going to university full time, had a part time job at a grocery store and a long term boyfriend. I had been with him since I was 15 and then, at 21, I had a kind of epiphany. While I was at work one day, I noticed my middle aged co-workers, and how unhappy they all seemed to be with their lives. That was going to be me if I didn't do something to change my trajectory. I could see what my life would be: I would marry my boyfriend, have kids and become the oldest living cashier in my little town. I used to have dreams of becoming a doctor, and now here I was. It scared me.

So I broke up with my boyfriend and then got together with another guy I worked with. He was so much fun to be around, so we hung out all the time. Soon after, the grocery store went on strike and there was a lock out. My plan was to quit my job, switch schools and move to the big city. My new boyfriend was moving to that city anyways to be a manager of a marketing company and I decided to go with him. I jumped the gun and quit my job one month before the buyout.

We moved to the city in the summer and by the time fall arrived, I wasn't sure if I wanted to go to school anymore. I still wanted to study, but I didn't know if I wanted to be a doctor or a teacher anymore, or what I wanted to be at all for that matter. I also felt bad that my parents were paying for it, so I withdrew from school. Well, that was my excuse anyway.

My mom told me that I was making the worst decision of my life. She said to me, "If you move back home, I will say I told you so!" As soon as I heard her say that, there was no way in hell I was ever going to let her know she was right.

Not long after we settled in our new place, my boyfriend was offered his own office division, which was a huge promotion, because he was such a fantastic salesman. The only catch was that it was in a different city, which meant we would have to move again. I moved with him and got a job at a bank. I wish I could have worked at the same grocery store chain I did back home. I used to make $23.80 an hour but they don't rehire old employees. It makes better business sense for them to hire new people at minimum wage. Because of that policy, I couldn't go back to work for them even if I wanted to.

My boyfriend said it would be better if I quit the bank and worked as a receptionist at the business he ran. He said it would be less money paid out to other employees and also keep the money within the business, and with us. I believed him and quit my bank job. Although our rent was only $500 per month, we never seemed to have any money. I found out quickly that he was a compulsive gambler and an alcoholic who was deceptive and conniving. By the time I figured out he was an addict, we were already pretty far in debt. One day he went into the bank and wrote a cheque for $400 and deposited it into the bank machine only to withdraw $400 cash. Then he ran off to the casino, thinking he would double the money. I had no idea this was happening until I got hauled into the manager's office the next day for fraud.

It gets weirder. At one point my boyfriend told me that he was gay and that he didn't need me in his life anymore. He turned out to be a very verbally and mentally abusive person. I discovered he frequented strip clubs all the time and spent money there in addition to his addictions. I was turning into a shell of a person having this toxic man in my life. One day he pointed to an ad in the paper for an amateur contest where a girl could win $500 first prize. Without batting an eye, he said, "You should do this."

By then, we just needed the money. I was pretty down on myself at that time in my life because of his abuse, so I thought what the hell. How much worse could my life get. I drove down to the strip club to talk to the DJ and find out what I needed to bring and what I needed to do. The contest was only a few days away and I wanted to be prepared so I stayed to watch one stripper just to see what she did. She was the first and only stripper I ever saw before my own feet hit a stage.

The night of the contest I got really drunk, went on stage and won! The only thing that really mattered to me at that time was that I could make my car payment because my car was the only thing left in my life that I still cared about. I didn't have school or even a job I enjoyed. So I took the prize money and made the car payment. He took the rest.

The contest was relatively easy. I didn't care that I was getting naked, I just didn't want to look stupid and embarrass myself. The agency called me up and wanted me to do another contest, but this time at a different club. I did that contest and won it, too. I was uncomfortable with that agency because they were pressuring me to go work out of town and I was adamant about not going.

I found an ad for another agency that was hiring girls and they told me to come down to the office so they could meet me. I later found out that the agent wanted to see if I really was stripper material and not some homeless wreck with missing teeth and a bad body. At the agency, I met with the agent and he told me how everything worked. I was told that the amateur contests are there for the girls to get some experience and the older girls usually let the newer ones win. Back then, when you entered a contest, you would get $40 just to participate but if you won, you got an extra $50. So, it was unusual that the prize money for the first contest I did was such a large amount.

My next contest after that went great so the week after, the agency sent me out for my first week of work on the circuit. Just travelling to my first booking made me grow as a person because I had to take the bus there by myself and leave my car at home. At this time, my slimy boyfriend was a top car salesman and he needed the car to get to work. I thought about the days when I was a lot younger and how easy it was to bus around by myself all the time. I realized that now at the age of 23, I was freaked out to do things by myself like jump on a bus. My eyes opened at that moment and I realized that my boyfriend was slowly killing my soul.

Working out of town was a good thing for me because the more I danced and the more time I spent away from him, the more confidence and strength I gained. I got the time to heal and to finally get away from him. With my new perspective, I realized how toxic of a person he was and I broke up with him shortly after I started dancing.

A few months after the breakup, he showed up at my apartment drunk. I had such a hatred for him that I didn't care if he froze to death because it was snowing and freezing outside. I had told the tenants that lived upstairs that if he were to ever show up, they should call the cops.

Dancing helped me get away from my boyfriend and I will always be grateful for that. A couple years later, I was at a pub with my older brother and my sister in law and I ran into him again. He told me that he just wanted me to know that he was really sorry for the way he treated me, the things he did to me and the abuse he put me through. When we were together he was a big believer and follower of spiritual books and tried to run his life by them, so I think that he basically wanted to free his conscience. I wasn't about to give him the satisfaction. I said to him, "Your apology doesn't fix anything, so I will never ever accept your apology. You have to learn to live with that!" That was the last time I ever saw him.

After being single for a bit, I met a new guy. We dated for almost a year but broke up because of some communication problems. We kept in touch with one another, and in the spring we talked about getting back together. It was May 2008 and I was thinking about quitting dancing because some of the local strip bars were starting to close down. There wasn't as much work now for all the girls and you had to travel further out of town more often to get work.

I was just about to drive out to see my ex-boyfriend because we were going to talk about getting back together again. He wasn't returning my phone calls but it wasn't uncommon for him to do this. He was known for shutting his phone off sometimes. The next day three of his best friends went to his house to see what he was doing. They saw his truck parked out front so they started banging on his door and yelling through the window but he didn't answer. One of his friends looked through the window and basically freaked out because she saw him laying on the couch with his head blown up to twice its normal size. He had died in his sleep. The coroner said that it was considered to be an accidental overdose. When I found out, my heart broke instantly. I loved him.

A part of me died that day. I didn't work for a month and when I did, I worked for only a week and I could barely get through it. After that, I would only work one day a week just to make enough money to pay my bills because I wanted to close myself up from the world and not leave my house. I was slowly dying. After a couple of months, my girlfriend came over and let herself in since she had keys to my place. She told me that she got me a job at a hardware store. She said I needed something to do in my life so I wouldn't just sit here and die. All I had to do was go meet with the manager and I basically had the job she lined up for me. So, I went, kicking and screaming. I got hired and worked for them for just over three years and I loved it! Two months ago I got a great job as a customer care liaison in a construction company because of this job.

Two years ago I had another tragedy in my life when my younger brother passed away. When he was born, I told my mom he was my baby and like a little doll, I took him everywhere and did everything with him. Where ever I was, I would go home to spend time with him every single Sunday. I was raised by my parents to always stand by and look after your family. Losing my baby brother was the worst thing that has ever happened to me in my life and it still hurts every single day.

My childhood was pretty normal and my parents are great people. They will be married 40 years next year. My dad is a logger and my mom was a stay at home mom. When my oldest brother was five, we moved to the town closest to the logging camp. Dad would work two weeks in camp and then have a week out. This is weird but I can remember being a little girl and always dancing around in my room, pretending I was a glamorous stripper.

When I was getting into dancing full time, I called up my parents because I wanted to be honest with them and I wanted them to know before they found out from someone else. My mother had one question – why. I told her not to worry. It's not like I was homeless and addicted to drugs.

"I can't talk to you right now," my mother said. "I'd rather you were homeless and addicted to drugs. Talk to your father."

Dad got on the phone. "So, you're stripping, hey. Call us when you quit." That was it. He hung up.

When I was in the business, the things I loved best about it was the freedom to be my own boss and to make my own schedule. I enjoyed the variety of different people and places every week. It was never stale; there was always something new and exciting going on.

On the other hand, I truly hate the stigma attached to dancing. I also hate the fact that I missed out on many important life events and family stuff like reunions because I had to work. It was really hard to do any last minute planning because it was mission impossible to get a girl to replace you for a Friday or Saturday shift. There were also the frustrating show price cuts. They would cut your show price whenever they felt like it. Funny, but it never seemed to happen when you would dance for a charity cause, just when they were over on their budgets for the week.

One of the hardest things about dancing is that you could go for weeks at a time where no one knows your real name or even cares that you have a personality. They just want to see you naked, day in and day out. It's hard on the brain. Sometimes it would actually take me a minute to respond to my real name! You don't know how nice it is to spend time with friends that know you by your real name first.

The worst club I worked at was completely disgusting. I only worked for a half day before I quit and left for good. I had worked five or six years on the circuit before deciding to book there, and it was a waste of time. I was disgusted and felt like a piece of trash while working there. All I can say is, I'm not a hooker but thanks anyways.

My first stalker was when I briefly lived with a girl who was from Alberta. She introduced me to a guy friend who was a small Chinese fellow. When she went back to Alberta, he would show up at the clubs I worked at to visit and ask me out for lunch. Slowly, he became a friend of mine too. He started buying me Christmas gifts and although I'm not sure how he found out about my birthday, he even got me birthday gifts.

When I needed a place to stay, he said I could move in with him in the two bedroom condo he owned. After I moved in, he would leave me flowers in random places like on my bed and in my bathroom. He would make dinner for me in the evenings and if I didn't come home at night, he would call me and ask me where I was. The situation was starting to get really uncomfortable and my imagination started to run away with me. I had thoughts of him sleeping in my bed and going through my underwear drawer when I wasn't home. I even had thoughts of him somehow videotaping me while I was undressing in the house. Most of all, I worried about leaving my poor cats at home with him alone.

After a few months of this, I started to date an ex-boyfriend and I spent the night at his place. When I came home the next day, I found the creeper packing a suitcase and he told me that he was going away for a romantic weekend with his girlfriend. I was thrilled and told him that I didn't even know he was seeing anyone. He left the house, only to return again the next day. I found out later that he never even left and he only wanted to see a reaction from me. Later, I found out that he consistently sent fan letters to another dancer out of town. By then I was totally creeped out by him. I told him that he wasn't normal and that he was scaring me. I told him that I would have to move out.

I woke up at 6:30 am on my birthday to the Backstreet Boys singing 'Happy Birthday' in the classic Marilyn Monroe style. Also, the creeper had spent the night decorating the house in streamers and decorations. He had a giant cake and presents (a pair of boots and a jacket) waiting for me as well. As I stood there in surprise, he appeared and tried to cut me a piece of cake. I told him I wasn't eating cake at 6:30 in the morning and he got upset by that.

That was it! I wrote him a letter that day and told him he was a psychopath who had mental issues and that I was moving out. The day I left, my boyfriend came over to help me. As he was grabbing my suitcases to carry them out to the car, creeper came running over and basically ripped them out of his hands. He said that he was going to take them out to the car for me. Then he turned to me and said, "I bought this place for you. I wanted you to be my girlfriend. This was supposed to be the place where we would have a relationship and start our life together."

When I moved out, I changed my cell number so I didn't hear from him for a while. I did run into him once at a bar but it was fine, I just ignored him. The last time I heard from him was when he sent me a Christmas card a few years ago. I'm still not sure how he got my address.

There are some other WEIRDOS (I'm not sure if that word is strong enough) that I have met over the years. One was a guy I was dancing for at a club out of town. He wanted me to wear my cat costume, then get on my hands and knees and lick milk out of a bowl. Another guy said he would pay me to tie his hands behind his back, duct tape his mouth, then kick him in the ass and stomp on his balls!

One time, I was walking down the hall to the bar to do my show when a dancer friend popped her head out of her room to call me inside. I didn't want to be late for my show but she said it would only take a minute. Inside her room, she had a guy tied up in the closet! He had his hands and feet tied and a gag over his mouth. His hands were tied up to the coat rack.

"It's fuckin stupid, isn't it?!" she said to me. "He gave me $1000 to leave him tied up there between my shows!"

I shook my head in disbelief.

She said to the guy, "You like this, don't you?" He nodded his head. It was creepy!

One of my scariest stories was when I was working out of town. There was a police raid in the building. The bar sold every drug known to man out of the office so this wasn't the first time a police raid happened there. All the dancers were told by the cops to stay in their rooms and not come out. I believe the place is gone now.

One of the weirder days I've had at work started when I got a call from my mom. She told me that she went to see her doctor that day and was diagnosed with skin cancer. It scared me so much. I was shaken and upset. After the call I had to go right on stage. It was a terrible show and I was not into it at all. A customer asked me why I wasn't smiling. I told him about the phone call from my mom and he said he was sorry. Later on, as I was doing my last show of the night, out of the corner of my eye I saw something roll across the stage. It was a dozen tiger stem blue roses with three foot stems. It was from the customer earlier on in the day.

Another gift I got from a customer was a digital camera after I told him mine had broke.

One time I traded some of my posters for salmon. I signed one of the posters, 'Love you more than 10,000 sockeye salmon.' Once, I got a cooler full of jars of pickled asparagus, three blocks of fancy cheese and prosciutto.

I haven't really gotten many gifts from customers over the years because I didn't really hang out with customers long enough in the bar. My dad always told me that nothing is for free and at the end of the day I should look after myself, so I never felt comfortable accepting gifts.

My best customer is a man that comes to the front row for every show with a big smile. He was one of my favourite people because he gave every single girl a $5 tip. He was very nice and would wave at you during your whole show (which was kind of funny by the third song). The biggest tip I ever got from a customer was $500.

My most embarrassing moment happened after a UFC pay per view. A friend gave me a pot cookie right before I went on stage. I had a hard time walking and I felt like I was in a Mario Technicolor world that was on fire. I kept telling customers around the stage, "I'm fucked. I ate a pot cookie." They just sat there and laughed at me.

A time that really scared me was when I accidentally snorted a drug that I thought was blow. My lips felt enormous and I felt like I had porcupine quills all over my body. It also felt like I was getting bigger and smaller at the same time and everything looked like it was outlined in black marker. I was on my computer and the keys looked like they kept jumping out at me and my computer looked puffy and round. I found out later that it wasn't coke, but a drug called Special K which is an animal tranquilizer!

My funniest story is when I got fired once because I didn't fit well in the line up for that week at the bar (I believe there were too many blondes) and after the bar replaced me, they wanted to fire the replacement and bring me back! I refused.

Another funny story is that my dancer name was a fluke. I was told by the agency that it would be a good idea if I changed my stage name because I got my boobs done and needed a new image. That same week, another dancer's cat had kittens.

She needed homes for the last two of them or else they would be taken to the animal shelter. I agreed to take them but since animals weren't allowed in the building, they had to be smuggled inside. The dancer put them in a suitcase and snuck them into the change room. It was a boy and a girl and I ended up using my female cat's name as the first part of my stage name after a friend suggested it. He also suggested the second part.

Something you would find interesting about me is that I am a logger's daughter and I made some of my own costumes. Also, when I danced, I would never ever take my shoes off while on stage because I think it looks horrible! Completely unsexy. Three things I would never leave home without are my stripper blanket, slippers and a can opener.

The one thing that surprised me about the industry is that it has a sense of family. We are in this together and should help each other out so dancing is not a competition. I was also surprised about the write offs. You can declare so many things because even our makeup is a tool of the trade.

I wish I knew how hard it would be to leave dancing behind. Because I was dancing for the money, I didn't want to go full circle in this business. What I mean by this is when a girl starts out, she usually starts by doing amateur contests on Sundays and at the end of her career, she doesn't want to end up doing amateur contests on Sundays. In the beginning, I thought that dancing would be a temporary job but it became a career for ten years. If I ever had to go back to it, I would do it because I still have all my gear and I can go work in Alberta.

People don't give dancers enough credit. I'm not ashamed to tell people that I was a stripper but I do edit my story according to company because it surprises them and changes their attitude. Not all dancers are addicted to drugs. There are not as many drugs in the change room as people think either. Five years after I started dancing, I tried coke for the first time and I did it on and off again for about four years. It was only for recreation and it didn't run my life. I only stopped doing it because I couldn't afford it.

My advice for new dancers getting into the business is to not do it at all because the money isn't there anymore. But if you do, be yourself and find your own style. We're on the same team so take as much advice as you can and don't let anyone in this business tell you that you're not worthy, EVER! Don't let them walk all over you or take advantage of you.

Bars are in the business to make money and so are we, so don't ever get naked for free, EVER! Once you do it, they will expect it. You won't make money that way. Unfortunately there is always someone more desperate who will work for less money. If you start agreeing to pay cuts in your show price, it's hard to get it back for future work. Look after yourself because no one else will.

I do not regret getting into this business because I wouldn't be who I am or where I am right now. Because of my job, I learned to stand up for myself and I gained a huge amount of confidence and independence. I also learned how to be assertive and how to say NO. It taught me a lot about the world. Also, some of the best people in my life, that I am still close to, I met when I was stripping. And they are friends for life.

# Strip Bar Etiquette

Most people already know the proper way to behave in a strip club, but after hearing some of the girls' stories I decided to enlist their help to create some guidelines for Strip Bar Etiquette.

## Common Courtesy

◊ Don't take photos or videos of me – EVER! If you want to see a stripper transform from your biggest fantasy to your worst nightmare, take a picture. Keep in mind I have seven inch spikes strapped to my feet.

◊ Poking, punching, grabbing or otherwise touching me is NOT the best way to get my attention. Saying my name or a simple 'Excuse me' will work just fine. Also, please don't try to hug me as soon as I get off the stage. I'm sweaty and wearing a clingy robe; I know you're just trying to cop a feel.

◊ Don't stereotype and assume that all dancers do drugs, drink alcohol, smoke pot or are sluts. And please don't assume that we want to party with you – most of the time we don't!

◊ If I let you near me for any reason, please do not see it as an opportunity to lick me. It's gross and it doesn't turn me on, EVER. It makes you seem sad, lonely, depressed, desperate and pitiful all at the same time. So don't.

◊ If you see me in public, don't approach me. I could be with my friends or my kids and for you to call me a strange name (my stage name), will confuse them and embarrass me.

The relationship we have inside a strip club doesn't exist in the 'real' world. Friendly, respectful smiles are acceptable though!

◊ If you come to the strip bar after work and you can't stand the stench of yourself, please go find the company of a hot shower before you try to get a private show. PLEASE. (Chicken Farmer Guy, this means you.)

◊ During a private dance, please refrain from dry humping me. You are a grown man, not a German shepherd. Just behave.

◊ Give love and cheer to all boobies, big and small.

## On Stage

◊ This should be obvious, but please don't touch yourself when I'm on stage and don't pull 'it' out. I don't want to see it, I don't want to touch it, I don't want to see you touch it, nothing. This includes covering it with your sweater only to flash me and say, "See what you do to me." Ew, ew, and EW.

◊ When I'm naked and crawling around on the stage, DO NOT blow on my vagina. It doesn't turn me on, and can actually transmit bacteria from your mouth to my nether regions! Gross!

◊ PLEASE do not steal pieces of my costume. I pay top dollar for custom costumes and if you steal my panties or bra, I have to pay a lot to have it remade (anywhere from $50-$100). Your trophy hunting costs me big $$$!

◊   Don't lean into the stage. Two things: One, I know you are trying to 'accidentally' touch me, and two, you are going to 'accidentally' get kicked. I'm onto you. A related offense is leaning in to smell me or breathe on me – don't do that. It's kind of a serial killer move.

◊   Please don't get up half way through my show and leave. Could you at least wait until I'm finished? Clap and show some appreciation. Smile if you like the show.

◊   Don't make gross suggestive faces such as licking the air or your fingers. It doesn't turn me on. It does, however, make me roll my eyes and move on to the next guy that can behave himself in public.

◊   Don't tell me what to do on stage. Examples of this delightful encouragement include but are not limited to: "Floss it," "Show me that pussy" (usually within the first 30 seconds of a 20 minute show), "Lick the pole," "Flash the starfish," and the now infamous, "Open it."

◊   Don't use your cell phone at the stage. I have caught so many guys pretending to be texting, only to discover halfway through my show that they are filming me (see above warning about high heels as weapons).

## Regarding Tipping the Dancers

◊   If you want to tip me, place the money on the stage and leave it there. Don't wave money at me and then take it away when I get close only to say, "So, what you gonna do for it?!" Money on the stage is money spent. You are not getting a refund.

◊ Tipping me $5 does not entitle you to sleep with me.

◊ If you appreciate what you see, drop a couple bucks on stage. I'm not saying to tip every single girl, but tip your favourite. It's nice to be tipped and we really do appreciate it.

◊ Don't throw change on stage! Not only is it degrading, it's a hazard. A stiletto heel and a mess of coins don't go together unless you are trying to injure me. Forgive me if I don't rush to collect your generous assortment of pocket change, but I don't have any health coverage if I bust a leg.

◊ Don't expect us to sit down and talk to you if you don't tip us. Money talks. If you want me to sit down and make a big fuss over your buddy's birthday, give me $20. My time is valuable.

◊ If you sit in the front row, tip the dancers! You are sitting in what is considered to be the best seat in the house. If you're sitting there and not tipping, you're taking up valuable space.

## Talking to Dancers

◊ Save the, "You could do so much better," speech for your children. The best part is guys usually whip this one out during a private dance. Draw your own conclusions.

◊ STOP ASKING US FOR EXTRAS. We don't do them.

◊ If you can't say anything nice, don't say anything at all.

◊ Spare me the details of how exactly you want to munch on my pussy all night long. Stop talking dirty to us. It doesn't turn us on. This includes telling me what you're going to do to yourself later while thinking about me. (ed. note: Yuck.)

◊ Don't compare me to your girlfriend. If she was that great (and not imaginary), you wouldn't be sitting in the front row at 2:00 pm.

◊ Just because I'm naked on stage, it doesn't mean I'm up for sale. It's a strip show, not an auction!

◊ Don't tell me your dick is the biggest I've ever seen. If it's that big, you wouldn't have to talk about it. I usually come back with, "no, mine is definitely bigger." That shuts them down pretty quick!

◊ Don't ask us if we're turned on when we are dancing. I was probably doing my grocery list in my head on stage.

◊ Don't say to me, "Do I get a free poster, or what?!" The answer is OR WHAT. It costs me money to make up my posters, so I will gladly give you one if you set $5 or more on the stage for me.

◊ Do not ask me to go on a date with you, be your girlfriend, marry you or go home with you. You don't even know me, just this fake persona. Wait, aren't you that guy that tried to tip me with coins earlier?? Seriously, I'm working, not looking for a boyfriend or a one night stand.

## Regarding Female Customers

◊ I don't care what sex you are, do not touch me – EVER! Girls are the absolute worst for this. They get drunk and assume that because they're not guys, it's open season.

They try to kiss, fondle and grab us off and on stage, all without asking permission or tipping a cent. And then of course they want a free poster!

◊　Don't sit there and snicker, whisper, point and laugh with your gal friends about me. Ladies, admit it, you're bad for this. Remember, I can hear you, and I'm someone's best friend, too.

◊　Don't bring your women to the strip bar if they will be bitchy. If you do manage to convince a woman to come, don't make her sit in the front row if she doesn't want to. We don't appreciate women who sit in the front row with their arms crossed while rolling their eyes at us anymore than they appreciate getting dragged there.

# Glossary

**Agency** – a company that hires dancers and books their jobs for them. The agency takes a percentage for the dancers' pay for this service. In Western Canada, most, if not all, strip clubs use an agency to book dancers. It is nearly impossible for dancers to work on the circuit without using an agency

**Agent** – the contact person between the dancers and the strip clubs. The agent books work for the dancers, hires new dancers, does the scheduling and determines pay rates

**Amateur** – a dancer that is fairly new to the industry

**Amateur contest** – a contest for new girls coming into the business and girls working in the business for less than a year. Often used by agents as an audition for prospective talent

**Ativan** – an addictive medication that controls anxiety, insomnia and in some cases schizophrenia

**Bald beaver** – a girl's shaved privates

**Baller** – a person who is flashy with his money

**Bang it** – to inject or shoot up

**Bar** – the club that the dancer works at for the week. Other terms: club, house, room and floor

**Bender** – consuming drugs and drinking alcohol for days straight (eg. eight day bender)

**Bitch** – an inferior; a servant

**Black and blues** – bruises

**Blacklisted** – when a dancer has been banned or denied bookings in the industry, usually due to a specific incident

**Blow** – slang term for cocaine

**Blowjob** – oral sex on a man

**Bong** – a glass device used for smoking drugs

**Boob job** – breast enhancement and breast implant surgery

**Booking** – getting hired to work at a club. It could be for the week or even as a replacement for a day

**Boot for us** – underage drinkers will persuade someone of legal age to buy alcohol for them

**Bumped from a show** – a girl's show given to another girl or cancelled completely

**Buy out a girl** – a customer pays a lump sum for the girl's time. Usually they will buy her time for the remaining hours the bar is open so she will sit with him and drink/talk/party/ dance. The bar gets a percentage of the money, just the same as if he had bought dances

**Cap** – the most a club will pay per show. More clubs are 'capping' their show prices due to a decline in the industry. It can also refer to a capsule of a drug

**Capsulotomy** – a procedure where the hardened or misshapen scar tissue surrounding a breast implant is removed or the tissue is altered in some way

**Change room** – a room where the dancers keep their clothing and get ready for their shows. Other terms: dressing room and dancer room

**Circuit** – usually refers to all the clubs the girls work in Western Canada, but some girls go as far east as Winnipeg and Ontario, or as far north as Yellowknife to work

**Cleaning house** – making lots of money in tips

**Club** – the bar

**Cocaine** – an illegal drug (in white powder form) that is a powerful addictive stimulant. It stimulates the body's central nervous system. Street terms: coke, crack, rock, dust, blow, snow and nose candy

**Coke** – short for cocaine

**Coke head** – a person who is a heavy user of cocaine

**Coked-out** – hyperactive and over-enthusiastic behaviour

**Contact sheet** – a print of all the negative images from a roll of film, so that all the images are the same size as the negative. It's a useful way of seeing which are the best images so you can decide which ones to make enlargements from

**Cookie** – slang for vagina. Other terms: pussy and hoochie

**Crack head** – a person who is addicted to crack cocaine

**Crack shack** – a small rundown house where drug deals occur

**Crystal meth** – a highly addictive, popular stimulant which increases alertness, concentration, energy. In high doses, increases euphoria, self-esteem and sexual excitement

**Dancer** – in the stripper world, it is a nice way of saying 'stripper'

**Dancer house** – a house where dancers stay for the week at that bar

**Dancer name** – a fake name all dancers use for privacy reasons. Other terms: stage name and stripper name

**Dancer room** – see Change room

**Dancing** – nice way of saying 'stripping' in the stripper world

**DJ** – the guy/girl in charge of music and introducing the dancers on the microphone before they step onto the stage

**Dope** – slang term for marijuana

**Downers** – slang for 'depressants.' It is a drug that decreases mental or physical activity, such as marijuana or alcohol

**Dressing room** – see Change room

**Drunk** – other terms: hammered, loaded, out of my tree, pissed, shitfaced, wasted and hammered

**E** – short for ecstasy

**Ecstasy** – an illegal drug that can generate euphoria, a feeling of intimacy and decreased anxiety. It has the same chemical structure and effects as a stimulant or hallucinogen

**Eight-ball** – an eighth of an ounce of drugs

**Feature** – the dancer for the week that makes the most amount of money per show. Other terms: feature dancer and feature girl

**Feature dancer** – see Feature

**Feature girl** – see Feature

**Fellate** – oral sex performed on a guy

**Fellatio** – see Fellate

**Fine** – a dancer can get fined for lateness, intoxication, missing a show, bad hair, no makeup, sets not long enough, etc

**Five car tail** – following a target car but keeping distance to avoid discovery

**Flapjacks** – saggy boobs

**Floated my boat** – slang for 'turns me on'

**Floor** – inside the bar (eg. I'm going to go work the floor)

**Forty pounder** – a bottle of alcohol that consists of 40 ounces

**Freebasing meth** – 'freebase' refers to the non-salt form of a drug. Drugs are usually converted to a water soluble salt so that they can be orally or intranasally consumed

**Freelancing** – freelancers are dancers that do not work on stage; they just work the floor selling private dances, usually the same bar every week. They do not go through an agency. Their income is generated by selling private dances

**Front row** – this is where customers sit at the stage where they can converse with the dancers and see them up close

**Full show** – a full show is usually 18 minutes long. The girls wear big costumes and sometimes have a themed set

**Getting booked** – see Booking

**Gig** – see Booking

**Girl** – see Dancer

**Grow-op** – shortened version for 'marijuana grow operation'

**Growing world** – see Grow-op

**Gyno** – see Front row

**Gyno row** – see Front row

**Half show** – a half show is usually nine minutes and the costumes are much less elaborate

**Hammered** – means to get really drunk

**Head** – oral sex

**Heroin** – a highly addictive drug typically used to treat severe pain. It has the same signs as morphine but usually preferred over morphine because of its lower side-effects

**High** – a euphoric feeling

**Hoochie** – slang for vagina

**House** – it can refer to the dancer house or even the bar

**House girl** – see Freelancing

**Hustle** – working the floor selling private dances, posters, magnets, anything to make money

**Hydromorph pills** – pain relievers given to cancer patients and eight times more powerful than morphine

**Ice** – see crystal meth

**Jezebel** – dictionary describes it as a 'wicked, shameless woman'

**Joint** – see Marijuana

**Kitten heels** – shoes with a short, slender heel no higher than 1 3/4

**Lap dance** – a customer pays for one-on-one time with a girl in a private dance booth. The lap dance ranges in price, contact, mileage and nudity. Also called a VIP dance, or a private dance

**Light rail transit** – sky train, c-train, tram, trolley, etc

**Lines** – powder cocaine is formed into lines and then snorted on a mirror or glass surface

**Loaded** – means drunk

**Magpies** – a nickname given to a group of regulars who meet daily at a popular BC strip club

**Making it rain** – when customers tip like crazy and throw tons of money on stage for a dancer

**Marijuana** – the most widely used illegal drug in the USA and Canada. Uses can be medicinal and recreational. Other terms: dope, weed, ganja, grass, mary jane, pot, and skunk

**Meth** – a drug that produces alertness, energy and concentration, and in higher doses can increase euphoria, self-esteem and sexual excitement. Commonly referred to as speed, crank, ice or crystal

**Moat** – a trench sometimes found around the perimeter of a stripper stage. By law, there must be no contact between customers and dancers, so a three foot moat around the stage ensures this rule is adhered to

**Narcotic** – this word comes from the Greek word 'narkos,' meaning sleep. They are drugs that induce sleep, such as heroin and morphine

**On the floor** – working the bar

**Out of my tree** – means drunk

**Oxycontins** – a highly addictive narcotic pain reliever that is similar to morphine. It's used to treat pain that is expected to last for an extended period of time

**Oxys** – short for oxycontin

**Pay cut** – a reduction in show price

**Percocets** – (generic drug name oxycodone with acetaminophen) is a combination narcotic painkiller used to treat severe short-term pain

**Percs** – short for percocets

**Pick** – a group of people get together and cut/clip mature marijuana plants for market

**Pimp** – a person that forces or encourages women to sell sex for money. He/she will collect all of the money the women earn

**Pissed** – means to get really drunk

**Platforms** – shoes with thick soles that are at least four inches in height where the heel and toes are raised

**Play the game** – when a girl fawns all over a customer with lots of flirting, smiles, innocent touching on the arm, etc

**Pot** – see Marijuana

**Private dance/ Private dancer** – see Freelancing

**Private show** – see Freelancing

**Promo** – dancers will give away items such as posters, key chains, magnets (to name a few) with her name and photo on it

**Promotion items** – see promo

**Prosciutto** – salted ham that has been cured by drying

**Pussy** – a woman's vagina

**Rack** – a woman's breasts

**Raining money** – see Making it rain

**Regular** – a customer who frequents the bar all the time

**Ride for Five** – a guy lays on his back on the edge of the stage with a five dollar bill in his mouth. The dancer sits/rides his face for a minute and then usually takes the bill out of his mouth with her breasts

**Rock bottom** – it means losing everything in your life such as friends and family, all your money, your job and respect

**Rookie** – a new girl fresh into the industry, up to a year

**Room** – the bar (eg. working the room)

**Set** – a stage dance is usually 9-18 minutes in length. Set lengths are determined by the club, the agency or the DJ. Fines can be given out to girls for short sets

**Shit faced** – slang for drunk

**Sketched out** – similar symptoms to 'coked-out,' but not necessarily due to drug intake. Generally suspicious or untrustworthy behaviour

**Slave** – a person entirely dominated by another

**Slutted me up** – made to look promiscuous (heavy make up, stilettos, short/tight clothing)

**Smashed** – slang for drunk

**Special K** – slang for Ketamine, a drug used in human and veterinary medicine, usually as an anaesthetic for dogs, cats, rabbits and even horses. Another slang name is Dorothy

**Squatted** – a squatter is a person who occupies someone else's property or premises without permission, lease or payment of rent

**Stage** – see Front row

**Stage dancing** – a dancer performing on stage for the whole bar, the opposite of a private dance which is one-on-one

**Stage name** – see Dancer name

**Stiletto** – a long, thin high heel found on some shoes and boots

**Strap-on** – a strap-on dildo in the shape of a penis with a harness that a female will wear during sexual activity

**Strip club** – other terms: strip bar, show lounge, exotic show lounge or gentleman's club

**Stripper** – other terms: peeler, exotic dancer, exotic entertainer, ripper, dancer

**Stripping** – taking clothes off for money

**Sunny side up** – exposing the contents of panties

**Twenty sixer** – a bottle of alcohol that consists of 26 ounces

**Turning tricks** – having sex with customers for money

**Uppers** – slang for 'stimulants.' It is a drug that improves mental and/or physical functions, such as cocaine or meth

**Veteran** – experienced dancer

**VIP** – VIP stands for 'very important people' but in the dancing community it is interchangeable with the term private dance. It can also mean freelancing (eg. I'm not on stage tonight, I'm just VIPing'). See Freelancing

**VIP dance** – see Freelancing

**VIP dancer** – see Freelancing

**VIP room** – the small room where private dancers occur. Also called private dance room, booth, etc

**Wasted** – slang for drunk

**Weed** – see Marijuana

**When it rains** – see Making it rain

Romana Van Lissum, a native of Karvina, Czechoslovakia, has been a fixture of the exotic dance industry and community in Western Canada for over 17 years. She plans to continue in her current position as a server in a popular Greater Vancouver strip club for as long as possible.

As an accomplished horsewoman and long-time animal lover, Van Lissum competes in 25 and 50 mile endurance rides and loves to spend as much time as possible training her horse on the trails near her home. Van Lissum is an advocate of treating all animals with kindness and respect. She also enjoys yoga, meditation, reading, travelling and spending time with her wonderful friends, her incredible husband of 21 years, and her beautiful daughter, Kelsey.

Van Lissum's first book, *How to Be a Waitress and Make Big Tips*, is available at **howtobeawaitress.com**.

She can be contacted through her websites, **howtobeawaitress.com** and **thelifeofastripper.com**.